HISTORICAL
ATLAS
OF
EMPIRES

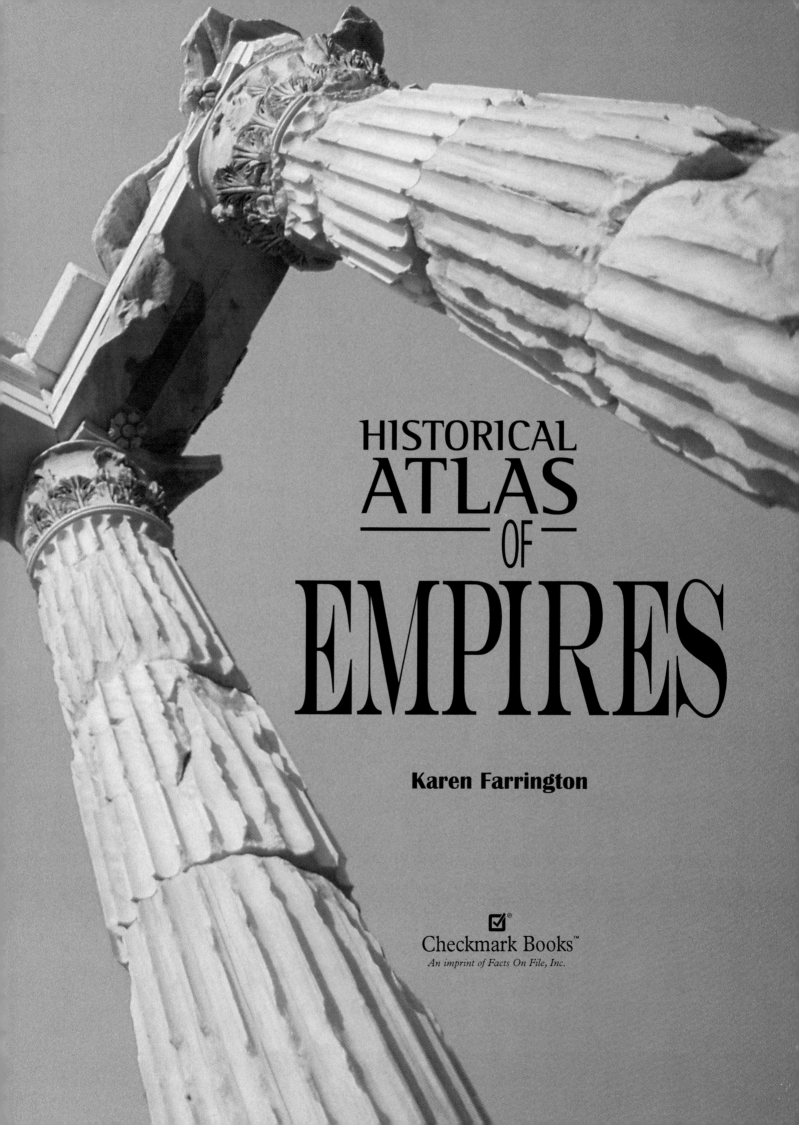

HISTORICAL
ATLAS
— OF —
EMPIRES

Karen Farrington

Checkmark Books™
An imprint of Facts On File, Inc.

HISTORICAL ATLAS OF EMPIRES

Copyright © 2002 by Thalamus Publishing

Checkmark Books
An imprint of Facts On File, Inc.
132 West 31st Street
New York, NY 10001

Library of Congress Cataloging-in-Publication Data
Farrington, Karen
    Historical atlas of empires / Karen Farrington.
    New York, NY: Checkmark Books, c2002.
        p. cm.
    Includes index.
    ISBN: 0-8160-4788-X
    1. Historical Atlas—Maps.   2. World History—Maps.
    G1030.F37 2002
    911 21   12648597

Checkmark Books are available at special discounts when purchased in bulk quantities for businesses, associations, institutions or sales promotions. Please call our Special Sales Department in New York at:
(212) 967-8800 or (800) 322-8755.

You can find Facts On File on the World Wide Web at:
http://www.factsonfile.com

For Thalamus Publishing
Project editor: Neil Williams
Maps and design: Roger Kean
Illustrations: Oliver Frey
Four-color separation: Michael Parkinson and Thalamus Studios

Printed and bound in Italy

10 9 8 7 6 5 4 3 2 1
This book is printed on acid-free paper

PICTURE CREDITS

Lesley & Roy Adkins Picture Library: 39, 40 (bottom), 114; Agence Photographique de la Réunion des Musées Nationaux/Lewandowski: 13 (left); Paul Almasy/CORBIS: 43 (top), 45 (top), 55 (right); Adrian Arbib/CORBIS: 79, 81; Archivo Iconografico S.A./CORBIS: 16, 36–37, 40 (top), 58 (top), 80, 105 (bottom), 117 (top), 120 (bottom), 139 (bottom), 149 (top), 163 (top); Yann Arthus-Bertrand/CORBIS: 82–83, 102; Asian Art & Archaeology, Inc./CORBIS: 48, 56; Austrian Archives/CORBIS: 128; Dave Bartruff/CORBIS: 62, 63 (top & bottom), 64; Morton Beebe/CORBIS: 133; Bettman/CORBIS: 123, 130, 139 (top), 167 (top), 177, 182 (top), 186 (bottom) Gary Braasch/CORBIS: 97; British Museum, London: 13 (right), 23 (bottom), 24 (top), 24 (bottom), 25, 29 (top), 33 (right), 34, 35, 45 (bottom), 50, 52, 54, 55 (left), 58 (bottom), 59, 65, 67, 71, 75 (right), 84, 89 (top), 90, 113 (bottom), 137, 148, 157 (bottom), 163 (bottom), 169; CFCL/Image Select/Ian Robinson: 106; Perry Clay/CORBIS: 6; Stephanie Colasanti/CORBIS: 101; Pierre Colombel/CORBIS: 51; Dean Conger/CORBIS: 86, 89 (bottom), 91 (bottom); CORBIS: 29 (bottom), 138, 153 (center), 176, 177, 178, 180 (top); Philip de Bay/CORBIS: 153 (top), 162; Araldo de Luca/CORBIS: 38; Leonard de Selva/CORBIS: 98, 172; Exley/Image Select: 113 (top); Gamma: 108, 131 (top), 146 (top), 146 (bottom), 173, 184, 187; Franz Geffels/CORBIS: 154; Christe Gerstenberg/CORBIS: 72, 141 (bottom); Todd Gipstein/CORBIS: 160; Angelo Hornak/CORBIS: 68 (right); Hulton-Deutsch/CORBIS: 148, 169 (top), 170, 179 (top), 180 (bottom); Image Select International: 1, 12, 15 (top), 20, 21 (top), 21 (bottom), 23 (top), 30 (top), 33 (left), 36–37, 53, 66, 70, 74, 75 (left), 88, 91 (top), 118, 132, 134, 135, 136, 141 (top), 144, 145, 147, 150, 152, 164, 167 (bottom), 182 (bottom), 185; ISI/Ann Ronan: 149 (bottom), 157 (top), 165, 179 (bottom), 183; Wolfgang Kaehler/CORBIS: 99, 107, 109 (top), 168; Earl & Nazima Kowall/CORBIS: 43 (bottom); Paul H. Kuiper/CORBIS: 117 (bottom); David Lees/CORBIS: 15 (bottom); Charles Lenars/CORBIS: 96 (bottom); Wally NcNamee/CORBIS: 189; Richard T. Nowitz/CORBIS: 2–3, 18–19; Diego Lezama Orezzoli/CORBIS: 30 (bottom) Gianni Dagli Orti/CORBIS: 31, 42, 73, 95, 96 (top), 116, 131 (bottom); Emzo & Paolo Ragazzini/CORBIS: 109 (bottom); Steve Raymer/CORBIS: 124–125, 171; Royal Ontario Museum/CORBIS: 57; David Samuel Robbins/CORBIS: 85; Kevin Schafer/CORBIS: 125; Juan Skylitzer/CORBIS: 115; Ted Spiegel/CORBIS: 78, 122; Vince Streano/CORBIS: 100; Thalamus Publishing: 8, 17, 19, 70–71, 105 (top); Thalamus/Martin Teviotdale: 19 (illustration); Peter Turnley/CORBIS: 7, 186 (top); Ruggero Vanni/CORBIS: 129; Francesco Venturi/CORBIS: 69; Patrick Ward/CORBIS: 9; Nik Wheeler/CORBIS: 14, 94, 103, 104; Roger Wood/CORBIS: 68 (left); Adam Woolfitt/CORBIS: 120 (top).

TITLE PAGE: Doorway to the Hall of Columns, palace of Darius I at Persepolis. Empires have always been a question of image—monuments to glorify the empire and its ruler in the eyes of its people and those subject to its power are the finest legacy of past eras.

PREVIOUS PAGES: Columns rise from the ruins of the Temple of Trajan at Pergamon, Turkey. Roman emperors undertook massive building programs in every province of the empire to benefit the conquered territories—and to remind the conquered that Rome was master.

RIGHT: The minting and issuing of coinage is another means of subjugating and regulating the lives of subjects. Coins bearing a portrait of the ruler have been used in almost all significant empires. In some cases, the ruler harks back on past glories to help establish a new dynasty. This coin of Charlemagne poses the Carolingian king as an ancient Roman emperor to justify his claim to be successor to the Roman Empire, which had been defunct for over 400 years.

Contents

Introduction—The Meaning of Empire 6

Chapter One—The First Empires 10
The Rise and Fall of Akkad 12
Egypt—Empire on the Nile 16
Assyria and the Age of Chaos 22

Chapter Two—Ancient Rivals 26
Achaemenid Persia 28
Alexander the Great 32
SPQR—Rome 36
Persia Rises Again 42

Chapter Three—The Glorious East 46
Out of Turmoil—Han China 48
India Flowers Under the Guptas 52
T'ang China—a Powerhouse 56

Chapter Four—Empires of Faith 60
Axum and the Ark 62
The Rise of Islam 66
The Carolingian Empire 72

Chapter Five—Steppe Empires 76
Raiders from the Steppes 78
Khazaria 82
The Mongol Khans 86

Chapter Six—To the Edge of the World 92
The Militaristic Toltec Empire 94
Srivijaya and the Trade Winds 98
The Almoravid Gold Road 102
The Inca State Machine 106

Chapter Seven—The Medieval World 110
The Byzantine Empire 112
The Angevin Dynasty 118
The Union of Kalmar 122

Chapter Eight—The Age of Discovery 126
The Holy Roman Empire 128
In Fortune's Eye—Venice 132
Spain in the Americas 136

Chapter Nine—Rivals in the Old World 142
The Ottoman Empire 144
From Muscovy to Behemoth 150
The Habsburg Empire 154

Chapter Ten—Rivals in a New World 158
Napoleon—General of Genius 160
The British Empire 164
French Colonialism 170

Chapter Eleven—The Modern Empires 174
The United States of America 176
Rising Sun—Japan 180
The Soviet Block 184

Conclusion—The State of Empire Today 188

Index 190

The Meaning of Empire

Another year!—another deadly blow!
Another mighty Empire overthrown!
And we are left, or shall be left, alone

From *National Independence and Liberty*, by William Wordsworth

The Parthenon, completed in 432 BC, was Athens' crowning glory. The city state was at its peak and had become history's first democratically run empire. The Athenian navy ruled the Mediterranean, keeping rival Sparta in second place. Yet Sparta won the Peloponnesian War (431–405 BC). One reason was that the demos (people) of Athens kept indicting their brightest military talents for fear that one would become a tyrant and impose an empire of absolute rule. Continued instability led to conquest by Alexander.

The definition of what constitutes an "empire" is open to debate. The Latin word *imperium*, from which the term "empire" derives, literally means "dominion" or "legitimate authority." Twentieth century political science has tended to restrict the term to a very precise model in which one state colonizes others for economic gain and political or cultural domination. Often cited is the 19th-century exploitation by European states (Britain, France, Holland, Spain, and Portugal) of most of the rest of the globe. Some historians also insist that a true empire must survive over many centuries. Yet to enforce this definition would be to ignore the dynamic and fascinating rule of a people such as the Inca, whose regime lasted only 80 years, or the achievements of Alexander the Great, whose empire barely outlived him in its entirety.

All empires share a number of characteristics. There is necessarily a ruling figurehead who utilizes a successful military arm to gain new territories and maintain existing ones. He (or occasionally she) fortifies key strategic ports and cities, exploits economic resources such as fertile land or mineral reserves, and keeps the masses in line through either fear or propaganda, or both. Laws—and sometimes a religion—are then imposed on a range of different cultures across a large geographical area. Grand public building works and monuments record the ruler's greatness. Wealth is pursued aggressively through any combination of diplomacy, cajolery, reward, and threat.

The typical empire is usually oppressive and ruthless, although it can be philanthropic, especially when it is firmly established and so is able to focus on the improvement of its society. Above all, it leaves its distinctive mark—for good or evil—on the peoples of its day and ultimately on history itself.

Empires are, by their nature, undemocratic, though even this depends on

one's definition of the term. The United States of America is the ultimate example of a democratic nation whose immense influence throughout the world arguably qualifies it as an empire. Another assumption that is open to question is that all empires strip conquered territories of their wealth, leaving them poorer. In the case of some European empires, such as the British Empire of the 19th century, the global trade increased not only Britain's wealth but also that of many of its colonies in a symbiotic relationship.

Definitions of the term "empire" can be further stretched by power politics. The "Emperor" Jean Bédel Bokassa's basis for declaring the Central African Republic an empire in 1977 was merely for self-aggrandizement. On the opposite extreme, successive leaders of the Union of Soviet Socialist Republics (USSR, or Soviet Union) always shunned the notion that they ruled an empire—even though the post-Cold War breakup of the USSR in 1991 provided the clearest possible evidence to the contrary.

For most people, an empire in the modern era is an anachronism and a vestige of ignorant times. Only a few decades ago, however, most British citizens believed that their empire was helping to civilize the rest of the world, and they saw it as a positive

structure serving the whole of humanity. Indeed, empires throughout history have brought huge benefits and the advancement of civilization. The British Empire gave the world a shared language, English; Napoleon's Empire swept away the old order in Europe and brought massive educational and legal reforms to the continent. Unfortunately, none of these changes came about peacefully and they were made by a relatively small number of individuals to the short-term detriment of many. Empires are, by their very nature, based on human greed and exploitation, and there is no room for them in today's crowded world.

DATE SYSTEMS

Dates in brackets after a person's name are shown in different ways in this book, depending on the information being given. Rulers of kingdoms or empires are given the dates of their reign, shown like this: (r.1745–67). When given, papal and presidential dates also show the period of the person's term, like this: (p.1590–1615). Birth to death dates are shown without a single-letter prefix.

The mighty are fallen. Despite referring to itself as a union of socialist republics, the collapse of the USSR in 1991 proved that it had indeed been an empire. The central power of a handful of Politburo "czars" kept many states in thrall to the Russian hegemony. But like so many empires before it, the autocratic rule of its communist leaders led to their own undoing. Joseph Stalin was an absolute ruler in life, but his image was soon destroyed after his death. By 1991, the feelings of ordinary Russians overflowed in an orgy of vandalism, as numerous Stalin statues were torn down, like this one lying in a park in Moscow—a reminder of the ephemeral nature of empires, and empire-builders.

Chaos, not Calculation

The dynamics behind what causes the rise and fall of empires has vexed philosophers throughout history. According to an ancient Chinese doctrine (known as *Heaven's Mandate*) their fortunes were governed by cosmic forces and natural cycles. There was a liberal sprinkling of Confucian moral teaching in this theory. Emperors who failed to conduct their lives in harmony with the "natural" laws were not expected to last long. Today, as we look back on the rise and fall of empires throughout history we can at last see the picture more clearly—that economic and military changes in developing societies created the impetus for empire-building. While the formation of individual empires was not necessarily inevitable, it is impossible to imagine how the modern world could have evolved in any other way.

The exchange of ideas from one society to another can have profound effects on the formation of an empire. The birth of the Soviet Union, for instance, was the direct consequence of ideas formulated by Karl Marx, not in Russia, but in England and Germany—and his ideas were intended for the industrial economies of the West (Europe) rather than for Asia. Even Marx would have been shocked if he could have seen the effects his ideas would have in the coming decades. For the Soviet Union, communist doctrine held its empire together, just as religion had done in earlier centuries for empires such as that of the Abbasids.

Due to their smaller populations and the difficulties of long-distance travel, ancient empires were generally much longer-lived than more recent ones. Certainly the three millennia that Ancient Egyptian culture was at its zenith is unsurpassed, and will almost definitely remain so. However any comparison with later regimes is not strictly fair, since for many centuries the Egyptians had no serious rivals and were conveniently shielded from intruders by the desert and sea. Later, the Romans and the Chinese Han empires dominated each end of Eurasia for many centuries.

The Romans and Han Chinese were two very different cultures who never directly encountered each other, but nevertheless shared much in common. They both governed huge areas over enormous spans of time; understood the importance of a good road network for communications; believed wholeheartedly that their respective empires were the greatest in the world. They were contemptuous of outside "barbarians" yet, paradoxically, were relaxed about assimilating these people into their

societies. Few people today realize, for instance, that by the third century AD the Romans were actually a minority in their own Senate! Rome had become the ancient world's melting pot, in much the same way as we think of the U.S. today.

Similarly Han China incorporated new peoples and assimilated them as its empire spread westward. This is the ultimate effect that empire-building creates—the bringing together of disparate peoples into a single political union. Although the leaders of history's empires could not possibly have foreseen the outcome of their actions, it is nevertheless a fact that our modern global society is the direct result of the empires of yesteryear.

The author's aim has been to chart the structure of empires from both a geographical and historical perspective. I have not sought to analyze or contrast the various leaders and dynasties, nor have I attempted to deduce some intricate formula for conquest down the ages. History is far more complex than that. This is a book of historical snapshots showing that chaos, rather than calculation, has been the ultimate ruler.

A SHORT GLOSSARY OF POWER TERMS

autocracy the absolute power of one person (see also **despot** and **dictator**)

democracy (Greek: *demos*, the people), government by the people through elected representatives

despot (Greek: *despotés*), lit.– a master, but also a king with unlimited powers

dictator a Latin term for a magistrate given temporary supreme power during emergencies. Appointed dictators during the last years of the republic became harder to remove, lending the word a newer, and more sinister meaning

emperor (Latin: *imperator*), lit.– commander in chief

hegemony (Greek: *hegemonia*), lit.– leadership, but especially when one state has dominion over others

oligarchy (Greek: *oligarchia*), a state ruled by a few persons

plutocracy (Greek: *ploutokratia*), government by the wealthy

tyranny government by a **tyrant** (Greek: *tyrannos*); a ruler who has seized power illegally and rules absolutely

The First Empires

The location of the first empires was no accident of history. Certain kings rose to prominence through intelligence, cunning, political astuteness, and military might but these individuals were just players in a much larger game. If King Sargon of Akkad had never been born there would have been others equally hungry for power in Mesopotamia. Early empires were born of geography, climate, water, the availability of food, and natural resources. All these factors were variable and some were hostile. The only unlimited ingredient was a supply of naked human ambition.

The first farmers began producing domesticated crops and animals by about 6,500 BC, allowing permanent settlements to replace the old, nomadic hunter-gatherer communities. These farming societies were split into separate tribes, each of a few thousand people, scattered among small villages and remote communities. The tribes were interlinked by family ties, language, and religion but they all existed independently as so-called "segmentary societies." In other words, although there were high-ranking families few individual leaders had the power to impose their will.

When agriculture became more intensive, this changed. Efficient food production allowed distinctive large-scale chiefdoms of 20,000 or more to flourish. On fertile river flood plains—such as the Nile valley and the Fertile Crescent of the Tigris and Euphrates—the first cities could be founded. Now chiefs and rulers sought craftsmen to bring trade and wealth, a religious ideology to keep order, large-scale construction projects to show off their greatness and, most important, armies to enforce grand plans for expansion.

UNITY AND POWER
This chapter examines the first true empires to flourish within this social

Pharaoh in his war chariot leads his army into battle.

environment. Among them Akkad, centered on what is now southern Iraq, is generally acknowledged as the first to unite different ethnic and cultural groups—a claim that could arguably be contested by the Old Kingdom of Ancient Egypt. It actually matters little which came first. These two superpowers co-existed in the third millennium BC, each characterized by strong central government, leaders revered as living gods, and healthy economies maintained by food surpluses.

Later rulers in the region would develop more bloodthirsty methods of control. This is particularly true of the Assyrians and specifically the Assyrian king Ashurnasirpal II, who came to power in 883 BC. He gloried in

cruel, unusual, and downright sadistic methods of publicly executing his enemies, although he did not have a monopoly on such methods since all leaders employed terror tactics. Paradoxically, he also rewarded loyal subjects and vassal states with flamboyant gifts—including a well-documented invitation to one of the biggest feasts ever recorded.

Assyria's downfall was typical of most world powers. Its brief victory over Egypt in 671 BC meant boundaries became unsustainable and uncontrollable—a salutary example to future empire-builders. As we shall see, it was a lesson few of them learned.

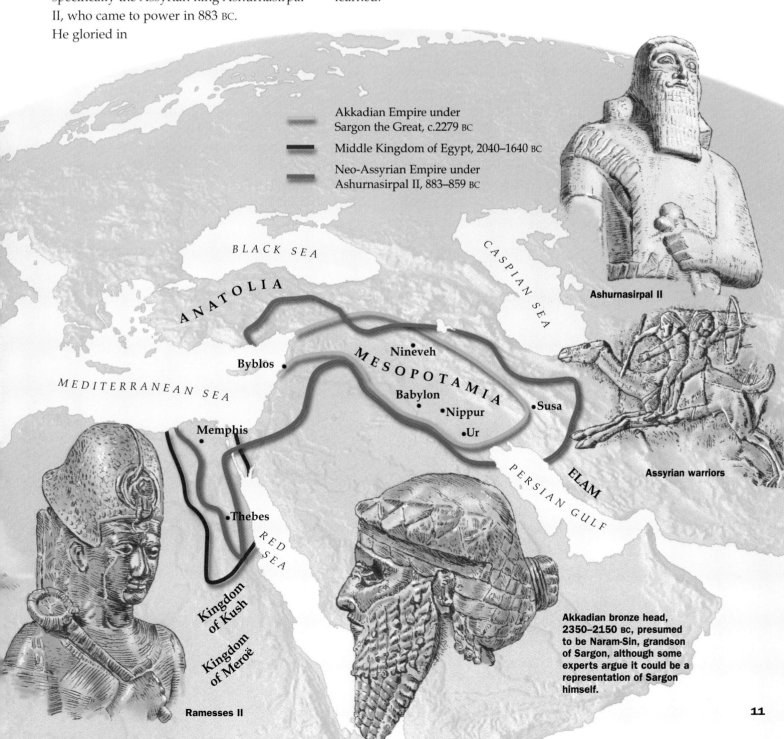

Akkadian Empire under
Sargon the Great, c.2279 BC

Middle Kingdom of Egypt, 2040–1640 BC

Neo-Assyrian Empire under
Ashurnasirpal II, 883–859 BC

BLACK SEA

CASPIAN SEA

ANATOLIA

Ashurnasirpal II

MESOPOTAMIA

Byblos

Nineveh

MEDITERRANEAN SEA

Babylon

Nippur

Susa

Memphis

Ur

Assyrian warriors

PERSIAN GULF

ELAM

Thebes

RED SEA

Kingdom of Kush

Kingdom of Meroë

Akkadian bronze head, 2350–2150 BC, presumed to be Naram-Sin, grandson of Sargon, although some experts argue it could be a representation of Sargon himself.

Ramesses II

The Rise and Fall of Akkad

The rulers of Mesopotamia's first urban centers began to look further afield to add grandeur to their names.

BELOW: Because Leonard Woolley, the excavator of Ur, thought this decorated object was carried on a pole as a standard, it became known as the Standard of Ur. In fact, its original function remains a mystery—it may even have been a musical sounding board. Measuring only 8 1/2 x 19 1/2 inches, the object was found in one of the largest graves in the Royal cemetery at Ur. One side of the main panels depicts War and the other Peace. It dates from c.2500 BC.

The study of ancient history can never be an exact science. This is particularly true of empires emerging at the very dawn of history; a time when written records were necessarily brief, often partial, and invariably open to later misinterpretation. Even so, we know enough about the rise of King Sargon of Akkad to credit him as founder of the world's first great empire—a leader who combined inspired military leadership with astute administrative skills.

The Akkadians first appear in written archives around 2700 BC in southern Mesopotamia (now Iraq), an area bordered by the Euphrates and Tigris rivers and known as the Fertile Crescent. A Semitic people, they lived alongside the Sumerians and along with them they built some of the world's first towns and cities. At this time the region was contested by several autonomous city-states and kingdoms, of which the most influential was the long-established civilization of Kish. It was as a humble cupbearer to the King of Kish, Ur-Zababa, that Sargon rose to prominence in about 2340 BC.

INTERPRETING ANCIENT RECORDS

Inevitably there is some dispute about the identity of the "real" Sargon. Some Biblical scholars say he is the Old Testament's King Nimrod—described as "the first on earth to be a mighty man" and "a mighty hunter before the Lord"—while original Akkadian texts give the meaning of his name as Sarru-kin or "the king is the true king." It seems unlikely that this was the name he was born with but the fullest surviving Babylonian account of his early years "The Legend of Sargon" (SEE BOX) casts little light on this issue, preferring instead to elevate him to mythical status alongside the goddess Ishtar. His place of birth is mostly guesswork, although traditional stories mention a mysterious origin in or

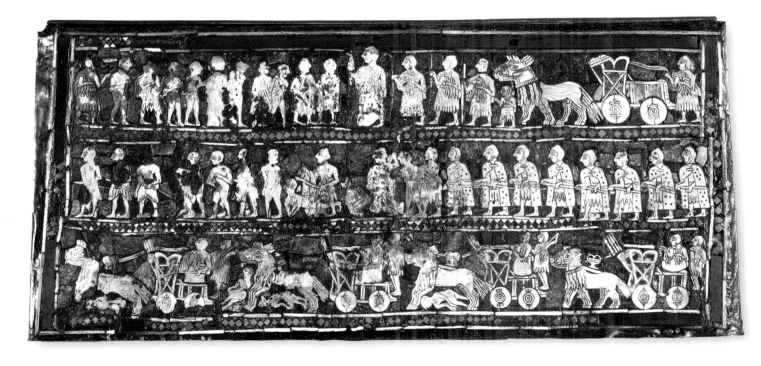

c.40000 BC	3500 BC	3000 BC	c.2675 BC	2400 BC	2350 BC	2334–2279 BC	2193 BC
First monumental religious structures begin to appear in the region around Nineveh	Sumerians arrive and settle in Mesopotamia	Trade links exist between Mesopotamia, Indus valley, and Arabia	Warrior-king Gilgamesh rules the Sumerian city-state of Uruk	Four-wheeled war chariots are used in Mesopotamia	Urukagina, king of Lagash, enacts the first known code of law	Reign of Sargon and founding of his Akkadian Empire	Gutian invasion leads to the fall of the Akkadian Empire

near the city of Azupiranu.

The text says Sargon did not know his father, though given that it was written to glorify the king we should not conclude that he was illegitimate. Rather, the dismissal of his father is a device to accentuate the social standing of his mother, "the high priestess," who by definition would have been from a noble or royal family. Priestesses had a sacred status and were not supposed to give birth—hence the reason this one concealed her pregnancy and sent her new-born child floating down-river in a rush basket.

There are of course echoes of the story of Moses here, though the connection is obscure.

The Israelite leader was born more than 900 years later at Goshen, in ancient Egypt, from where his mother consigned him to the Nile as a way of protecting him from mass infanticide. It is possible the two stories later became intertwined as a way of emphasizing Sargon's Semitic roots. Certainly the political influence he won was later venerated by Semitic Babylonians (Babylonia was a Mesopotamian kingdom between the 18th and 6th centuries BC), who regarded him as something of a national hero.

THE LEGEND OF SARGON

Sargon, the mighty king, king of Akkad am I
My mother was a high priestess, my father I knew not
The brother(s) of my father loved the hills
My city is Azupiranu, which is situated on the banks of the Euphrates
My mother, the high priestess, conceived me, in secret she bore me
She set me in a basket of rushes, with bitumen she sealed my lid
She cast me in the river that rose not over me
The river bore me up and carried me to Akki, the drawer of water
Akki, the drawer of water, took me as his son and reared me
Akki, the drawer of water, appointed me as his gardener
While I was a gardener, Ishtar granted me her love
And for four and (obscure) years I exercised kingship.

LEFT: This sandstone stela celebrates the victory of Naram-Sin c.2230 BC (see caption below) over the Lullubu, a tribe from the Zagros Mountains. At some point later, after a conquest by Elamites, the stela was stolen and taken to the Elamite capital of Susa, where it was discovered by archaeologists.

This Akkadian greenstone seal depicts the struggle between wild animals and heroes, which was a popular design on seals of the period about 2250 BC. The cuneiform inscription giving the owner's name is unclear, but describes him as the servant of Bin-kali-sharri, a prince, one of the sons of Naram-Sin, king of Agade or Akkad (2254–2218 BC). King Naram-Sin was the grandson of Sargon, founder of the Akkadian dynasty. He was succeeded by another son, Shar-kali-sharri (2217–2193 BC), after which a period of instability brought the empire to its end.

2112 BC	2100 BC	2037 BC	2004 BC	c.2000 BC	c.1750 BC	1595 BC	1550 BC
Ur-Nammu founds the Third Dynasty of Ur	The first ziggurats are built at Ur and related settlements	The Multi defensive wall is built to protect Mesopotamia from invasion	The Elamites, invaders from the East, sack Ur	Domesticated horses are introduced into Mesopotamia	Babylonian warrior-king Hammurabi establishes code of law in Mesopotamia	Babylon is sacked by the Hittites	The Mittani kingdom is founded, a people who commence attacks against Egypt

Sargon's wars

It is unclear quite how Sargon became King of Kish but it seems fair to assume that he was already an influential voice at court with a reputation for efficiency and strong leadership. The main sources documenting his dynasty come from copies made by Old Babylonian scribes in the city of Nippur, who used a mix of Akkadian and Sumerian scripts to summarize what must once have been an extensive records library.

According to the Sumerian list of kings, the first five rulers of Akkad—Sargon, Rimush, Manishtusu, Naram-Sin and Shar-kali-sharri—together reigned for 142 years, of which 56 could be attributed to Sargon alone. This implies that Sargon lived to an untypically ripe old age, though there is no particular reason to doubt the source. A similar list of kings for the city of Ur, though written 250 years later, ascribed dates which have proved remarkably accurate under archaeological analysis.

The Nippur texts tell how Sargon set up his court at Akkad (sometimes called Agade), a city in northern Sumeria that has not yet been located but probably stood between Sippar and Kish on the Euphrates. From here he launched a devastating and merciless series of raids on the Sumerian cities of the south; battering down defensive walls, imprisoning senior administrators, and—so we are told—ultimately cleansing his army's weapons in the "nether sea," or Persian Gulf.

Sargon humiliated one enemy ruler, Lugalzagesi of Uruk, by forcing his neck beneath a yoke and driving him to the sacred gate of the god Enlil at Nippur. In conquered cities he left behind trusted governors to collect taxes and tributes, while the deployment of a permanent army emphasized his ambition to create a true empire rather than some short-term occupation of vassal states. Neither was his aggression confined to the 34 battles recorded in the South. There were successes in northern Mesopotamia at Mari, northern Syria, where he worshipped the god Dagan, Ebla (which he destroyed), the Lebanon, and the foothills of the Zagros mountains. All the while Akkad's trade links grew wider, boosting the King's war chest and treasury. Ships from Magan (possibly a port in

BELOW: Part of the excavated Sumerian ruins at Uruk, which Sargon conquered during the Akkadian expansion.

Tepe Gawra, near Nineveh, is thought to be the world's oldest monumental structure, built about 4000 BC.

The first cities of the "fertile crescent"—Mesopotamia—between 4300–2330 BC.

first Sumerian settlements
Earliest dynastic Sumerian culture
Extent of the Akkadian Empire 2371–2230 BC
ancient coastline in Persian Gulf

Oman), Meluhha (on the Arabian Sea coast) and Dilmun (Bahrain) made regular voyages up the Persian Gulf.

A LARGE BUT UNSTABLE EMPIRE

According to eighth century BC sources, Akkad's empire extended as far as Crete in the west, Magan in the east, and through 65 of the region's major cities. The problem however lies in assessing what, in this context, is meant by "empire." It is far from certain that such a vast area of Western Asia was ever a single entity under Sargon's dynasty. Much more likely is that areas moved in and out of Akkad's influence according to shifting balances of power at the time. The kings succeeding Sargon all report large-scale rebellions and since three of them—Rimush, Manishtusu and Shar-kali-sharri—died violent deaths it is clear that Akkad did not enjoy an unchallenged status.

This is not to belittle the achievements of Sargon's dynasty. Inscriptions extolling the reign of Naram Sin, for instance, have been located at sites more than 600 miles apart—right down the Tigris river, along much of the upper Khabur and throughout Babylonia. Whether or not this was ever a "single empire," it is a persuasive indication of the dynasty's influence. Inscriptions show that Akkadian language and literature prospered under these kings, that there was a "golden age" of art, particularly sculpture, and a general broadening of outlooks and attitudes within Mesopotamia.

The decline of Akkad about 2200 BC is as perplexing as its rise. Few royal inscriptions seem to have been made in the years after Shar-kali-sharri's death and central power became ineffective. The nomadic Amorites' invasion from the northwest and the expanding population of the Gutians to the east accentuated this demise.

Sumerian warrior's ceremonial helmet made from a single sheet of beaten gold weighing about 110 pounds. Ur, dating from c.2500 BC.

BELOW: Ziggurat and ruined walls of Ur. The ancient Sumerian city in modern-day Iraq is also traditionally believed to be the birthplace of the biblical Abraham.

Egypt—Empire on the Nile

Isolated from other cultures by arid deserts, the Red Sea, and the Mediterranean, Egypt remained free from invasion for centuries, and developed its own unique civilization.

It is tempting to place ancient Egypt in a neat historical chronology, as a stand-alone civilization in which power was passed through family dynasties in seamless

By general academic agreement (as opposed to undisputed fact) Egyptologists have segmented the region's history into 34 separate royal dynasties. Their approximate dates extend from the pre- and early dynastic periods (5000 to 2625 BC), through the Old Kingdom (2625—2134 BC) the Middle Kingdom (2040–1640), and the New

succession, interrupted only by the occasional power struggle. This may be convenient, but it creates a misleading view. The history of ancient Egypt spans at least 3000 years, from c.3000 BC to the Roman conquest in 30 BC. This continuity is unparalleled, but it does not mean that Egypt successfully isolated itself from the turmoil in the outside world. Its kingdoms rose and fell, and the apparent stability is an illusion.

Despite this cautionary note it is still legitimate to see ancient Egypt as an empire—albeit one constantly re-inventing itself amid changing religious views, internal wars, and the influence of outside cultures.

Ritual execution of vanquished enemies was common. This detail from the Palette of Narmer shows King Narmer (Menes) presiding over a ceremony with his priests. At the right lie two rows of five beheaded bodies, their heads arranged neatly between their legs. Such rituals would have occurred frequently as the first pharaoh of the first dynasty conquered all of Egypt along the Nile.

Kingdom (1539–1075 BC). In-between are the First, Second, and Third Intermediate Periods, followed by the Late Period (664–332 BC), and finally the death throes of the empire at the hands of the Romans. There is no consensus, sadly, over the names of some rulers. For instance King Khufu (who built the Great Pyramid at Giza) is often referred to by his Greek name, Cheops.

The life-blood of Egyptian civilization was, unquestionably, the River Nile. It was a powerful natural ally for early farmers (c.6000 BC), flooding in the late summer but receding in fall to leave damp fields with a new layer of silt ready for sowing. Crops flourished through the warm winters and

3500 BC	**3100 BC**	**2800 BC**	**2686–2160 BC**	**2585–2560 BC**	**c.2500 BC**	**c.2500 BC**	**c.2455 BC**
Dawn of Egyptian history with unification of Upper Egypt	Egypt's Upper and Lower kingdoms are unified by Pharaoh Menes	Expeditions are sent via the Red Sea to the land of Punt (probably in East Africa)	Egyptian Old Kingdom	Fourth dynasty reign of King Khufu; Great Pyramid constructed in this period	Egyptian army develops the phalanx (a tight formation of soldiers)	Egypt develops seagoing vessels capable of crossing the Mediterranean	Death of Egyptian fifth dynasty king Reneferef

could be harvested in late Spring before the rains returned. It was a cycle that produced high yields, grain surpluses for trade, and ultimately the wealth to maintain an effective army. The Nile was, and is, also a superb natural highway. The prevailing wind blows north-to-south, allowing boats to travel upstream by sail and down with the flow. Settlements were built close to the river—which meant garrisons could be quickly reinforced—while the surrounding desert acted as a formidable natural barrier to would-be aggressors. From the historical record, it seems that Egyptian civilization existed for 1,300 years before it even suffered an invasion.

UNITING THE TWO LANDS

By 3000 BC settlements in the Nile region had evolved from hundreds of disparate subsistence farming communities into a series of small towns and chiefdoms, all competing for the limited fertile land available. In Upper Egypt (the south of the country) these eventually amalgamated into a single kingdom and around 2920 BC its ruler, King Narmer, conquered the whole of Lower Egypt as well. Narmer consolidated his fledgling empire by founding a new capital, Thebes, on the Nile delta some 600 miles down-river of his southern powerbase of Hierakonopolis.

As the first pharaoh of the first dynasty, Narmer's name is heavily bound up in Egyptian folklore with the legendary king Menes. This was a time when the foundations of state government were being laid, written records (in the form of hieroglyphs) created, and religion used to cement royal supremacy. Ancient Egypt was a theocracy, a state managed by administrators beneath a divine king or living god. To defy the king was blasphemy. Yet kingship itself was never totally secure. Early rulers had to prove that they were physically fit by running a set course through each of the nomes (regions) they governed. If they failed the test, they risked ritual sacrifice.

A tantalizing glimpse of Narmer's empire has been deduced from his Palette, a single piece of carved slate found at Hierakonopolis. It glorifies the unification of the Two Lands, and shows Narmer wielding a mace above a kneeling, bearded prisoner (beards often denoted foreigners or enemies) and being escorted by a high priest, servant, and standard bearers. A further bas-relief depicts ten bound and beheaded corpses, their heads placed beneath their feet, laid out as if for inspection following execution. Mutilation of dead enemies, including the removal of genitals, was a common practice among victorious Egyptian armies.

BELOW LEFT: In the reign of King Zoser (Djoser, 2630–2611 BC) the first true pyramids marked the beginning of the golden age of monumental tomb construction. Zoser probably began work on his tomb at Saqqara on his accession. Not only was its design of six stepped levels revolutionary, but it was the earliest complete building of hewn and dressed stone in Egypt. The Stepped Pyramid dominates a large complex of courtyards and buildings, many containing superb examples of early wall paintings.

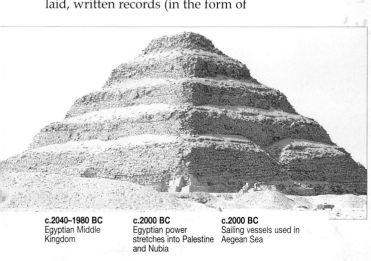

c.2040–1980 BC
Egyptian Middle Kingdom

c.2000 BC
Egyptian power stretches into Palestine and Nubia

c.2000 BC
Sailing vessels used in Aegean Sea

Mediterranean Sea

• Buto

LOWER EGYPT

Tanis

• Bubastis

• Heliopolis

Abu Rawash •
Memphis •
Dahshur •

• Giza
• Saqqara

• Maidum
• Seila

Faiyum

Herakleopolis •

Nile

• Kom-el-Ahmar
Sawaris

Western Desert

MIDDLE EGYPT

Eastern Desert

Beni Hassan •
• Sheikh Sa'id
• El-Amarna

Meir •
Dara •
• Asyut

El-Hammamiya •
Qaw-el-Kebir •

Nag el-Deir
•

Naquada (Ombos)

Abydos •
Dendara •

• Karnak
• Thebes (Luxor)

Border between Upper and Lower Kingdoms 2134–2040 BC

UPPER EGYPT

Gebelan •
Hierakonopolis •

• El-Kab
• Edfu

Border of Kingdom of Upper Egypt c.3000 BC

1st Cataract and southern border of Old Kingdom

Elephantine •

• Syene (Aswan)

Shoreline of modern Lake Nasser

Red Sea

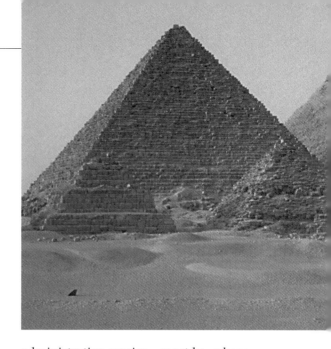

The Old Kingdom Pyramids

The beginning of the Old Kingdom heralded the golden age of pharaonic rule. In Snefru (c.2573–2549 BC) it saw the emergence of a great warrior king, a ruler who enjoyed prosperity at home and the fruits of empire-building abroad—south into the gold-rich lands of Nubia, west into Libya, and east into the Sinai. Snefru is thought to have built the earliest Egyptian pyramid, at Dahshur, but it was his son Khufu who turned these monumental tombs into gigantic symbols of godly supremacy. It is Khufu's Great Pyramid at Giza, on the apex of the Nile Delta, which remains today the most impressive testament to ancient Egypt's superpower status.

The Great Pyramid is flanked by a slightly smaller neighbor, that of Khaefre, and the much more modest tomb of Menkaure. Alongside the Great Sphinx, they comprise the central area of an awesome royal cemetery for fourth-dynasty rulers, viziers, and senior administrators. It is estimated that Khufu's pyramid alone employed some 18,000 laborers during the pharaoh's lifetime and involved the manhandling of 2.3 million limestone blocks. The pyramid shape is linked to worship of the Sun God Ra, or Re, and helped the king's ka (spirit) to climb up and accompany him on his voyage across the sky. A secret chamber containing the barque Khufu would use for these daily trips was discovered in 1954. It was in kit form ready for Khufu's servants to reassemble in the afterlife.

ULTIMATE STATUS SYMBOLS

The building of the Great Pyramid was a massive drain on the empire's resources. However, there is no hard evidence to support the Greek historian Herodotus's claim that Khufu had to strip treasures from temples and prostitute one of his daughters to pay for its completion. Even so, the economic wealth and strong central government of the Old Kingdom—in which citizens could be compelled into armed or

administrative service—must have been crucial to turn Khufu's dream into reality. By the time of the New Kingdom, pyramids were merely symbols of the distant past. Religious views had changed, threats from foreign enemies had increased, and the sheer scale of such projects was discouraging. Above all, New Kingdom pharaohs were aghast at the way robbers had plundered the gold-laden graves of their forefathers. They switched tactics, preferring to site tombs in the remote Valley of the Kings, near Thebes.

By around 2400 BC the empire was on the wane. Fifth-dynasty kings were too ready to grant land gifts and favors to the nobility

SOLDIERS OF THE PHARAOHS

Egypt's military prowess was founded on a disciplined, full-time army. Garrisons were established near the traditional royal capitals, such as Thebes and Memphis, at strategic points along the Nile, and in conquered trouble-zones like Nubia and the borders with Asia. Each infantry platoon comprised 10 men, 20 platoons formed a company which was headed by a captain and standard-bearer, and 25 companies formed a division. Archers, specialist javelin throwers, and a fast-chariot cavalry (after c.1600 BC) served to support the skilled swordsmen of the infantry.

RIGHT: The Great Pyramids of Giza form the centerpiece of a massive royal funerary complex. The pyramid of Menkaure (Mycerinus in Greek) is nearest (218 feet), with smaller structures in front of it, then the pyramids of Khaefre (Chepren, 471 feet) and Khufu (Cheops, 479 feet) beyond.

FAR RIGHT: A relief of Queen Hatshepsut that originally decorated a wall in the temple of Karnak, Thebes, was defaced on the orders of her successor, Tuthmosis III. The erasing was so carefully done that the relief's shape is still clearly visible. This form of propagandist vandalism was common after the succession of a new pharaoh.

c.1900 BC	c.1550–1075 BC	c.1550 BC	1482 BC	c.1460 BC	1353 BC	c.1350 BC
Work begins on Amun temple in Karnak	Egyptian New Kingdom	Tomb workers' village of Deir el-Medina founded by Pharaoh Tuthmosis I	Death of Tuthmosis I, founder of Valley of the Kings burial ground	Tuthmosis III reconquers Egypt	Akhenaten becomes Pharaoh of Egypt	Syrians become multi-lingual, learning Hittite and Babylonian languages

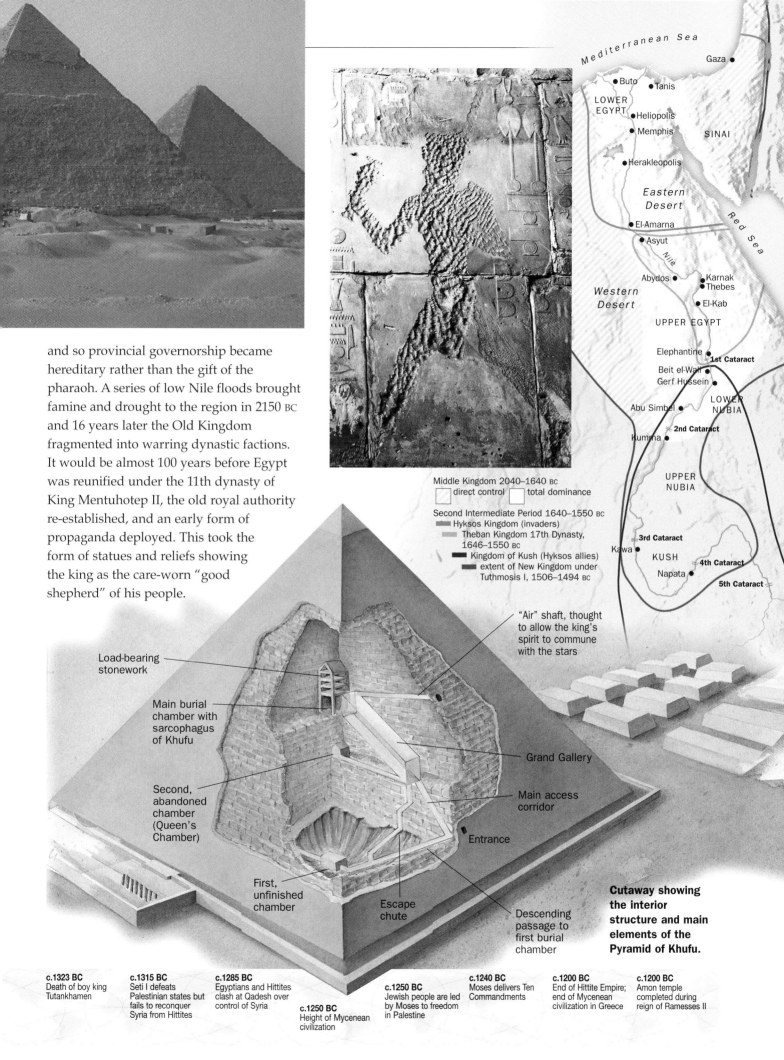

and so provincial governorship became hereditary rather than the gift of the pharaoh. A series of low Nile floods brought famine and drought to the region in 2150 BC and 16 years later the Old Kingdom fragmented into warring dynastic factions. It would be almost 100 years before Egypt was reunified under the 11th dynasty of King Mentuhotep II, the old royal authority re-established, and an early form of propaganda deployed. This took the form of statues and reliefs showing the king as the care-worn "good shepherd" of his people.

Mediterranean Sea

Gaza

Buto ● ● Tanis

LOWER EGYPT
● Heliopolis
● Memphis

SINAI

● Herakleopolis

Eastern Desert

Red Sea

● El-Amarna
● Asyut

Nile

Abydos ●
● Karnak
● Thebes

Western Desert

● El-Kab

UPPER EGYPT

Elephantine ●
1st Cataract

Beit el-Wali ●
Gerf Hussein ●

Abu Simbel ●
LOWER NUBIA

2nd Cataract
Kumma ●

UPPER NUBIA

3rd Cataract
Kawa ●
KUSH **4th Cataract**
Napata ●
5th Cataract

Middle Kingdom 2040–1640 BC
☐ direct control   ☐ total dominance

Second Intermediate Period 1640–1550 BC
▬ Hyksos Kingdom (invaders)
▬ Theban Kingdom 17th Dynasty, 1646–1550 BC
▬ Kingdom of Kush (Hyksos allies)
▬ extent of New Kingdom under Tuthmosis I, 1506–1494 BC

"Air" shaft, thought to allow the king's spirit to commune with the stars

Load-bearing stonework

Main burial chamber with sarcophagus of Khufu

Grand Gallery

Second, abandoned chamber (Queen's Chamber)

Main access corridor

Entrance

First, unfinished chamber

Escape chute

Descending passage to first burial chamber

Cutaway showing the interior structure and main elements of the Pyramid of Khufu.

c.1323 BC
Death of boy king Tutankhamen

c.1315 BC
Seti I defeats Palestinian states but fails to reconquer Syria from Hittites

c.1285 BC
Egyptians and Hittites clash at Qadesh over control of Syria

c.1250 BC
Height of Mycenean civilization

c.1250 BC
Jewish people are led by Moses to freedom in Palestine

c.1240 BC
Moses delivers Ten Commandments

c.1200 BC
End of Hittite Empire; end of Mycenean civilization in Greece

c.1200 BC
Amon temple completed during reign of Ramesses II

ABOVE: New Kingdom pharaohs preferred remoter sites to their predecessors. One such is the Valley of the Kings near Thebes. Even further south at Abu Simbel, Ramesses II built this tomb from the rock face.

FAR RIGHT: While digging foundations for a fort at el-Rashid (Rosetta) in 1799, Napoleon's soldiers discovered a stone carved with writing. The inscription of 196 BC is an affirmation of the royal cult of King Ptolemy V. The Stone's importance , however, lies in the fact that the inscription is repeated in three languages: hieroglyphics, demotic (a native script used in daily life), and Greek. As a result, Egyptologists were able for the first time to decipher the meaning of Egyptian hieroglyphic writing from the Greek.

New Kingdom, New Wars

Egypt in the early Middle Kingdom became a much more aggressive state. The empire needed to re-assert supremacy over its ambitious neighbors and under the reign of Amenemhet I (1991–1962 BC) Lower Nubia to the immediate south was conquered and garrisoned. Later Senwosret III pushed Egyptian influence into the Levant (eastern Mediterranean), forcing local rulers into line.

This expansionist policy had two key consequences. First, it produced a burgeoning democracy in which effective power passed from the pharaoh to his viziers. Second, it encouraged large-scale immigration from the Levant—particularly by the Hyksos. This Semitic people gradually took over Lower Egypt, establishing a capital at Avaris, while the "true" Egyptian court ruled Upper Egypt

Map:
Crete
Cyprus
Mediterranean Sea
Tyre
Jerusalem
Alexandria
Pelusium
Memphis
SINAI
Siwa
Sahara Desert
EGYPT
Red Sea
Thebes
Nile

☐ boundary of Alexander's empire in the region at 323 BC

▨ kingdom of Ptolemy

from Thebes. According to one contemporary record, *The Admonitions of Ipuwer*, Egypt became a chaotic and demoralized state in which "foreigners have become [native] people everywhere."

From around 1640 BC the Theban court became sandwiched between foreign settlers. To the north the Hyksos cemented their presence by embracing imported technology such as bronze, war chariots, composite bows, and scale armor. To the south the revitalized kingdom of Kush re-took Nubia. The Theban ruler Seqenenre II began a spirited fightback but it was not until 1532 BC and the reign of Ahmose I that the Hyksos were finally expelled and the New Kingdom was born. Now Egypt once again embraced an overtly militaristic role and the warrior-pharaoh Tuthmosis I began an unprecedented assault on neighboring states, conquering the entire Levant, establishing a frontier along the Euphrates river, re-taking Nubia, and controlling Kush beyond the Fourth Cataract of the Nile.

AKHENATEN'S HERESY

The empire's slow final slide into the abyss probably began with the rule of Amenhotep IV, the "heretic king" who later changed his name to Akhenaten. Akhenaten rejected the god Amon as Egypt's ruling deity and replaced him with the sun god Aten—

devoutly followed by his wife Queen Nefertiti. This caused outrage among the high priests based in the great Temple of Karnak, who later desecrated Akhenaten's temples and the artwork that graced the new capital he built in middle Egypt (now called el-Armana). Fortunately one of the true masterpieces of Egyptian sculpture, the painted limestone head of Nefertiti, survived this purge and was discovered by archaeologists early in the 20th century AD.

Akhenaten was succeeded by his son-in-law, Tutankhamen, in c.1343 BC. Little is known about this pharaoh's reign, though the discovery of his intact tomb stuffed with treasures has been of incalculable importance to Egyptologists. Tutankhamen's gold death-mask remains one of Egypt's most instantly recognizable ancient artifacts.

The last millennium of the empire was marked by gradual retrenchment. A war against the Hittite Empire (based in modern-day Turkey) dragged on for three generations until a peace deal was finally concluded under Ramesses II. There were increased incursions into the Nile delta by the Sea People—tribes from the Aegean, Turkey, and the Middle East—and by c.1180 BC the New Kingdom was at an end. Libyan power meanwhile had increased dramatically and the founder of the 22nd dynasty emerged as Shoshenq I, known as the Great Chief of the Meshwesh Libyans.

From 760 BC onward, what we think of as Egyptian culture disintegrated. The Kushite kingdom again grew powerful—actually subsuming the country for a time—the Persians invaded and occupied territory on two occasions, and in 332 BC Alexander the Great stamped his authority on the region. This Hellenistic period, ruled by the Greek Ptolemies, led to a climactic end of the empire in 31 BC with the Roman emperor Augustus's victory at Actium.

ETHNIC CLEANSING IN NUBIA

Self-sufficient farmers proud of their warrior tradition, the Nubians were a thorn in Egypt's side. They suffered appallingly whenever the pharaohs decided to flex some military muscle. One Egyptian minister of c.2000 BC, Antefoker, noted: "I slaughtered the Nubians on several occasions. I came north, uprooting the harvest and cutting the remainder of the trees and torching their houses..." He described his duty as "setting the fear of Horus (the God-king)" among the southern foreign lands to pacify (them)."

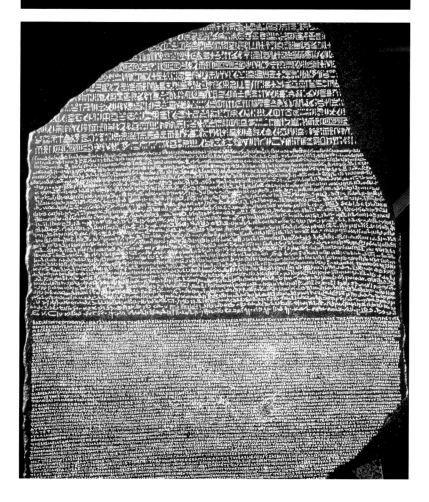

Assyria and the Age of Chaos

The vacuum caused by the collapse of the Mesopotamian Akkadian Empire in about 2200 BC remained unfilled for over 300 years; and then two competing empires clashed.

BELOW, FAR RIGHT: Late in the reign of Sargon II (721–705 BC), the Assyrian king built himself a new capital, which he called "the fortress of Sargon" (Dur-Sharrukin), known today as Khorsabad. This is one of a pair of colossal human-headed winged bulls that guarded an entrance to the magnificently sculptured palace at the heart of Dur-Sharrukin.

The end of the Akkadian Empire (SEE PAGES 14–15) heralded a chaotic and confusing period of Mesopotamian history. There were many reasons for the instability, not least that the region had few defensible borders. Kingdoms would rise or fall according to the strength of individual rulers and this "power lottery" was exacerbated by the arrival of new settlers such as Kassites and Amorites—groups eager to exploit the fertile plains.

The great city of Ur (in the extreme southwest of the old Akkadian Empire) re-emerged briefly as a significant power in 2112 BC. The first king of this city's third dynasty, Ur-Nammu, held sway throughout the old kingdoms of Akkad and Sumer, and commissioned the building of the first ziggurats—distinctive, high temple

platforms. Ur was sacked by the forces of Elam in 2004 and for two centuries the region's political structure dissolved into the familiar pattern of competing minor states and cities. It was from this uneasy and uncertain background that two great new empires emerged at roughly the same time— Assyria and Babylonia. Because of disputes surrounding the precise timescale of subsequent events, all dates have a margin of error of up to 120 years.

Over the next 12 centuries these two politically distinct regions would share laws, art styles, languages, and cultures. Yet there was much shuffling of rulers and a mutual suspicion that flared periodically into all-out war. The great cities of Assyria were concentrated in what is now northern Iraq— Ashur (now Sharqat), Nineveh (now an archaeological site called Kuyunjik), Calah (now Nimrud), and Dur Sharrukin (now Khorsabad). Babylonia centered on its capital city, Babylon (south of modern Baghdad)

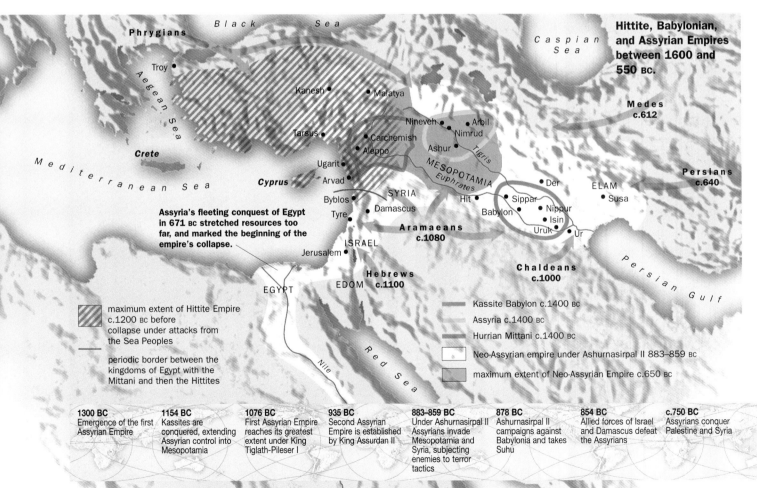

Hittite, Babylonian, and Assyrian Empires between 1600 and 550 BC.

Assyria's fleeting conquest of Egypt in 671 BC stretched resources too far, and marked the beginning of the empire's collapse.

maximum extent of Hittite Empire c.1200 BC before collapse under attacks from the Sea Peoples

periodic border between the kingdoms of Egypt with the Mittani and then the Hittites

Kassite Babylon c.1400 BC

Assyria c.1400 BC

Hurrian Mittani c.1400 BC

Neo-Assyrian empire under Ashurnasirpal II 883–859 BC

maximum extent of Neo-Assyrian Empire c.650 BC

1300 BC	1154 BC	1076 BC	935 BC	883–859 BC	878 BC	854 BC	c.750 BC
Emergence of the first Assyrian Empire	Kassites are conquered, extending Assyrian control into Mesopotamia	First Assyrian Empire reaches its greatest extent under King Tiglath-Pileser I	Second Assyrian Empire is established by King Assurdan II	Under Ashurnasirpal II Assyrians invade Mesopotamia and Syria, subjecting enemies to terror tactics	Ashurnasirpal II campaigns against Babylonia and takes Suhu	Allied forces of Israel and Damascus defeat the Assyrians	Assyrians conquer Palestine and Syria

and included important cities such as Isin, Larsa, and Eshnunna (now Tell Asmar).

For chronological and ethnic reasons, experts on Assyria like to distinguish between Old and Neo (new) Babylonia. Old Babylonia is generally considered to begin with the rule of Hammurabi in 1787 BC and end in 1595 BC with the sacking of Babylon by the Hittites, a people originally from northern Greece. Under Hammurabi the kingdom was at its zenith. Here was an unusually gifted administrator, a ruler who was sufficiently organized to order the

between 1813 and 1781 BC. His Amorite dynasty stepped into a power vacuum left by the collapse of Akkad and took control of a region stretching from the Zagros Mountains to the Eastern Mediterranean. Shamshi-Adad imposed all the trappings of a centrally organized empire, including regional governors and local councils, but this structure fell to Hammurabi's Babylonia within 20 years of his death.

For the next 350 years Assyria was drawn under the influence first of the Hurrians, expanding their territory from the north, and

Carved in limestone in about 875 BC, this relief from the Palace of Nimrud shows a battle scene. Soldiers armed with bows and arrows oppose each other across a river or a moat. Three more soldiers can be seen swimming across, two holding onto inflated animal bladders for extra buoyancy.

clearing of irrigation canals and the insertion of an additional month into the calendar to make it more effective. His greatest legacy was the CODE OF HAMMURABI, one of the most important ancient legal documents known.

A DISPUTED KINGDOM

Neo-Babylon began much later, around 612 BC, and lasted for barely 85 years, following the final demise of the Assyrian Empire. In between the Old and the Neo- sits a great slab of Middle Eastern history in which Babylon was controlled at various times by Hittites, Kassites (a non-Semitic people), Elamites, and Assyrians.

The Assyrian Empire itself was effectively founded by Shamshi-Adad I, who reigned

later their offshoot—the Mittani. The region did not regain independence until around 1400 BC, expanding under Tukulti-Ninurta I, who briefly forged a revitalized Assyria. However he was murdered by aggrieved noblemen and after yet another wave of inward migration, driven in part by the retracting Hittite and Egyptian empires, Assyria was once more plunged into chaos. It was not until the revival of the monarchy in 934 BC, and the ascendancy of a particularly ruthless and bloodthirsty ruler in 883 BC, that Assyria would expand to control the entire Middle East. This ruler was the Emperor Ashurnasirpal II.

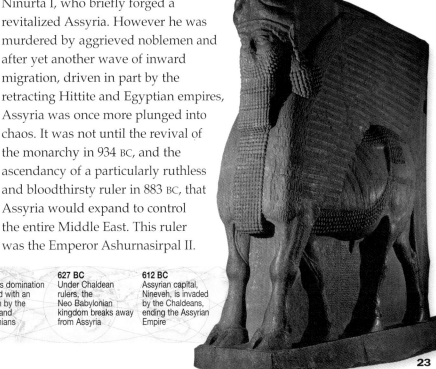

724-722 BC
Israel revolts against the Assyrians

689 BC
Assyrians reconquer rebel provinces of Palestine, Syria, and Babylonia

663 BC
Assyrians sack Thebes to end Egyptian revolt

616 BC
Assyria's domination is ended with an invasion by the Medes and Babylonians

627 BC
Under Chaldean rulers, the Neo Babylonian kingdom breaks away from Assyria

612 BC
Assyrian capital, Nineveh, is invaded by the Chaldeans, ending the Assyrian Empire

Feasting and flaying

When Ashurnasirpal II (883–859 BC) became king, he inherited an Assyrian Empire that had recovered much of its former glory. It dominated northern Mesopotamia and received tribute from minor states as far away as Tyre, on the eastern Mediterranean coast. Yet the threat of rebellion was ever-present and Ashurnasirpal rose to the challenge with relish. A brilliant military commander and tactician he spent the first six years of his reign confronting enemies

FLAYED ALIVE

Ashurnasirpal records in unflinching detail the punishments meted out after he re-took the rebel city of Suru, Bit-Halupe. "Azi-ilu I set over them as my own governor," he notes. "I built a pillar against his city gate and I flayed all the chief men who had revolted and I covered the pillar with their skins: some I walled up within the pillar, some I impaled upon the pillar on stakes and others I bound to stakes around about the pillar: many within the border of my own land I flayed and I spread their skins upon the walls and I cut off the limbs of the officers, of the royal officers who had rebelled. Ahiababa (the rebel leader) I took to Nineveh. I flayed him. I spread his skin upon the wall of Nineveh."

and subjecting their leaders to appallingly cruel and unusual executions.

Ashurnasirpal seems to have taken great pride in his reputation as a monster. In the inscriptions recovered from his ruined palace at Calah—the main source of our knowledge about him—he speaks with total frankness of the atrocities he inflicted. These annals tell how early in his reign he publicly flayed the rebel governor of Nishtun, Arbela (near Irbil in Iraq) and brutally suppressed Aramaean uprisings in their mountain stronghold northeast of modern-day Lebanon. He terrorized the land of Nairi (Armenia) and later stormed through the west of his empire to the Mediterranean, extracting tribute from major cities, including some Phoenician strongholds. By the 870s BC he was undisputed master of what is now called the Neo-Assyrian Empire.

Among his more dreadful acts of revenge were the punishments inflicted on leading rebels from the city of Suru (SEE BOX), led by Ahiababa "the son of a nobody." Yet Ashurnasirpal was also at pains to record his generosity and hospitality—character traits he regarded as equally important evidence of his greatness. After completion of his grand new palace at Calah—built with the slave labor of his captives—he threw a grand banquet to celebrate his move from the traditional Assyrian capital Nineveh. Ashurnasirpal sacrificed 200 cattle and 1,000 sheep to his goddess Ishtar, and then served up astonishing quantities of food including 15,000 lambs, 500 geese, 500 gazelles, 10,000 doves, 10,000 fish, 10,000 eggs, 10,000 [containers of] beer, 10,000 skins of wine, and 1,000 crates of vegetables.

WEAKNESS IN LUST FOR POWER

If this suggests he over-catered, the guest list reveals otherwise. According to the Calah inscriptions, 69,574 guests were present at the ten day feast—among them delegates from all the Assyrian vassal states and cities, 1,500 palace officials, and thousands of ordinary men, women, and children. "I provided them with the means to clean and anoint themselves," says Ashurnasirpal proudly. "I did them due honors and sent them back, healthy and happy, to their own countries."

It was under the eighth century BC kings Tiglath-pileser III, and later Sargon II, however, that the new Assyria reached its zenith. The empire was divided into provinces, nominal independence of vassal states was abolished, and administrators were appointed (subject to regular royal inspections). Central power was bolstered by improved communications—such as a postal system—and the axing of all hereditary positions.

As is usually the way with empires, Assyria's downfall lay in the lust of its rulers for more influence. The fleeting conquest of Egypt in 671 BC stretched resources too far and by 609 BC Assyria had fallen—this time to a resurgent Babylonia under Nabopolassar and his successor Nebuchadnezzar.

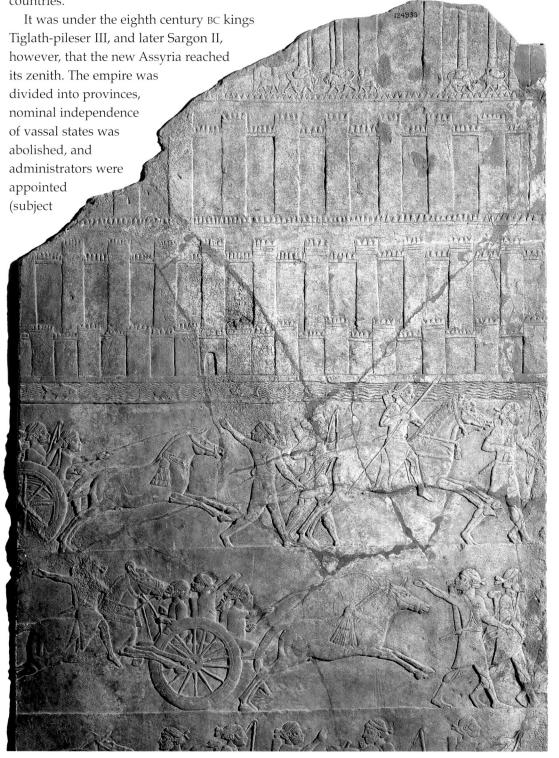

Some 200 years after Ashurnasirpal II, Ashurbanipal was the Assyrian king (668–626 BC). He was known to the Old Testament as the "great and honorable Ashurbanipal" [EZRA 4:10]. Soldier, hunter, and scholar, he was known to the Greeks as Sardanapalus, and his capital was the city of Nineveh. This Stone panel (c.645 BC) is from the king's palace. The top half of the panel depicts a city, which is thought to be Nineveh, last capital city of the Assyrian Empire. Colossal human-headed winged bulls decorate the building behind the massive triple walls. The soldiers shown are possibly Elamites. Usually, Elam and Assyria were enemies, but in this case the panel appears to show a scene in which Assyrian soldiers are accompanying a band of Elamites. Since the tribes of Elam frequently warred with each other, it is likely that in this case the Assyrians are acting as supporters of one faction to "liberate" another.

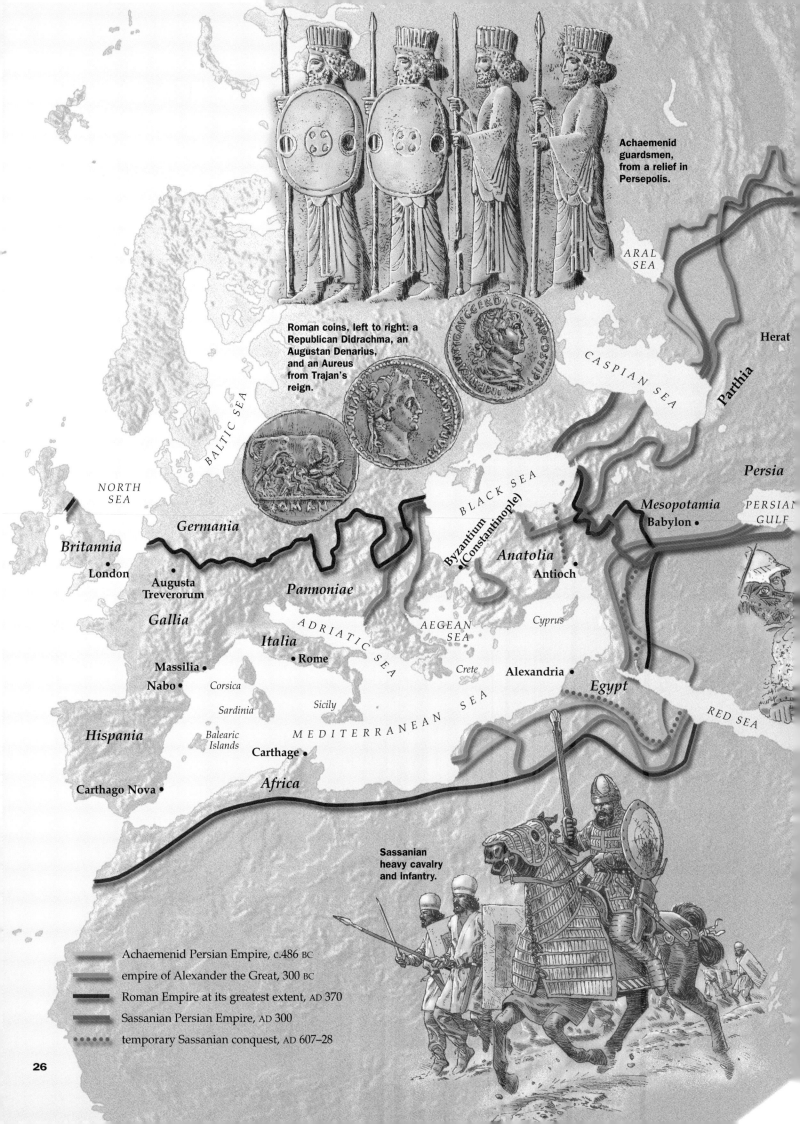

Achaemenid guardsmen, from a relief in Persepolis.

Roman coins, left to right: a Republican Didrachma, an Augustan Denarius, and an Aureus from Trajan's reign.

ARAL SEA

Herat

CASPIAN SEA

Parthia

BALTIC SEA

NORTH SEA

Germania

Britannia

London

Augusta Treverorum

Gallia

BLACK SEA

Byzantium (Constantinople)

Anatolia

Antioch

Persia

Mesopotamia

Babylon

PERSIAN GULF

Pannoniae

ADRIATIC SEA

AEGEAN SEA

Cyprus

Italia

Rome

Massilia

Nabo

Corsica

Sardinia

Sicily

Crete

Alexandria

Egypt

RED SEA

Hispania

Balearic Islands

Carthage

MEDITERRANEAN SEA

Carthago Nova

Africa

Sassanian heavy cavalry and infantry.

Achaemenid Persian Empire, c.486 BC

empire of Alexander the Great, 300 BC

Roman Empire at its greatest extent, AD 370

Sassanian Persian Empire, AD 300

temporary Sassanian conquest, AD 607–28

Ancient Rivals

Alexander the Great at the battle of Issus.

For most people if they are asked to think of an empire the first to spring to mind is Rome. The Roman Empire is remembered for having the world's best armies, the most impressive culture, and the most enduring architecture, the remains of which still litter the European continent today. Yet other mighty empires co-existed with Rome, spreading their cultures and ideas and ultimately benefiting the whole of humanity through their advancement of civilization.

The Persian Achaemenid dynasty was such an empire, coming onto the stage of history while Rome was still in its infancy. Under the leadership of Darius I, the Achaemenid Persians built the great city of Persepolis, the finest city of its time, and created an empire that stretched from the Indus River in modern-day Pakistan to Egypt and Greece. In the 1830s a British army officer, Henry Rawlinson, translated the strange symbols on the Behistun Rock in modern-day Iran. The script took years to decipher but became the foundation for knowledge about the Achaemenid dynasty. The glories of Persepolis, burned down by Alexander the Great in 330 BC, became apparent through excavations undertaken in the 1920s.

The destruction of Persepolis by Alexander's forces ended Persian dominance of this huge region, and replaced it with Greek hegemony. The creation of Alexander the Great's empire was a true turning point in history, when a small army of Greeks put an end to the dominance of Middle Eastern cultures and—as they saw it—the tyranny of the Persians, although it was replaced with a tyranny of their own making. Alexander's empire soon disintegrated, but his achievement was nevertheless profound and Greek culture was spread across the Middle East and Asia as a consequence of his few years of conquest. Alexandria, the city he founded in Egypt, was to become the ancient world's seat of learning and culture.

THE GREATEST EMPIRE

Soon, Rome eclipsed Ancient Greece, and Europe was dominated by the largest and greatest of the ancient empires. Under the Romans, the Celtic tribes were civilized and a Latin culture came to encompass most of Europe. Rome gave its empire a common language, a common currency, and a common code of civil law. In the empire's final centuries, the new faith of Christianity spread throughout its territories and the foundations of modern Europe were created.

In the third century AD the Persian Sassanian Empire—successors to the Achaemenids—under the leadership of Shapur I, harassed the Romans and even took the emperor Valerian prisoner in battle. This rivalry was ultimately in vain, however. Both the Roman and Persian empires were living on borrowed time. Barbarians gathered at Rome's northern and eastern borders, soon to overrun the empire; Sassanid Persia faced the Arab armies of Islam, as a new age dawned.

Kabul

Achaemenid Persia

A new dynasty arose in Mesopotamia after 550 BC named after an obscure earlier ruler, but history knows the dynasty better by the Greek name: Persais, or Persians.

FAR RIGHT: After his amalgamation of the Medes and Persians, Cyrus the Great moved west, defeating the Lydians and their king, Croesius, in 547 BC. The Lydians had a tradition of minting coins, and the Persians adopted the system. The gold daric, named after Darius I, and the silver siglos (shekel) were the main coins. This gold daric bears the figure of an archer, representing the king, on the front. The reverse consists of a rectangular punch mark.

Persia under the Achaemenids became known for its remarkable traits of religious tolerance, fair taxes, clear lines of communication, and local representation, and these characteristics kept the regime stable for nearly two centuries. The Persians borrowed some notions from the Assyrians, refined them, and lent them in turn to the Romans, who would ultimately inherit the mantle of empire in the region.

From about 550 BC the Achaemenid dynasty ruled the land of Persia and made numerous conquests until it crumbled before the might of Alexander the Great in 330 BC. It was named for Achaemenes, also known as Hakhamanish, an obscure ruler of a minor region. But the founder of the empire was in fact one of his descendants, Cyrus the Great.

Although knowledge about his brief life is limited, it is known that Cyrus (r.559–530 BC) brought the Medes, the Lydians ruled by the fabulously rich King Croesus, and the

Babylonians into the Persian fold. It was the enlightened Cyrus who wisely set the tone for liberal thinking, permitting other religions beside his favored one, Zoroastrianism. He is particularly noted for his support in the reconstruction of the Jewish State and for this he receives favorable comment in the Old Testament. In the absence of overt oppression the desire among the subjugated nations to rebel was largely muted. One surviving inscription allegedly made on behalf of Cyrus proclaims: "I am Cyrus, King of the world, the great and just king… my countless soldiers roamed Babylon in peace and sincerity, I forbade harassment and terror all over Sumer and Akkad. I strove for peace in Babylon and in all other cities… I tried to preserve their habitat…" Cyrus's tomb is located at Parsagadae, where he built his royal palace, which can still be seen today.

His son and successor was Cambyses who added Egypt to the empire but died during a dispute among his relatives, leaving the throne open to an imposter. A nephew of Cyrus intervened to re-establish the

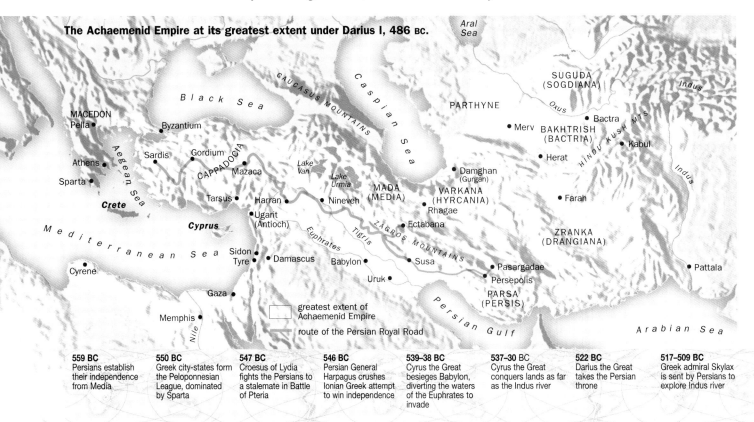

The Achaemenid Empire at its greatest extent under Darius I, 486 BC.

559 BC	550 BC	547 BC	546 BC	539–38 BC	537–30 BC	522 BC	517–509 BC
Persians establish their independence from Media	Greek city-states form the Peloponnesian League, dominated by Sparta	Croesus of Lydia fights the Persians to a stalemate in Battle of Pteria	Persian General Harpagus crushes Ionian Greek attempt to win independence	Cyrus the Great besieges Babylon, diverting the waters of the Euphrates to invade	Cyrus the Great conquers lands as far as the Indus river	Darius the Great takes the Persian throne	Greek admiral Skylax is sent by Persians to explore Indus river

Achaemenid claim to the crown. Darius I (r.521–486 BC) finally suppressed the civil unrest that threatened the empire and imposed a new order in which his organizational skills came to the fore.

AN EFFICIENT INFRASTRUCTURE

Each nation that the Persians overwhelmed was appointed its own satrap (royal governor). To insure against the satrap's possible disloyalty, an army general, who answered directly to the king, was stationed alongside the satrap. In addition, a system of observers—or spies—monitored events in the furthest reaches of the empire on the king's behalf. A sophisticated system of roads was a key to the empire's success because these allowed for the relatively swift communication of news as well as the movement of troops.

There was even a postal service, which took advantage of the road network—although mail was subject to imperial censorship. Darius sponsored a judiciary, a uniform weights and measures system, and also a sound monetary system, including a standard coin. A canal was also constructed to link the River Nile with the Red Sea;

a forerunner of the Suez Canal.

Further additions were made to the empire in the north and east during Darius's reign. And yet, despite his astonishing achievements, Darius is better remembered by history for his inability to quell the Greeks. The Greek city-states were constantly bickering among themselves and appeared to be easy pickings for Achaemenid ambitions. However, repeated attempts failed to bring them to heel. Most memorably Darius's numerically superior forces were soundly beaten at Marathon in 490 BC, from where the Greek runner Pheidippides raced to Athens to bring news of the battle and request support.

LEFT: The tomb of Cyrus the Great at Pasargade, Iran, is a surprisingly modest and unadorned monument to the founder of the Achaemenid dynasty.

513 BC	511 BC	c.500 BC	491 BC	480 BC	479 BC	470 BC	466 BC
Persian forces cross the Hellespont between Asia Minor and Europe	Darius the Great invades southeastern Europe, including Thrace and Macedonia	Persians develop composite bows, sturdier than wooden ones	A Persian fleet heading for Greece is destroyed in a storm, saving Greece from invasion	Persians invade and sack Athens, although most of the Athenian population had already been evacuated	Athens builds city walls, preserving peace for two decades	Spartan general Pausanias charged for treason for communicating with Persian king; walled into a temple to die	Cimon of Athens defeats Persian army in Anatolia, ending Greco-Persian conflict in the Aegean

RIGHT: The doorway to
the Hall of Columns in the
palace of Darius I at
Persepolis. The relief,
harking back to earlier
Akkadian times, depicts
King Sargon I (see pages
12–15) with an attending
servant.

FAR RIGHT: Detail of a
bas-relief from the Palace
at Persepolis. Doubt
remains as to whether this
portrays Darius I or his
son Xerxes seated on the
throne receiving an
embassy of Medes. Darius's
legacy to the Persians was
the formation of a vast,
well-equipped, and highly
trained army.

BELOW: The ruins of
Persepolis.

Sibling Rivalry

Darius I made his capital at Susa, then began
construction of a new city at Persepolis.
Here he had built an impressive palace in
which he could relax, or receive guests in
considerable style. At the city's center a
mighty stone terrace, accessed by sweeping
staircases, formed a platform on which stood
the civic and religious complexes, often on
their own taller platforms. As a result,
Persepolis boasted considerable height for
the period and for the fact that the site was
not built on a large hill for effect.

When the all-conquering Alexander took
Persepolis some 150 years later, the victor
enjoyed one night of celebrations in the city
before torching it. This uncharacteristically
drastic action was probably revenge for the
burning of Athens by the Persians some five
generations previously. The ruins were
battered by the elements and partly
swallowed by shifting sands. Only when
archaeologists got to work in the 1920s did
the extent of the city become apparent. Some
of its riches were also revealed, including
fine sculptures and gold artifacts.

Another fascinating legacy bequeathed by
Darius is the inscription he left on the great
rock of Behistun in western Persia. The text
is cut into rock some 400 feet above the
ground, measuring 150 by 100 feet, in three
languages—Old Persian, Elamite, and
Babylonian. It proved to be a
"Mesopotamian Rosetta stone," giving
archaeologists an insight into these three
mysterious cuneiform scripts.

On his death in 486 BC, Darius was
succeeded by his son Xerxes. Darius's tomb
is close to his city, carved into a sheer rock
face and made to look like a palace.

ENEMIES WITHOUT, STRIFE WITHIN

Like his father, Xerxes had little early success
in incorporating the Greeks into the
Achaemenid Empire. Eventually, victory
seemed assured when he assembled in

his brother for the throne. The two sides met at Cunaxa, near Babylon. Cyrus lost and was killed. Xenophon, an Athenian officer, recorded the details of the grueling march over the Armenian Mountains endured by the surviving Greek mercenaries, many of whom lost their sight to snow blindness and their toes to frostbite. The resulting book, *Anabasis* (Journey Upward) became a classic Greek text.

A perceived weakness in the leadership sparked a series of revolts around the empire, including in Egypt. By the time Artaxerxes III took power, the wisdom displayed by empire-founder Cyrus the Great had been consigned to history and callous cruelty coupled with savage ambition was rife.

Greece an army of some 200,000 supported by a fleet of 1,000 ships. Indeed, the soldiers crossed from Asia into Europe at the Hellespont (the Dardanelles) across a bridge supported on a row of boats. However, on the other side the Persians met a Greek army that was well-trained, disciplined, and desperate to defend its homeland. Ironically, the very size of the Persian army proved a handicap. It was unable to obtain sufficient supplies, or move its troops rapidly enough in battle. The combined Greek forces won a decisive victory after Xerxes returned home with half of his army.

Artaxerxes succeeded his father. Little distinguished historically, he did, however, die from natural causes—a rarity in such violent times. Coming to the throne through the murder of his brothers, Artaxerxes' son Darius II fared no better than his father. He married an aunt, Parysatis, whose penchant for poisoning people and having those who displeased her skinned alive earned her a fearsome reputation and hardly improved the king's image.

The theme of brother against brother returned to haunt the Achaemenids with the death of Darius II. His eldest son became Artaxerxes II, but disgruntled Prince Cyrus, Satrap of Sardis, raised an army of Greek mercenaries and challenged

Alexander the Great

The most enigmatic general of the ancient world was also the most successful. At the end of his short life, Alexander of Macedon bestrode the known world from west to east.

RIGHT: Since the Greeks held Macedonians in some contempt as being unsophisticated northern barbarians, Philip II determined that his son should be exposed to the best in Greek thinking. His chosen tutor was the Athenian mathematician, poet, and philosopher Aristotle, who set up an academy in Macedonia for Alexander and his companions.

The empire forged by Alexander the Great was fleeting, but its spontaneity and dynamism swept away the old order— from Greece to India—in a grueling march of conquest and cruelty. Alexander's empire was founded entirely through military initiative and was the result of sheer brilliance by Alexander—small in stature but highly charismatic—who remains one of history's most fascinating characters.

Alexander (356–323 BC) was the son of the ambitious Macedonian king Philip II and his wife Olympias, who was deeply immersed in the occult. Macedonia was something of an outpost among the Greek states, generally considered less cultured and civilized than its neighbors. However, in common with other Greek states, Macedonia had long suffered incursions from nearby Persia in its bid to increase its sphere of influence.

Philip (r.359–336 BC) used his skills as a diplomat to forge alliances with the more compliant Hellenic states. Those who resisted his overtures found themselves subject to invasion. By 337 BC he had formed a confederacy with himself as protector and was casting greedy eyes toward Persia, knowing that the united Greek states were at last a match for Achaemenid forces. However, Philip was assassinated before he could put his grand plan into action. Alexander took the reins of power and embraced his father's goals. At 20 years old, he had already benefited greatly from tuition by Aristotle in areas including philosophy, physics, and poetry. Furthermore, he inherited his father's tactical genius and instantly proved his mettle by ruthlessly quashing unrest in Thebes. His army destroyed everything in the city except the temples and the home of the poet Pindar. His mother's wholehearted belief in mystical powers proved fundamental. Only after a priestess at the Oracle in Delphi assured Alexander that he was invincible did he proceed with his invasion.

STARK REVENGE

By 334 BC Alexander had amassed an army of 35,000 and crossed the Hellespont (Dardanelles) in the opposite direction to that of Xerxes almost 150 years earlier. The first confrontation with the Persians took place near Troy. Despite ranks of hoplites— Greek mercenaries—fighting alongside the Persians the victory went to Alexander. Legend has it that he lost just 110 men.

En route to Issus, scene of the next battle, Alexander visited the Gordian (Gordium) Knot in Phrygia. According to mythology the knot had been intricately tied by the

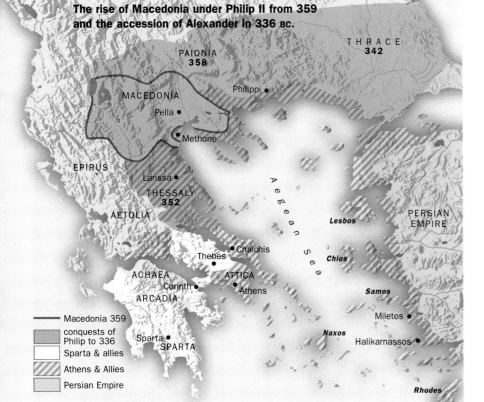

The rise of Macedonia under Philip II from 359 and the accession of Alexander in 336 BC.

THRACE 342
PAIONIA 358
MACEDONIA
Pella
Philippi
Methone
EPIRUS
Larissa
THESSALY 352
AETOLIA
Lesbos
PERSIAN EMPIRE
Aegean Sea
Chalchis
Thebes
Chios
ACHAEA
ATTICA
Corinth
Athens
ARCADIA
Samos
Miletos
Naxos
Sparta
SPARTA
Halikarnassos
Rhodes

— Macedonia 359
conquests of Philip to 336
Sparta & allies
Athens & Allies
Persian Empire

356 BC	340–339 BC	338 BC	336 BC	335 BC	334 BC	333 BC	332 BC
Alexander born at Pella, son of King Philip of Macedonia	Acting as regent, Alexander defeats the Thracians and Illyrians	Leads Macedonian cavalry against the Athenians at Battle of Chaeronea	At the age of 20, he succeeds his father, Philip	Campaigns in Thrace and on the Danube; destroys rebellious Thebes	Across Hellespont into Asia. Wounded that year at Battle of Granicus. Takes Miletus, Halicarnassus	Fights king Darius III of Persia at Battle of Issus, where he is again wounded	Takes Tyre and Gaza. Reinforced in Eygpt and Syria by troops from Greece

father of Midas. Whoever undid it was destined to rule all Asia. Unable to pick the knot open, Alexander drew his sword and sliced through it.

For the second battle, King Darius III commanded the Persians at Issus, and once again the Achaemenid force was numerically the superior. However, the Persian king's leadership lacked his rival's innovation and inspiration, for Alexander was the convincing victor. Alexander now turned south toward Egypt, and conquered Tyre and Gaza along the way. Grateful for freedom from the Achaemenids, the Egyptians welcomed him as a liberator. He was crowned pharaoh and founded the city of Alexandria, which would one day be home to Cleopatra and serve as the cultural capital of the ancient world.

Despite the adulation accorded him, Alexander had unfinished business. He forged back up the Mediterranean coast for a final conflict with Darius at Guagamela, which occurred on October 1, 331 BC. For the third time, Alexander was triumphant; Darius fled in disgrace and was later murdered by his own generals.

The mighty Persian Empire was arrayed before Alexander. Centuries of Persian abuse of the Greeks had been avenged. He went to Babylon and the capital Susa before plundering and burning Persepolis. Then the Greek host, with many new allies, swung north and then east. Alexander determined to battle his way through the inhospitable Hindu Kush Mountains, the Khyber Pass, to the Indus river… and beyond.

Most busts of Alexander were made after his death. This one was found in Alexandria and probably dates from the 2nd–1st centuries BC. Alexander is always shown clean-shaven in his images, which was an innovation; the previous royal fashion had been for beards. Alexander's trend-setting would last well into the Roman imperium.

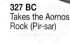

331 BC
Battle of Guagamela. Enters Babylon and then takes Susa

330 BC
Storms Persian Gates, enters Persepolis and pursues Darius. Campaigns south of the Caspian Sea.

329 BC
Operations near Samarkand and in Afghanistan.

328 BC
Campaigns in Bactria and Sogdiana (Russian Turkestan); marries Roxanne.

327 BC
Takes the Aornos Rock (Pir-sar)

326 BC
Invades India. Defeats King Porus at Battle of the Hydaspes. Puts down troop mutiny at the river Hyphasis.

325 BC
Sails down Indus, crosses Makran Desert, meets fleet near Hormuz

324 BC
During that summer he stops the mutiny of the Macedonian veterans at Opis.

Death of a God

After reaching the borders of India, Alexander was keen to push on still further into uncharted territory, but the mutinous reluctance of his battle-worn troops forced him to undertake the awesome return to Macedonia. Alexander divided his army into three groups: the sick and wounded would march overland directly to Persia; the fit were to march with him along the uncharted desert shore of the Arabian Sea through what is now southern Pakistan and Iran; and the third group would hastily construct ships and sail along the same coast, as a form of naval support. Those making the desert trip with Alexander faced hideous deprivation in harsh conditions, and there were numerous deaths. Yet the final rewards of the 25,000-mile trek were monumental.

From Greece in the west to the Indus valley in the east, and from Bactra in the north to Thebes in the south, the boundaries of Alexander's empire took in all the former Persian territories and more besides. Although Alexander had been reckless, he nevertheless succeeded through sheer daring and military skill. After the Persian army's elimination there was no organized resistance since the peoples on the Persian periphery were tribal and unorganized. Only when he reached India did Alexander face real opposition, and this must have contributed to his soldiers' refusal to go further.

Alexander was deeply committed to fusing Persian culture with that of Greece. In one direction he encouraged his generals to take Persian wives and adopt some local customs. In the other Greek attitudes and language was superimposed on the conquered. At least 17 new cities were founded, all bearing the name of Alexandria, some of which still exist today.

PERSONALITY CULT

Increasingly Alexander became convinced of his own infallibility. His mother had told him that he had been sired by a god in the form of a snake. He earned the enmity of fellow Macedonians shortly before his death when he ordered that he was to be worshipped as a god. His men had been loyal and were inspired by his extravagant gestures; in the Persian deserts he had spilled the last of his own fresh water into the sand when his troops were thirsty, to show solidarity with them. But they grew wary of his alcohol-fueled binges, during which he was capable of great cruelty. He was drunk when he killed one of his childhood friends, a man who had once saved his life. Only the swift actions of his generals prevented Alexander from taking his own life in remorse when he realized what he had done.

Historians have speculated that Alexander was homosexual. Although he married and fathered a son, the close friendships he made with fellow fighters may have been more than comradely. His best friend Hephaestion is on record as saying: "Alexander means more to me than anyone." There is no absolute clarification about his sexuality, however.

Documentary maker Michael Wood followed the path taken by Alexander,

A silver tetradrachm of Alexander the Great. When Crenides came under Macedonian sway after 359 BC, Philip II took control of one of Europe's richest gold mines. Crenides was renamed Philippi, and went on to produce so much gold that Philip was able to produce enough coins that they became one of the staple currencies of all Europe. At first, Alexander continued minting his father's coins, but the need for a wider silver currency led to this coin. With the head of Herkles on one side and a seated Zeus (above) on the other, it was in widespread use throughout the empire.

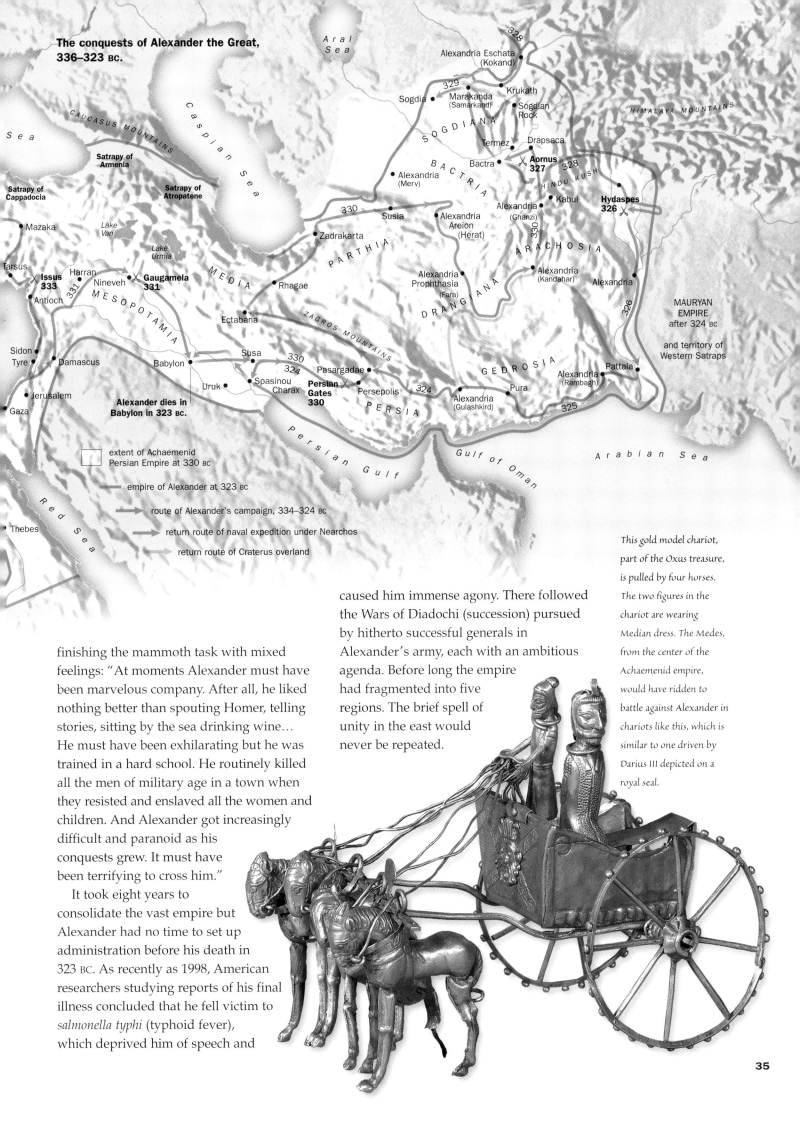

The conquests of Alexander the Great, 336–323 BC.

Aral Sea

Alexandria Eschata (Kokand)
328
329
Sogdia
Marakanda (Samarkand)
Krukath
Sogdian Rock
SOGDIANA
Termez
Drapsaca
BACTRIA
Bactra
Aornus 327
328
HIMALAYA MOUNTAINS

Caspian Sea

CAUCASUS MOUNTAINS
Sea

Satrapy of Armenia

Satrapy of Cappadocia

Satrapy of Atropatene

Alexandria (Merv)
330
Susia
Zadrakarta
PARTHIA

Alexandria Areion (Herat)

HINDU KUSH
Alexandria (Ghanzi)
Kabul
330
Hydaspes 326

ARACHOSIA

Mazaka
Lake Van
Lake Urmia
MEDIA

Tarsus
Issus 333
Harran
Ninveh
331
Gaugamela 331
Antioch
MESOPOTAMIA
Rhagae
Ectabana
ZAGROS MOUNTAINS

Alexandria Prophthasia (Fara)
DRANGIANA
Alexandria (Kandahar)
Alexandria
326
MAURYAN EMPIRE after 324 BC

and territory of Western Satraps

Sidon
Tyre
Damascus
Babylon
Susa
330
324
Pasargadae
Uruk
Spasinou Charax
Persian Gates 330
Persepolis
324
PERSIA
GEDROSIA
Pura
Alexandria (Gulashkird)
Alexandria (Rambagh)
325
Pattala

Jerusalem
Gaza
Alexander dies in Babylon in 323 BC.

Persian Gulf
Gulf of Oman
Arabian Sea

extent of Achaemenid Persian Empire at 330 BC

empire of Alexander at 323 BC

route of Alexander's campaign, 334–324 BC

return route of naval expedition under Nearchos

return route of Craterus overland

Red Sea

Thebes

finishing the mammoth task with mixed feelings: "At moments Alexander must have been marvelous company. After all, he liked nothing better than spouting Homer, telling stories, sitting by the sea drinking wine… He must have been exhilarating but he was trained in a hard school. He routinely killed all the men of military age in a town when they resisted and enslaved all the women and children. And Alexander got increasingly difficult and paranoid as his conquests grew. It must have been terrifying to cross him."

It took eight years to consolidate the vast empire but Alexander had no time to set up administration before his death in 323 BC. As recently as 1998, American researchers studying reports of his final illness concluded that he fell victim to *salmonella typhi* (typhoid fever), which deprived him of speech and

caused him immense agony. There followed the Wars of Diadochi (succession) pursued by hitherto successful generals in Alexander's army, each with an ambitious agenda. Before long the empire had fragmented into five regions. The brief spell of unity in the east would never be repeated.

This gold model chariot, part of the Oxus treasure, is pulled by four horses. The two figures in the chariot are wearing Median dress. The Medes, from the center of the Achaemenid empire, would have ridden to battle against Alexander in chariots like this, which is similar to one driven by Darius III depicted on a royal seal.

CHAPTER TWO

SPQR—Rome

Over the course of a thousand years the village, and then city, of Rome extended its influence over the entire known western world. The language Romans spoke—Latin—still influences our world today.

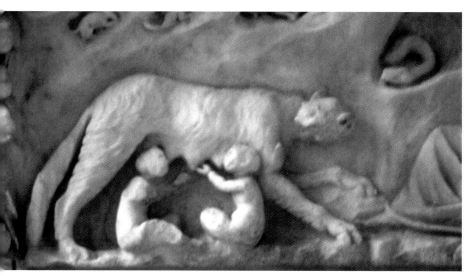

ABOVE: Rome celebrated its humble origins through the myth of Romulus and Remus, the abandoned twins suckled by a she-wolf. Through numerous early political struggles, Romans eventually arrived at a quasi-democratic republic centered on the Forum Romanum (FACING, TOP RIGHT), under the legend SPQR— Senatus Populus Que Romanus (The Senate and the People of Rome).

RIGHT: As the republic matured toward empire, it was Roman engineering that lubricated expansion, particularly in building roads. This is a reconstructed portion of the Via Appia, near Rome.

According to legend, Rome was founded in 753 BC by Romulus and Remus, twins who had been cast adrift on the River Tiber by a jealous uncle—to be rescued and suckled by a she-wolf and finally adopted by a shepherd. Recent findings by archaeologists unsurprisingly dash this romantic theory. Four graves discovered beneath the famous Roman Forum have been dated to the tenth century BC, and appear to be those of villagers from the small settlement that would later become Rome.

The truth of the actual founding has been lost in the mists of time. However, we do know that Rome—for some six centuries the capital of the civilized world and the benchmark of empires—had humble beginnings and its star was slow to ascend.

For some time Rome was a tiny community in the shadow of its more sophisticated Etruscan neighbors. Built upon seven hills next to the River Tiber, Rome had plenty of geographical advantages, as the historian Livy (59 BC–AD 17) pointed out: "Not without good reason did gods and

men select this place for founding a city; these most healthful hills; a commodious river, by means of which the produce of the soil may be conveyed from the inland countries, by which maritime supplies may be obtained; close enough to the sea for all purposes for convenience and not exposed by too much proximity to the dangers of foreign fleets."

Following a scandal, the Etruscan kings who had held power in Rome were ejected in about 510 BC. Royal rule gave way to the admirable Roman republic. If equality and justice were not always achieved, there was at least general recognition of their importance. Given the domestic strength offered by the government, its rulers—limited in power and length of tenure—cast acquisitive eyes abroad to increase Roman territories and, accordingly, Republican wealth.

BARBARIAN CELTS THREATEN

Romans soon learned a painful lesson when marauding Celts sacked the city in 390 BC and exacted tribute. After finally beating off the invaders the government appreciated the

c.700 BC	c.600 BC	c.540 BC	509 BC	509 BC	508 BC	498–493 BC	405–396 BC
Romans engage Etruscans in frequent battles and develop powerful military	Italian cities found the League of Twelve Cities	Etruscans allied with Carthaginians defeat Greeks and increase naval power in Mediterranean	Roman Republic is established following overthrow of Tarquin monarchs	Treaty between Carthage and Rome defines their spheres of influence	Tarquins attempt to regain power	Rome recognizes autonomy of Latin cities but is established as dominant	Romans besiege city of Veii, eventually conquering and annexing it

value of extending its borders to protect the city. First on the Roman agenda were the Samnites who were brought to heel soon after the Celtic incursion. Other tribes on the Italian Peninsula succumbed to Roman advances and there were scuffles with the long-established Greek states on the Italian mainland.

Rome's power steadily grew. The city-state possessed just 350 square miles of territory in 500 BC. Yet within 250 years it had gained some 10,000 square miles and exerted influence in a further 42,000 square miles around the Mediterranean Sea.

Inevitably conflict between Rome and Carthage, the other significant power in the region, ensued. The Punic Wars are best remembered for the exploits of Hannibal, who traveled through Spain and southern France before crossing the Alps with soldiers and elephants. He notched up some impressive victories before overstretched supply lines took their toll. He was ultimately beaten by a brilliant Roman general, Publius Cornelius Scipio, and by 146 BC Carthage was defeated.

Roman leaders recognized the need for an infrastructure to support the infant empire.

Romans were, of course, famous for building roads and it is along these arrow-straight tracks that soldiers, supplies, and information swiftly moved, enabling Rome to keep control of distant outposts. Following the capture of a Carthaginian ship, Roman engineers quickly copied its design and built a fleet. Thereafter Rome dominated the Mediterranean, which assisted both conquest and trade.

Macedonia came into the Roman fold in 146 BC, in the same era as Sardinia, Spain, Epirus, Galatia, and North Africa. The city of Carthage was razed, as was the previously powerful Corinth. Greek architecture, art, and literature was soon subsumed by Rome as it eclipsed the older classical society to become the premier power in Europe.

BELOW: Hannibal (247–182 BC) posed the worst threat to Rome when the Carthaginian general invaded Italy after crossing the Alps.

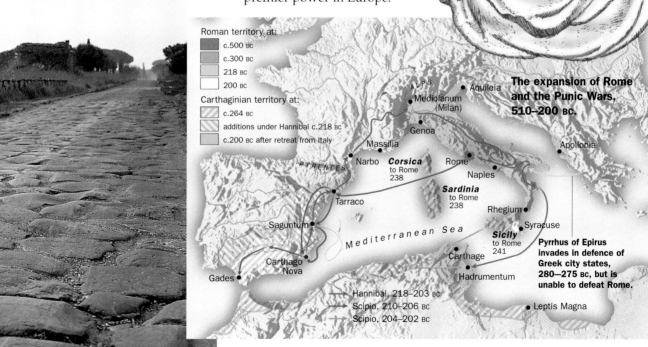

Roman territory at:
- c.500 BC
- c.300 BC
- 218 BC
- 200 BC

Carthaginian territory at:
- c.264 BC
- additions under Hannibal c.218 BC
- c.200 BC after retreat from Italy

The expansion of Rome and the Punic Wars, 510–200 BC.

ALPS
Aquileia
Mediolanum (Milan)
Genoa
Massilia
Apollonia
PYRENEES
Narbo
Corsica to Rome 238
Rome
Naples
Tarraco
Sardinia to Rome 238
Rhegium
Saguntum
Syracuse
Mediterranean Sea
Sicily to Rome 241
Carthago Nova
Carthage
Gades
Hadrumentum

Pyrrhus of Epirus invades in defence of Greek city states, 280—275 BC, but is unable to defeat Rome.

Hannibal, 218–203 BC
Scipio, 210–206 BC
Scipio, 204–202 BC

Leptis Magna

380 BC	367 BC	282 BC	203 BC	146 BC	73–71 BC	55 BC	50-44 BC
Romans build defensive fortifications around their Seven Hills area	Romans under Marcus Camillus repel second invasion of Gallic Celts	Etruscans and Gauls are defeated in their attempt at rebellion	Hannibal is recalled to Carthage following defeat	Carthage is destroyed, and all its residents killed or enslaved	Spartacus leads a slave revolt against Rome and holds out against several Roman armies until capture in the south	Caesar's armies kill a reported 400,000 Germans and simultaneously undertake first invasion of Britain	Great Roman Civil War is triggered by power-struggle between Caesar and the Senate headed by Pompey

By the era of the emperor Constantine, the "marbled" Rome Augustus left was at its peak. In this model, the Colosseum is at the lower center; the Arch of Constantine is at its upper left rim. Beyond is the Forum and Capitoline hill. Right of the Forum at an angle lie the Forums of Augustus and Trajan. The Theater of Marecellus sits below this caption.

From Republic to Autocracy

Despite Rome's military successes its government faced internal pressure. Successful military men sought to carve out political careers at the end of their service and they often commanded a loyal following among soldiers. Poorer people—plebeians—had become disillusioned with the iron grip on power maintained by the patrician class. All attempts to devise fairer distribution of land were thwarted by the conservatives. Rome was ripe for revolt.

The Republic's first significant challenge came from Cornelius Sulla (138–78 BC), who took power by force after a murderous campaign against his political rivals. When his rule ended in 79 BC a savage struggle for power ensued. One of the candidates, Marcus Crassus, brutally put down a rebellion of slaves led by Spartacus in 71 BC —and ordered that the 6,000 captured former slaves be crucified. Cicero recorded the excesses of the era.

The First Triumvirate brought about some measure of stability. This included Crassus, Gnaeus Pompeius (known as "Pompey"), and the lesser-known Julius Caesar. Pompey had already made Syria and Jerusalem into Roman provinces. Now it was Caesar's turn to make his name by gaining prizes for Rome. He focussed on Gaul where the resident tribes were in perpetual rebellion. Within six years he had the region of present-day France under Roman control, finally defeating Vercingetorix in 52 BC. Caesar made two forays into Britain but was unable to establish himself there permanently. An account of his exploits called the *Gallic Wars* also demonstrated Caesar's abilities as an early journalist.

Now Caesar became engulfed in a feud with Pompey. Cicero summed it up as follows: "Pompey is determined not to allow Gaius Caesar to be elected consul unless he has handed over his army and

42 BC Roman leader Mark Antony meets Egypt's Queen Cleopatra and follows her back to Egypt

30 BC Antony and Cleopatra commit suicide

AD 30 Widespread riots in Judea following crucifixion of Jesus Christ

43 Roman forces invade southern Britain

61 Boadicca's revolt in Britain is put down by Roman consul Paulinus

114 Roman Empire under Trajan reaches its greatest extent

132 Emperor Hadrian crushes Jewish rebellion and initiates Diaspora (dispersal) of Jews from Judea

249–251 Widespread persecution of Christians is carried out in Rome under Decius

provinces; Caesar on the other hand is convinced that there is no safety for him if he quits his army…" Caesar took over the Italian peninsula and Rome itself, finally defeating the fleeing Pompey in a battle in Thrace. Continuing to rout his enemies Caesar went to Egypt where Cleopatra beguiled him. She bore his son, who became Ptolemy XV. Caesar was finally murdered in 44 BC—but not before he had introduced the Julian calendar which has held fast for more than 2,000 years.

NEW STABILITY AND PROSPERITY

There followed more alliances, betrayals, and battles until Octavian, Caesar's adopted son, took power. He drew a line under Republican Rome, making himself emperor and initiating 400 years of Imperial rule. His timing was immaculate. The populace was heartily sick of the internal strife that had afflicted Rome for a century. Now was the time to capitalize on the riches of empire, as Roman merchants and entrepreneurs thrived. After consolidating his position with the Senate and army, Octavian had himself proclaimed the Emperor Augustus. Rome was finally an empire in the true sense. In the peace that characterized Augustus's rule a massive building program commenced and the emperor later claimed that he had found Rome in brick and left it in clothed marble.

As sole ruler, Augustus was able to instigate a concerted strategy for the empire—for the first time in its haphazard history. Understanding well the difficulties of maintaining Roman territory, he aided the legions by defining borders along rivers. He seized more foreign territory than any other Roman ruler, including the lands today known as Switzerland, Austria, Hungary, Belgium, and Holland.

Augustus's ambitions suffered a serious setback, however, with the humiliating defeat in the Teutoburg Forest. Through incompetence, the general Varus lost three legions when a coalition of Germanic tribes

ambushed them. Still, a census in 29 BC proclaimed that Rome had more than 4,063,000 citizens— testament to its huge success. That number excluded slaves and the inhabitants of occupied countries who had yet to earn Roman citizenship. A wise and respected ruler, Augustus died in AD 14.

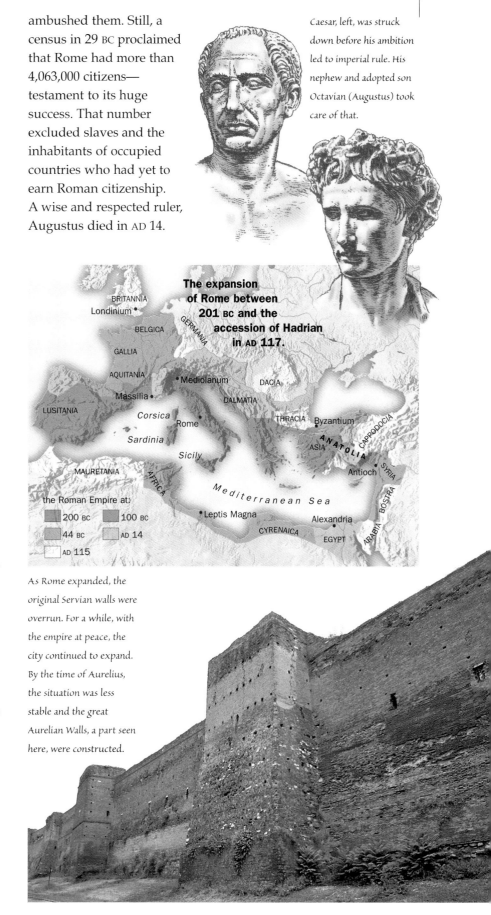

Caesar, left, was struck down before his ambition led to imperial rule. His nephew and adopted son Octavian (Augustus) took care of that.

The expansion of Rome between 201 BC and the accession of Hadrian in AD 117.

BRITANNIA
Londinium
BELGICA
GERMANIA
GALLIA
AQUITANIA
Mediolanum
DACIA
Massilia
DALMATIA
LUSITANIA
Corsica
Rome
THRACIA
Byzantium
Sardinia
ANATOLIA
CAPPODOCIA
ASIA
Sicily
Antioch
SYRIA
MAURETANIA
AFRICA
Mediterranean Sea
BOSTRA
the Roman Empire at:
200 BC   100 BC
44 BC   AD 14
AD 115
Leptis Magna
Alexandria
ARABIA
CYRENAICA
EGYPT

As Rome expanded, the original Servian walls were overrun. For a while, with the empire at peace, the city continued to expand. By the time of Aurelius, the situation was less stable and the great Aurelian Walls, a part seen here, were constructed.

260	286	303–311	311	391	405	410	476
Emperor Gallienus ends persecution of Christians by enacting the Edict of Toleration	Emperor Diocletian splits the empire into Eastern and Western, with separate emperors	Christians are again strongly persecuted under Diocletian	Another Edict of Toleration is enacted to protect Christians	Christianity becomes the state religion of Rome, with other religions suppressed	Huge migration of European tribes puts increased pressure on Roman Empire	Visigothic leader Alaric becomes first to successfully invade Rome	Revolt by mercenaries in Roman army effectively ends the Western Roman Empire

Decline and fall

ABOVE: *Roman soldiers battling barbarians. Detail from Trajan's Column.* BELOW: *The beautiful Arch of Constantine.*

Reflecting the weaknesses of autocratic rule, Roman emperors ranged from robust and ruthless to downright feeble. Still, Imperial rule held firm, even in the face of the crises caused by barbarian attacks throughout the empire. Indeed, the Roman Empire still had not reached its zenith under Augustus although it was the first emperor himself who engineered the delay. Stung by his failure to extend the border in Germany from the Rhine to the Elbe, Augustus instructed his successor Tiberius not to seek further gains but to cement those already in his possession.

Claudius added Britain to the empire in AD 43. Physically impaired, he was deemed to be a puppet ruler under the evil influence of his wife Agrippina, and his exploits in Britain were believed to be a vain attempt to boost his prestige. However, more recently historians have overhauled Claudius's image, citing the smart reforms he made in the system of state finances.

Despite the acquisition of England, Claudius's wife poisoned him in favor of her son Nero. A bon viveur little interested in affairs of empire, Nero has the unsettling distinction of killing his mother and two wives, allegedly setting fire to Rome, and persecuting the early Christians. He was ultimately murdered and finally replaced by Vespasian, who in turn was succeeded by sons Titus and Domitian. Further territories were added to the empire in Germany while frontiers in the east were strengthened. As the reputation and wealth of the empire grew, neighboring peoples were often more easily pacified and some even joined the empire by consent.

The empire expanded once more under the Spanish-born Emperor Trajan (r.98–117) to include Mesopotamia, Dacia (modern-day Romania, named after the Romans), and tracts of Arabia. However, his new conquests exacerbated the difficulties of maintaining an empire. Frontiers were once again blurred. He invested in a system of fortifications in central Europe—known as limes—yet still skirmishes in the hinterlands of the empire were commonplace.

By now, legionaries were rarely Italian-born, and some retained dangerous loyalties to their home regions (for instance, the Roman soldiers stationed in northern England to guard the border with the Caledonian tribes were often Caledonian themselves, and are known to have encouraged unsanctioned migration into the empire). Non-Roman soldiers often only joined the army to try to win Roman citizenship and a service pension, so their motivation was often dubious.

GOLDEN ERA PRECEDES THE FALL
Nevertheless, Roman respect for the army remained key. On his deathbed in England in 211 the Emperor Septimus Severus told his sons Caracalla and Geta: "enrich the soldiers, and despise all the rest." In a bold move Caracalla improved on his father's advice. Not only did he foster strong links with the army but in 212 he extended Roman citizenship to all free-born peoples in the empire, in an enlightened definition of citizenship not equalled until modern times.

Trouble was on the horizon, however. Two decades later, the armies in the provinces tried to install their own commanders as emperors, dubbed the "Thirty Tyrants." Successive emperors regained control but the episode simply bolstered autocracy and stifled the reforms that could have allowed Rome to progress even further. As barbarian attacks and incursions increased in the third century the empire's fabric began to unravel. Economic as well as military pressure began to build and Rome suffered a series of reverses that just a century before would have been unthinkable. The end finally came in 476 with the death of Emperor Romulus Augustulus. A barbarian general, Odoacer, became king of Italy, and the remnants of the empire relocated to Byzantium (Constantinople).

Western civilization eventually recovered, but not for many centuries. It is interesting to speculate what would have happened if the Roman Empire had survived and continued to mature rather than falling into the long, icy grip of the Dark Ages.

Arguably the last of the great Roman emperors, Constantine paved the way in 313 for Christianity to become the state religion.

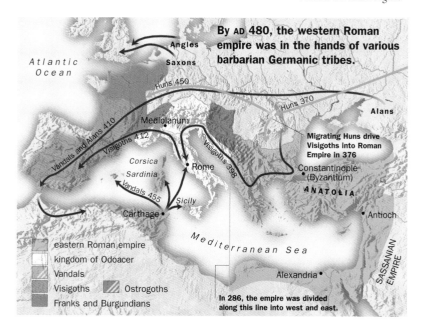

By AD 480, the western Roman empire was in the hands of various barbarian Germanic tribes.

Atlantic Ocean

Angles

Saxons

Huns 450

Huns 370

Alans

Vandals and Alans 410

Visigoths 412

Mediolanum

Visigoths 398

Migrating Huns drive Visigoths into Roman Empire in 376

Corsica

Sardinia

Rome

Constantinople (Byzantium)

ANATOLIA

Vandals 455

Sicily

Antioch

Carthage

Mediterranean Sea

eastern Roman empire
kingdom of Odoacer
Vandals
Visigoths
Ostrogoths
Franks and Burgundians

Alexandria

SASSANIAN EMPIRE

In 286, the empire was divided along this line into west and east.

THE SPREAD OF CHRISTIANITY

The Christians were cruelly persecuted by several emperors, until Constantine (r.306–337) adopted the faith (*see pages 112–3*). Jews were also periodically harassed, especially since they were prone to rebellion. Celtic Druids in France and Britain were persecuted because of their (Rome-alleged) predilection for human sacrifice. After Constantine adopted Christianity, it became the official religion of Rome and this was instrumental in spreading the faith throughout Roman Europe. Christianity was well-established—even among some barbarian tribes—by the time Rome fell and would continue to grow even during the Dark Ages.

Persia Rises Again

Always eager to replicate the success of Alexander the Great, Roman pragmatism failed to defeat the new Sassanian power that had arisen in Persia—and the new Persia kept Rome out.

Above: This rock-carved relief shows Ardashir I receiving his crown from the god Ahura Mazda, the main deity of the Zoroastrian faith.

BELOW, FAR RIGHT: Iranian Pharsis visit Qal'eh-ye Khamushan (Tower of Silence). Zoroastrians leave their dead in such places for vultures to consume. The practice also spread to Pharsis in areas of northern and western India.

After the death of Alexander the Great the Parthians emerged as the dominant power in Persia. Roman forces with ambitions in the region were usually stopped in their tracks by Parthia's fearsome archers. However, frequent skirmishes between the two weakened the Parthians. The ruling Arsacid dynasty came to grief in AD 226, when Ardashir, king of the neighboring Fars, staged a coup and founded the Sassanian dynasty (named after Ardashir's grandfather, Sassan).

The Sassanians were far more aggressive than the Parthians, both at home and on the frontiers. Ardashir looked back to the halcyon days of Achaemenid rule and sought to replicate that era. While Parthia had aspired to include Armenia within its boundaries, the Sassanians intended to achieve an empire similar to that of their forebears, Cyrus the Great and Darius I.

The stated Sassanian aim was to eradicate Hellenistic culture from the region. This had flourished at the expense of Persia's indigenous customs since Alexander's conquest and his insistence on merging the two societies. (*see page 34*). Soon, a centralized system of administration was established, with a revived Zoroastrianism as its official faith (Ardashir's grandfather, Sassan, had been a prominent Zoroastrian high priest). Although there is little historical evidence regarding Sassanian Persia, its society appears to have had four distinct classes: a priesthood, the military, civil service, and the proletariat. Nobles were permitted to keep their own cavalry and sometimes had elephants at their disposal.

AD 226	253	297	328	337–349	349–358	363	484
Ardashir I overthrows Parthian dynasty and founds the Sassanian dynasty	Sassanians sack Roman city of Antioch, in present-day Syria	Romans defeat Sassanians but give them monopoly over silk trade in Rome	Emperor Shapur II defeats King Thair of Arabia (Yemen)	Shapur II fights Romans in Mesopotamia	The Sassanians subdue Scythian peoples in northeastern Persia	Emperor Julian is killed in battle against the Sassanians	Ephthalites attack Persia and kill King Peroz

HARASSING THE ROMANS

Ardashir was repelled from Armenia, so he turned his attentions to Roman Mesopotamia. Rome responded but the battles that followed between 230 and 244 were by no means conclusive. However, the Persians made sufficient impression to negotiate a peace treaty that gave them fresh territory in the west. Ardashir's son and successor Shapur I notched up an astonishing victory against the time-honored Roman enemy. In 260 he ordered his army into Syria and succeeded in taking Antioch, timing his invasion for when most of the city's citizens were at the theater.

Outraged, the Roman emperor Valerian (who co-ruled with his son Gallenius) gathered together his army to respond. Alas, Valerian was outmaneuvered and found himself cornered at Edessa. He was taken prisoner and paraded in chains by the triumphant Shapur. It was a humiliation hardly known by Romans. Valerian became one of a rare breed of Roman emperors not beaten by enemies at home but by those overseas (the others are Decius, who was killed by Goths nine years previously; Julian killed by Persians in 363; and Valens who was slaughtered a century later by Visigoths at Adrianople). The Persian victory is commemorated in a stone relief at the tomb of Darius I at Naqsh-e-Rostam.

Valerian died in captivity, crushed by his experiences. Shapur adopted the title "King of kings of Persia and non-Persia," emphasizing the intent of the new Persian order.

A NEW RELIGION

Shapur I patronized Mani (AD 216–74), a prophet who traced a link between Buddha, Zoroaster, and Jesus and portrayed himself as the greatest of these. His new religion—Manichaeanism—experienced some considerable success, just like Christianity at the time. It spread from Persia as far as Spain and China, before being suppressed by a subsequent Sassanian king, Bahram I. Although he ruled for less than three years, Bahram's reforms were startling. In a fit of ruthlessness he had Mani and as many of his priests as he could find crucified.

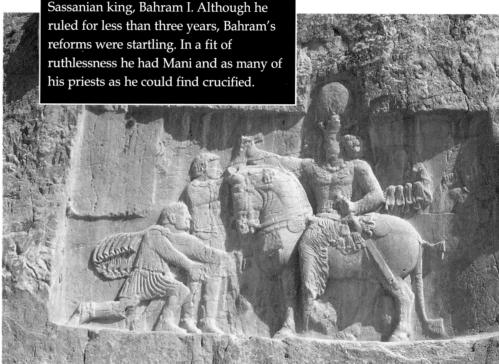

A Sassanian rock sculpture on a cliff face at Naqsh-e-Rostam, near the site of Persepolis, depicts the Roman emperor Valerian kneeling in submission before the victorious Shapur I after Edessa.

500	505	540	562	612–615	627	633	642
Ephthalites expand their territories in Persia	Eastern Roman Empire and Sassanians become allied against Ephthalites	Antioch is once more sacked	Sassanian and Turkish forces crush the Ephthalites	Under King Khosru II, Sassanians conquer Asia Minor, Syria, and Palestine	A Byzantine army sacks the Sassanian capital of Ctesiphon	The revelations of Mohammed are first published in the *Koran*	The Arabs invade Persia, ending the Sassanian Empire

Triumph and Defeat

Despite the pressures within the Roman Empire which were bringing it to breaking point, emperors never forgot Shapur I's stinging exploits and sought to avenge them. In 298, Roman forces defeated the Persian king Narses. The Upper Tigris became a Roman province once again.

Narses abdicated and his son became Hormizd III. An enlightened man, his keenest interests were in architecture and the legislature. Within seven years his untimely death had deprived the Sassanian Empire of one of its most steadfast rulers. Before his death, his queen became pregnant, and the robes of power were ceremonially placed on the queen's swollen belly. On his birth the baby was already known as Shapur II.

Shapur's tenure was somewhat overshadowed by the accomplishments of Constantine I, the Roman emperor who moved his capital to Byzantium (renamed Constantinople in 330). Constantine was a great advocate of Christianity—although he molded the faith to his own advantage. Responding to Roman Christianity, Shapur instituted a purge against Christians in Persia in 339. Yazdegerd I, who took the Persian throne just as the fourth century gave way to the fifth, later became even more notorious for the persecution of Christians.

In 409 Yazdegerd had appeared conciliatory by issuing an edict of tolerance that permitted churches to be rebuilt. Suddenly he reversed his stance and launched a four-year campaign that claimed the lives of numerous practicing Christians within his empire. These exploits earned him the name of "The Sinner," but probably did not contribute to his overthrow by nobles in 420. His son Bahram V rapidly seized power back for the Sassanians and continued the blood-soaked policies. Christians in Armenia and Mesopotamia were likewise harassed and harried by his successor, Yazdegerd II.

FLUX IN THE OLD ORDER

Religious rivalry gave renewed impetus to the conflict between Persia and Rome, although both suffered the penalties of having extended borders maintained by large and costly armies. In addition to their problems in the west with Rome—and later Byzantium—the Sassanian kings had to contend with aggression from the Ephthalites, or White Huns, pressing in from the east. There were many wars and much loss of life, but despite the bloodshed the borders remained largely intact.

The reign of Kavadh I, which began in 488, was characterized by experiments in a

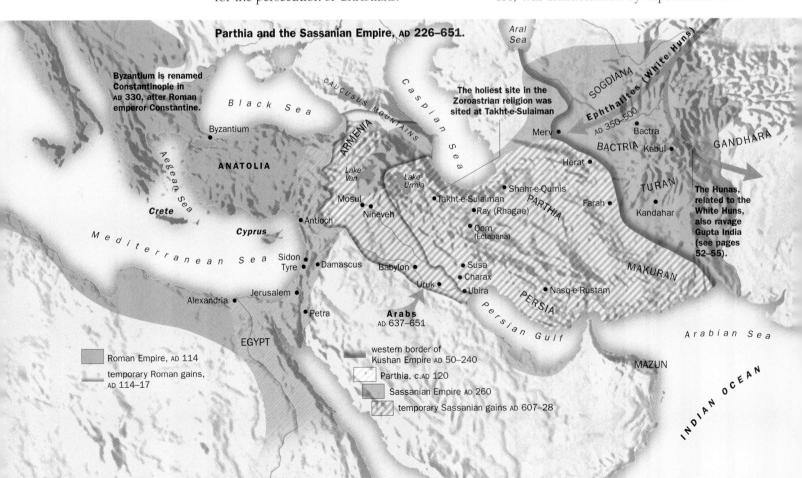

Parthia and the Sassanian Empire, AD 226–651.

Byzantium is renamed Constantinople in AD 330, after Roman emperor Constantine.

The holiest site in the Zoroastrian religion was sited at Takht-e-Sulaiman

The Hunas, related to the White Huns, also ravage Gupta India (see pages 52–55).

Roman Empire, AD 114

temporary Roman gains, AD 114–17

western border of Kushan Empire AD 50–240

Parthia, c.AD 120

Sassanian Empire AD 260

temporary Sassanian gains AD 607–28

Aral Sea · Black Sea · Caspian Sea · Aegean Sea · Mediterranean Sea · Persian Gulf · Arabian Sea · INDIAN OCEAN

Byzantium · ANATOLIA · ARMENIA · CAUCUSUS MOUNTAINS · Lake Van · Lake Urmia · Mosul · Nineveh · Antioch · Crete · Cyprus · Sidon · Tyre · Damascus · Babylon · Jerusalem · Alexandria · Petra · EGYPT · Arabs AD 637–651 · Takht-e-Sulaiman · Shahr-e-Qumis · Ray (Rhagae) · Qom (Ectabana) · Susa · Charax · Uruk · Ubira · PARTHIA · Merv · Herat · Farah · Nasq-e-Rustam · PERSIA · SOGDIANA · Ephthalites (White Huns) AD 350–500 · Bactra · BACTRIA · Kabul · GANDHARA · TURAN · Kandahar · MAKURAN · MAZUN

very early form of communism. Influenced by a radical religious leader called Mazdak who preached liberty and equality, the idealistic young king attempted to put the theories into practice. He was hounded out by priests and outraged nobles and replaced by his brother Jamasb. Assisted by the Huns, Kavadh returned to claim the throne once more, toning down his commitment to infant communism. When he encountered further difficulties—not only with the aristocrats but also with Mazdak's followers—he turned about and repressed the revolutionary ideas.

Perhaps the most celebrated Sassanian ruler was Khosru I (r.531–579), also known as Anushirvan the Just. In sweeping reforms, he overhauled the tax system, the civil service, and reorganized the army. Aligned with him were the village lords or petty nobility, who enforced his new systems of tax collection. He invested in better buildings in the capital Ctesiphon and founded new towns outside the city. With his active support, books were brought into Persia from India and translated. He also annexed Ethiopian Axum, previously a Christian state.

His namesake, Khosru II (r.591–628) is remembered with considerably less affection. He formulated a foolishly robust foreign policy that took Sassanian armies into Jerusalem, Palestine, Egypt, and Cyrene in Africa. It was only a matter of time before the Byzantines countered the aggression. Striking in Armenia in 627, the opposing armies met at Nineveh, and Khosru was soundly beaten. He fled the battlefield, only to be deposed and finally crucified by his own people.

A succession of Sassanian emperors followed but they were weakened by the failures of Khosru, unpopular taxes, a rigid social structure, and religious divide. The last of the line, Yazdegerd III, was defeated by the Arabs in 651 and later assassinated. The stage was set for a takeover of the region by Arabs, bringing with them the new religion, Islam.

This silver coin of King Hormizd IV (r.579–90) is proof that Sassanian Persian influence spread far and wide. It was found in the mouth of a person buried in the Astana cemetery, near Tufan, northwestern China. Documents also found in the same tombs indicate that Sassanian coins were widely used as a currency in this part of China. Even further east, over 1,500 Sassanian silver drachms have been found in China, part of a commerce that belonged to what would later be called the Silk Road (see pages 50–51).

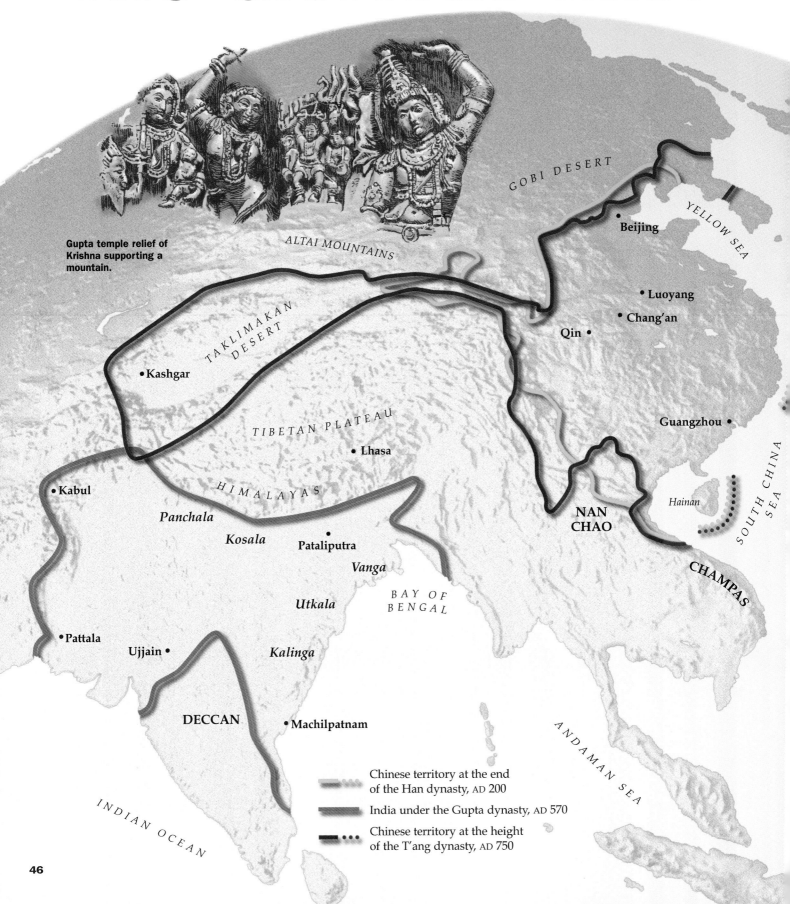

CHAPTER THREE

The Glorious East

Gupta temple relief of Krishna supporting a mountain.

GOBI DESERT

YELLOW SEA

ALTAI MOUNTAINS

• Beijing

• Luoyang

• Chang'an

Qin •

TAKLIMAKAN DESERT

• Kashgar

TIBETAN PLATEAU

Guangzhou •

• Lhasa

• Kabul

HIMALAYAS

SOUTH CHINA SEA

Hainan

Panchala

NAN CHAO

Kosala

Pataliputra

Vanga

CHAMPAS

Utkala

BAY OF BENGAL

• Pattala

Ujjain •

Kalinga

DECCAN

• Machilpatnam

ANDAMAN SEA

INDIAN OCEAN

Chinese territory at the end of the Han dynasty, AD 200

India under the Gupta dynasty, AD 570

Chinese territory at the height of the T'ang dynasty, AD 750

The years between 200 BC and AD 900 produced three of the great classical empires of Eastern Asia. Two of these, the Han and T'ang dynasties, dominated Chinese culture to such an extent that some elements of their administration survived into the 20th century. The third, the Gupta regime of northern India, presided over major advances in human knowledge, particularly science, medicine, philosophy, and the arts.

During this period two great religions expanded their influences: Hinduism (already an ancient religion by this time) and Buddhism. In China the Confucian philosophy also quickly spread. New intercontinental trade routes flourished and the Silk Road—a route across the wastelands of central Asia—gave Chinese and Indian merchants access to the lucrative markets of the Roman Empire

via Persian wholesalers. Trade brought wealth, and wealth encouraged royal patronage of religious institutions. Under the Gupta king Chandragupta II (r.AD 380–414), some monasteries established themselves as investment bankers in addition to their traditional role as farm and land managers.

THE POWER OF FAMILY

The Gupta leaders maintained control by combining strong central leadership with a form of local democracy, although they were not above securing the empire's borders by marrying-off princesses to powerful neighbors. For the Han and T'ang dynasties the pursuit of stable rule was a much bigger political minefield. It was easy enough for an emperor to accept as wife or concubine the daughter of a strong regional leader, so keeping him on-side. But the vastness of China ensured there were many such leaders often co-existing in an atmosphere of mutual suspicion. The system of arranged marriages created large and extended families with a multitude of competing heirs. It meant the royal courts were plagued by backstairs intrigue as wives and concubines plotted the advancement of their own families and the downfall of their rivals'. For the most intelligent and cunning such as the ruthless Wu Zetian (who rose to become China's only woman emperor), this environment was the fast track to power.

The male-dominated Confucian establishment bemoaned the influence of women who dogged the royal court with ambition, yet male intrigue was just as great. Despite the constant friction and internal conflict, art, literature, science, and philosophy all flourished at this time.

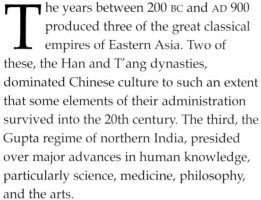

Taiwan

Funerary statuette of a Han warrior.

A ceramic T'ang equestrian archer.

Members of emperor Qin Shi Huangdi's funerary terra-cotta army.

Out of Turmoil—Han China

When the last Qin ruler, Zheng (r.246–210 BC) completed the seizure of all China that the war-like Qin had begun in 360 BC, he called himself Shi Huangdi, the "First Emperor."

The death of Shi Huangdi, in 210 BC ended the Qin dynasty and plunged China into eight years of bloody civil war. In 206 BC, the surviving royal family was beheaded, and it seemed the region would revert to its old, haphazard political profile with rival feudal states perpetually jockeying for power. Yet, remarkably, the

This sculpture of a man holding an umbrella is part of a wide tradition in grave goods. It dates from a time in the Western Han dynasty (206 BC–AD 9) and is unusual in that the earlier Han period tended to prefer models of buildings to human figures (with the notable exception of the many military figures which continued to be buried with nobles in imitation of the Qin ruler Shi Huangdi).

empire passed intact, in 202 BC, to a peasant farmer and former Qin official called Liu Bang (posthumously called Gaozu), founder of the Han dynasty.

Han China would flourish for the best part of four centuries—an eastern contemporary of the Roman Empire—in an era of previously unknown prosperity, strong central government, intercontinental trade links, and academic development.

The Han dynasty splits into two periods. The Former or Western Han (206 BC–AD 9) centered on Liu Bang's new capital city of Chang'an. This period ended when the throne was usurped by Wang Mang, a senior courtier. Wang's violent death 14 years later marked the end of the interregnum and the emergence of the Later or Eastern Han under Liu Xiu, the 15th Han emperor, who moved the capital to Luoyang. The Later Han Empire survived until AD 220, when it fragmented into the appropriately named Three Kingdoms.

Han China's initial outstanding achievement was to embrace the sound political and administrative institutions of the Qin while abandoning its severe totalitarian tendencies. Thus the Qin ideology of book-burning, heavy taxes, and harsh laws was replaced by a more just administrative and legal system, based on the teachings of the great Chinese philosopher Confucius. Essentially this "Han Confucianism" was underpinned by the notion that sound government could be achieved only through consent—a principle said to have been based on the Confucian saying: "An empire can be conquered on horseback—but not governed from a horse." It won popular support; not least for its hounding of loan sharks or merchants found guilty of profiteering. People found guilty of such offenses faced punitive taxes and humiliating personal restrictions which forbade them to wear silk gowns, ride in carriages, or hold public office.

BRASH BUT EFFECTIVE

Liu Bang was a complex and charismatic leader—intelligent and accepting of advice from his educated ministers, yet also contemptuous of academics as impractical theorists. He once graphically illustrated this by urinating in a scholar's formal hat. Generally, his rural accent and colorful language won him few friends among the upper classes.

Liu's good example did not mean, however, that Han government would be free of manipulative politics. When Liu was killed by a stray arrow during a frontier battle in 195 BC, his ambitious widow, Lu Hou, arranged for his two young grandsons to become joint puppet rulers, with herself as the real power broker (although her military aggression in the west and south failed). Her example started a worrying

c.403 BC	202 BC	160 BC	136 BC	115 BC	111 BC	102 BC	AD 8
Start of Warring States period as rival states jostle for control	Liu Bang declares himself emperor of China; start of the Han dynasty	Wu Ti becomes emperor and begins a campaign against the Huns	Confucianism is adopted as state ideology in China	Chinese envoy Zhang Qian travels to Parthia to trade silk for horses	China occupies Vietnam	As it expands westward, China obtains control of strategic oases in central Asia	Emperor Wang Mang begins series of radical state reforms; end of Former Han Dynasty

trend for the future. A widowed empress could try to advance her own relatives, only to leave them vulnerable to competing factions when she died. This led to a culture of backstairs intrigue in the royal palaces.

The long reign of the Emperor Wudi (141-87 BC) saw both the zenith and nadir of Han power. Territory was extended south of the Yangtse, close to China's modern border, and into Annam (central Vietnam). Rebels in southern Manchuria and northern Korea were brought into line, and in the north and west major

advances were made against the nomadic Hsiung-nu tribes, as far west as Kazakhstan. Yet these ventures sucked huge resources from the economy. The nationalization of the iron and salt industries, currency devaluation, and a booming population caused the major internal feuding that brought Wang Mang briefly to the throne in AD 9. His death in Chang'an during the "Red Eyebrows" peasant rebellion set the stage for the Later Han dynasty.

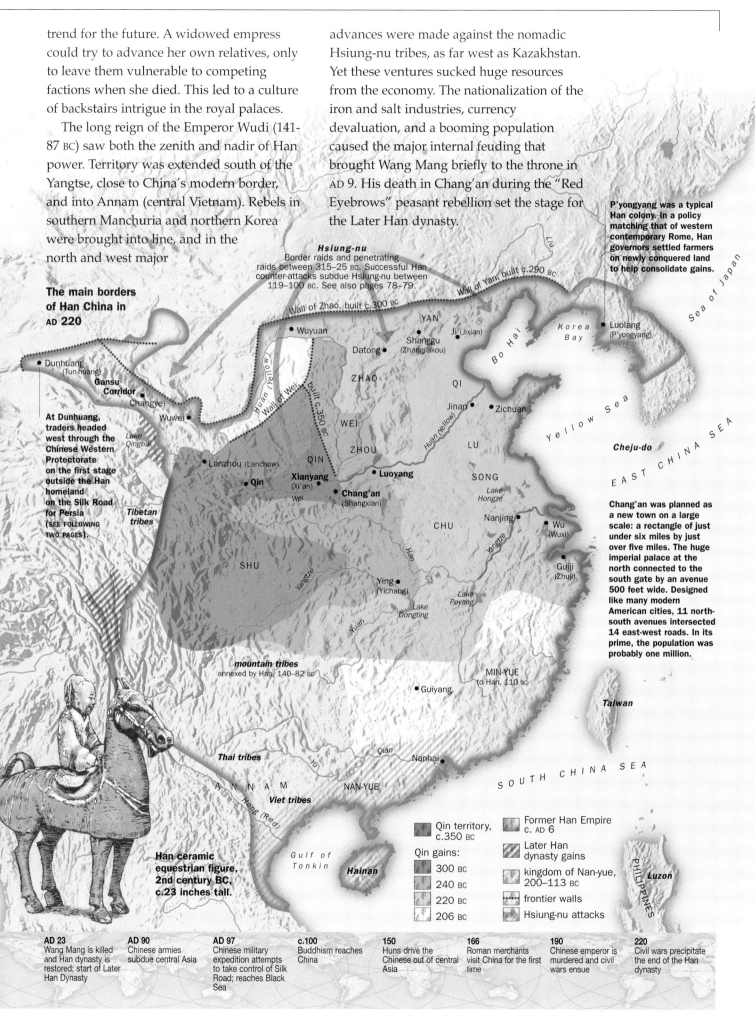

The main borders of Han China in AD 220

At Dunhuang, traders headed west through the Chinese Western Protectorate on the first stage outside the Han homeland on the Silk Road for Persia (SEE FOLLOWING TWO PAGES).

Hsiung-nu
Border raids and penetrating raids between 315–25 BC. Successful Han counter-attacks subdue Hsiung-nu between 119–100 BC. See also pages 78–79.

P'yongyang was a typical Han colony. In a policy matching that of western contemporary Rome, Han governors settled farmers on newly conquered land to help consolidate gains.

Chang'an was planned as a new town on a large scale: a rectangle of just under six miles by just over five miles. The huge imperial palace at the north connected to the south gate by an avenue 500 feet wide. Designed like many modern American cities, 11 north-south avenues intersected 14 east-west roads. In its prime, the population was probably one million.

Han ceramic equestrian figure, 2nd century BC, c.23 inches tall.

Qin territory, c.350 BC
Qin gains:
300 BC
240 BC
220 BC
206 BC
Former Han Empire c. AD 6
Later Han dynasty gains
kingdom of Nan-yue, 200–113 BC
frontier walls
Hsiung-nu attacks

AD 23	AD 90	AD 97	c.100	150	166	190	220
Wang Mang is killed and Han dynasty is restored; start of Later Han Dynasty	Chinese armies subdue central Asia	Chinese military expedition attempts to take control of Silk Road; reaches Black Sea	Buddhism reaches China	Huns drive the Chinese out of central Asia	Roman merchants visit China for the first time	Chinese emperor is murdered and civil wars ensue	Civil wars precipitate the end of the Han dynasty

Massacre of the Eunuchs

Guang Wudi began a 32-year reign in AD 25, triumphing as the strongest of 11 rival claimants. The first of the Later Han emperors, it took him a decade to subdue his opposition fully. He was obliged to shore up his position by agreeing political marriages with wives and consorts from the regions, appointing their

sons as provincial kings and princes. Once secure, Guang Wudi watered down their power, and relied instead on the advice of favored family members.

This tactic would eventually prove a

Machiavellian nightmare. The death of an emperor resulted in consort families plotting against each other to secure the succession. Soon, emperors were turning to the eunuchs—palace guards who became a powerful and secretive faction—to protect them from their own wives. The eunuchs predictably increased their influence and assumed total control under the ineffective child emperor Huandi, who reigned between AD 146 and 168. For the wives and consorts it became vital to ensure easily-manipulated children were placed on the throne. After Zhangdi, who died in AD 88, all nine of the Later Han emperors were minors.

LEGACY OF THE HAN

The downfall of the Han Dynasty was hastened in 184 by two rebellions at opposite ends of the empire. Corruption, anger at eunuch power, floods, and an agricultural

The Silk Road c.112 BC–AD 100
Routes under control of:
Chinese Han Empire
Kushan Kingdom
Persian Empire
Roman Empire

After c.950 AD, Venice is Europe's terminus for the Silk Road

Routes north under no central control

crisis resulted in the Yellow Turbans rising in the east and the wonderfully-named Five Pecks of Rice sect (after the tribute they paid to their Daoist religious leaders) forming an independent state in the southwest. With no effective central armies, provincial warlords now began to amass their own. One of them, Dong Zhou, used the death of the Emperor Lingdi in 189 as an excuse to attack and destroy Luoyang, slaughtering 2000 eunuchs in the process. The last Han emperor, Xiandi, survived precariously for 31 years before his abdication turned China into three separate kingdoms.

Despite the curse of royal scheming and in-fighting, the Han dynasty gave China some of the country's greatest legacies. Paper was invented, and by AD 121 it was being mass-produced from tree bark, hemp, and linen. In Confucianism and Daoism, Han China bequeathed two enduring philosophies to the world and many of the foundations for medicine and astronomy were laid. Sculpture—especially the terracotta figurines used in tombs to recreate familiar surroundings for the dead—is outstanding in its clarity and simplicity, while the royal tombs themselves rank among the most important archaeological treasures in the world.

One such site, discovered at Mancheng, Hebei province, in 1968, turned out to be the tomb of Prince Liu Sheng, who died in 113 BC. The remains of the prince and his wife were encased in suits made of some 2,500 individual jade plaques, sewn together with gold thread, in a labor of love thought to have taken ten years to produce. The importance of this royal couple is underlined by the size and grandeur of their vault. It was created by removing around 2,700 cubic yards of rock and soil from a hillside and the interior contained more than 2,800 of their possessions—including six carriages with sacrificed horses.

FACING: In the Eastern, or Later, Han dynasty it was common for the tombs of ordinary people to contain burial goods representing daily life. The figures in this group are playing Liubo, a gambling game.

BELOW: Jiaohe was a Han garrison town on the Silk Road. The remains of Buddhist temples, stupas and pagodas have been uncovered in the ruins.

THE SILK ROAD

The Silk Road trade route was a defining aspect of the Han Empire in that it created an overland trade link between China (SEE MAP, LEFT) and the Classical civilizations of the Mediterranean. It led from the western Han capital of Chang'an and ran through a natural corridor west of the Yellow river before splitting into northerly and southerly routes around the unforgiving deserts of the Taklimakan. On the other side the routes merged again at Kashgar, from where the Road crossed Central Asia to Afghanistan, Iran, and finally Europe. The route derives its name from the luxurious Chinese silks bought by Persian merchants for sale to wealthy Roman households.

India Flowers Under the Guptas

For just over two centuries a dynasty with humble origins presided over the blooming of Indian culture. As with their contemporaries to the west, Huns brought about their end.

The Gupta kings were architects of the first truly great Indian Empire. They rose to power around AD 320 amid the political uncertainty that had dogged the subcontinent since the fall of the Kushan kingdom in northern India a century earlier. Although the Kushans and their predecessors the Mauryans had each carved out large territories, neither quite managed to bind their empires effectively.

The Mauryans had insisted on a rigid central bureaucracy with harsh penal laws—a model that left large internal tracts of India only nominally acquiescent, or worse, in a perpetual state of rebellion. The Kushans were more flexible, relying on regional support from minor kings known as YAGHBUS, but their overall authority tended to diminish away from their northwestern heartland.

Gupta rulers trod a middle path. Officially, their word was law and they liked to remind their subjects of this fact by assuming grandiose titles such as *maharajadhiraja paramabhattaraka* (Great King of Kings, the Supreme Lord). On the other hand, they actively promoted a form of devolved power, and many city councils were made up of craftsmen, artists, and merchants, as opposed to state officials. This encouraged government by consent, which in turn created sustained economic growth and allowed literature, music, and art to flourish. The Hindu religion also began to re-establish itself under Gupta rule.

Dynasty founder Chandragupta I (not to be confused with Chandragupta Maurya who established the Mauryan Empire 600 years earlier) was from a quite unremarkable branch of the nobility. However, his shrewd marriage to a princess from the long-established and respectable Licchavi tribe allowed him to be crowned king of the Maghada kingdom, in the heartlands surrounding the River Ganges.

The throne passed to his son Samudragupta 15 years later. He quickly set about extending the borders. Our knowledge of Samudragupta rests heavily on an inscription composed by one of his senior aides on a stone pillar. It refers to defeated kings, expanded northern territories, and a long military campaign in the south. Also mentioned are tributes received from the western Sakas region, Ceylon (Sri Lanka), northwest Iran,

The Gupta kings minted beautiful coins, usually with the purpose of showing the king to emphasize his status as great ruler and heroic warrior. This gold dinara of about AD 415–50, minted by Kumaragupta I, measures only 1/4 inch in diameter, and is also shown here lifesize.

FAR RIGHT: A scene of young women relaxing, c.5th century, from one of the frescoes on a cave wall at Ajanta. The caves contain many frescoes, which are remarkably well preserved considering their age, as well as royal inscriptions of the Guptas.

AD 320	360	395	450	495	535
Accession of King Chandragupta marks beginning of Gupta dynasty.	King Samudragupta conquers most of northern India	King Chandragupta II conquers western India; empire at greatest extent	The Hunas (White Huns, or Ephthalites) invade Punjab but are stopped there by Gupta armies	Huns succeed invading central India	Gupta dynasty is ended when Huns invade rest of Gupta India

and the population of all the islands (probably a reference to trading posts strung out across southeast Asia and the Indian Ocean). Samudragupta's Empire minted beautifully-crafted gold coins which depicted him as both conqueror and musician. Yet he never exerted absolute control much beyond the Ganges valley.

SCIENTIFIC REVOLUTION

It was left to his heir, Chandragupta II (sometimes called Vikramaditya) to turn the Gupta dynasty into a true superpower. He benefited from an alliance struck late in the fourth century AD in which a Gupta princess was given in marriage to a prince of the Vakataka dynasty, a powerful kingdom in the south of India. This blood tie ensured that Chandragupta had a friendly southern neighbor—safeguarding his territory in the Deccan Plateau and freeing his armies to annex the Sakas and the rest of western India. The years between Chandragupta II's accession in AD 380 and his death in AD 414 saw the Gupta Empire at its peak.

The stability of the dynasty produced a spectacular cultural, economic, and scientific windfall. Chandragupta II was a staunch patron of the arts, science, and philosophy, and his policies encouraged an intellectual elite to blossom under the guidance of the

Hindu Brahman (priests), using the classical Sanskrit language.

Scientific research was classified and recorded, medical knowledge increased exponentially, and metalworking was so advanced that even today the quality of Gupta iron is difficult to reproduce. By AD 499 the astronomer Aryabhata had calculated the value of *pi* to 3.1416 and noted that the Earth was probably a sphere revolving on its own axis around the sun.

Statue of Avolakiteshvara dating from the 6th century. Hindus found that they were able to elaborate the pantheon of gods under the Guptas.

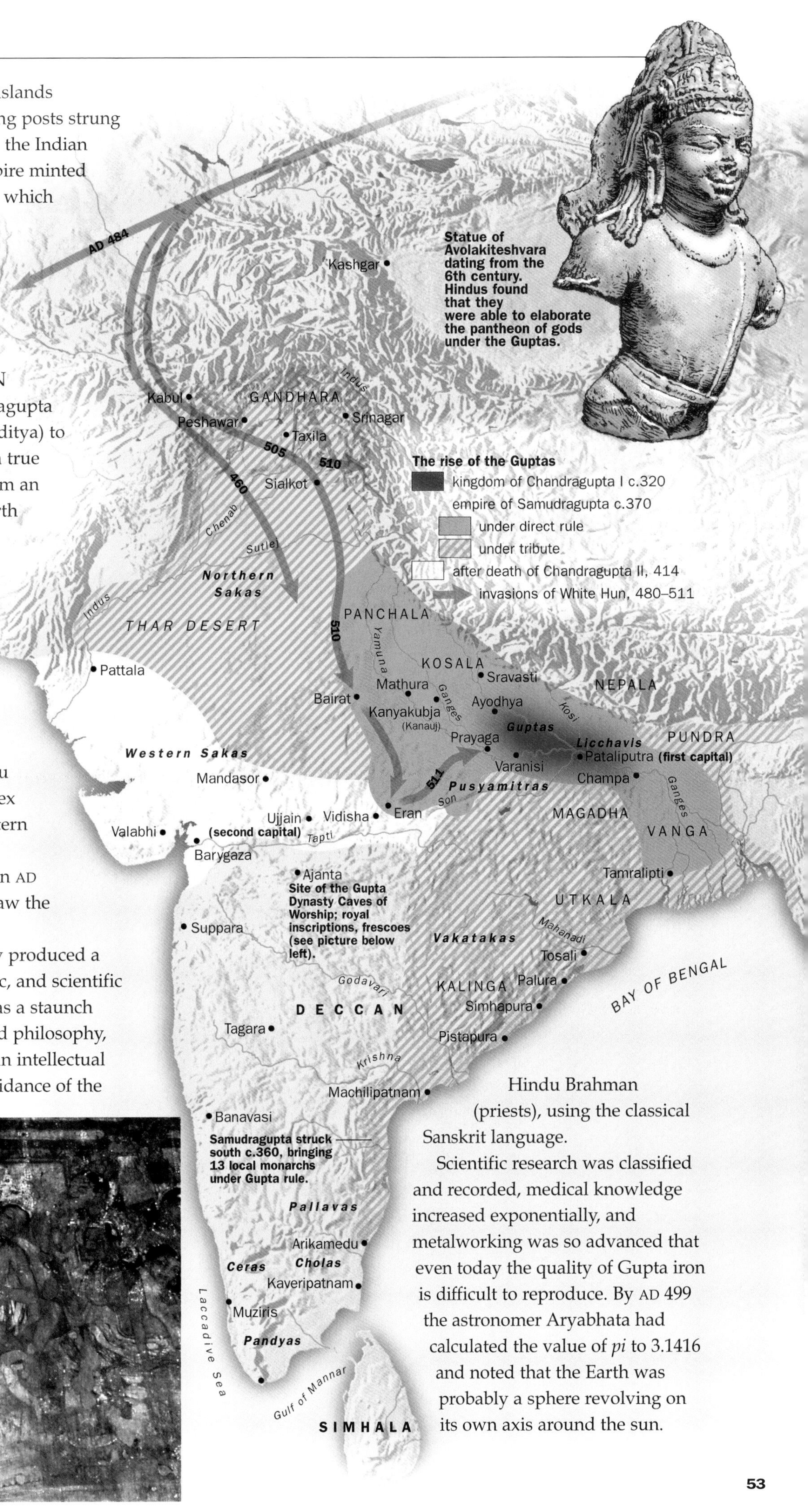

The rise of the Guptas

kingdom of Chandragupta I c.320
empire of Samudragupta c.370
under direct rule
under tribute
after death of Chandragupta II, 414
invasions of White Hun, 480–511

AD 484
Kashgar
Kabul
GANDHARA
Peshawar
Srinagar
Taxila
505
510
Sialkot
460
Indus
Chenab
Sutlej
Northern Sakas
THAR DESERT
Indus
510
PANCHALA
Yamuna
Pattala
KOSALA
Mathura
Sravasti
Bairat
Kanyakubja (Kanauj)
Ayodhya
NEPALA
Ganges
Kosi
Guptas
Prayaga
Licchavis
PUNDRA
Varanisi
Pataliputra (first capital)
Champa
Ganges
Western Sakas
Mandasor
511
Pusyamitras
Son
MAGADHA
VANGA
Valabhi
Ujjain
(second capital)
Vidisha
Eran
Tapti
Barygaza
Tamralipti
Ajanta
Site of the Gupta Dynasty Caves of Worship; royal inscriptions, frescoes (see picture below left).
UTKALA
Mahanadi
Vakatakas
Suppara
Tosali
Godavari
KALINGA
Palura
BAY OF BENGAL
Tagara
DECCAN
Simhapura
Pistapura
Krishna
Machilipatnam
Banavasi
Samudragupta struck south c.360, bringing 13 local monarchs under Gupta rule.
Pallavas
Arikamedu
Ceras
Cholas
Kaveripatnam
Laccadive Sea
Muziris
Pandyas
Gulf of Mannar
SIMHALA

53

Life Under the Guptas

Political mastery of India produced bumper dividends—and not just for the Gupta kings. Local officials grew wealthy through their cut of land taxes. Merchants amassed fortunes by capitalizing on relatively secure trade routes between China and the Mediterranean. And with a burgeoning export market, craft industries, farming, and spice houses provided plenty of lucrative employment for the lower classes. As a result ivory, stone, jewelry, metal, perfume, sandalwood, spices, fine cloth, pepper, indigo, and herbs all became key components in the Indian economy.

The institutions which perhaps gained most from this trade boom were the Buddhist and Hindu monasteries. Wealthy businessmen provided generous endowments; so much so that the monks progressed from running small-scale farms employing local labor to acting as venture capitalists and bankers. The more important monasteries housed some of the most stunning murals found anywhere in the ancient world while, relieved of financial worry, Buddhist philosophers were able to establish schools of excellence.

A RESURGENCE OF HINDUISM

This presented an intellectual challenge to the Hindu Brahmans (priests). By the Gupta period they had already largely rejected sacrifice in favor of personal devotion toward the two principal gods—Vishnu and Shiva. Senior Brahmans began to reinterpret ancient texts in line with their own vision of society, claiming essentially non-religious works such as the *Mahabharata* and the *Ramayana* were sacred literature. Gradually Hindusim, and the Brahman language Sanskrit, became identified with "Classical" India. It allowed the priests—already guardians of the caste system—to control the expansion of knowledge.

In one sense this was helpful to Gupta society because it created a scholarly

tradition in which teaching was valued and "thinkers" flourished. On the other hand it reinforced a clique that was inward-looking and isolated. Over the years important practical and technical skills were devalued, diminishing the role of the craft guilds. This was accentuated by a caste system in which towns were divided into various social sectors. The "untouchables"—considered the lowest form of human life, whose jobs included scavenging and leather-making—could "pollute" the body of a high-caste member simply through touch. Travelers such as the Chinese Buddhist pilgrim Hsuan Tsang were often baffled by this rule.

The trappings of wealth among the upper classes also produced a kind of dilettante set;

The two powerful—yet markedly divergent— religions on the Indian sub-continent grew wealthy within the prosperous empire. The Buddhists expanded their monasteries and exported teachers. The face of this monk (RIGHT), carved in the 4th to 5th centuries AD, was found in Gandhara, yet has the features of a person from much further south. The serenity of this face contrasts with the exuberant force of Hindu sculpture. The fragment of sandstone from a doorjamb (CENTER) is a fine example of Gupta workmanship. The left-hand vertical section shows ganas—demons and spirits who are part of Shiva's army—frolicking. A fat dwarf squats down at the bottom of the right-hand section. The floral scroll coming out of his mouth, full of movement and life, symbolizes the energy of the god (in this case Shiva, because of the ganas) whose temple lay beyond the doorway. Temples to Shiva sprang up everywhere in the Gupta period, none more famous than that at Elephanta, an island in Mumbai (Bombay) harbor. The bust here (FAR RIGHT), intended to inspire awe, displays all the vigor that the doorway panel pictured indicates.

fashion-conscious, high-living individuals who sought to create perfection around them. They surrounded themselves with flowers, exotic furnishings, subtle perfumes, and high-art—particularly in the form of terracotta figurines. One of the most fascinating glimpses of this lifestyle is depicted in the *Kama Sutra*, which—although best known for depicting many and varied sexual positions—also shows the fashionable Gupta gentlemen pursuing contentment in their day-to-day routine.

END OF THE DYNASTY

By the fifth century AD, the Gupta Empire was crumbling. In part this was driven by a relaxation of central control on land and taxes—where once a nobleman's land revenue had been the gift of the king, now the nobleman was seen as landowner by right. This inevitably led to stronger regional rulers and a more loosely-knit empire.

A more sinister threat, however, was rising unexpectedly in the north. The Hunas, related to the White Huns or Ephthalites (*see pages 44, 79*), settled in Bactria and gradually migrated across the mountains of northwestern India. By AD 454, there was open warfare on this border and the Guptas were unable to hold back the tide. Early in the sixth century they lost control of Kashmir and the Punjab to the Huna kings Toramana and Mihirakula, and soon the chaos brought an end to the Gupta dynasty. India became divided once again among provincial local rulers.

T'ang China—a Powerhouse

When the Han Empire collapsed in 220, China split into three rival states until reunited by the tyranical Wen (r.589–604). His ineffective successor Yang (r.604–17) was deposed after a popular rebellion by the general Li Yuan, who became Emperor Gaozu (r.618–26), first of the T'ang dynasty.

The Chinese regard the period of the T'ang dynasty as one of the most glorious: prosperity, territorial expansion, and artistic brilliance mark the 288 year-span. Even the grave goods of common folk were touched by a simple elegance, like this model of a lady.

Ancient China only ever had one woman emperor. Her name was Wu Zetian and the fact that she held power for more than half a century speaks volumes for her political skills in an empire plagued by family cliques, dubious alliances, and outright treachery. She was politically astute, fiercely independent, and a sound judge of character. Above all, she inspired loyalty in her advisers, and—thanks to an utterly ruthless streak—a climate of fear among her enemies.

Wu Zetian was born in AD 625, barely seven years into the fledgling T'ang dynasty. At this time the new emperor Gaozu was fighting a war of attrition against regional warlords and was heavily reliant on the military and diplomatic genius of his son, Li Shimin. When, in 626, Gaozu abdicated in favor of Li, it proved to be a turning point in T'ang fortunes. Li became the Emperor Taizong and brilliantly manipulated his opponents to render them ineffective. Using inter-tribal rivalries he changed northern Asia's balance of power—wiping out the Eastern Turks, seizing the Ordos and Inner Mongolian regions, subjugating Central Asia, and garrisoning key trading centers such as Kucha, Kashgar, Tukmak, Khotan, and Yarkand. He secured Tibet's goodwill by sending its powerful king a T'ang princess and for four years China's supremacy seemed beyond challenge.

Unfortunately, supreme power clouded Taizong's judgment. By the mid-630s (with Wu Zetian now a favored member of his harem) he avoided affairs of state to pursue long and expensive hunting expeditions. He ordered a grand public building program with little thought for the cost involved and even ordered the destruction of a palace that had taken laborers two million man-days to complete. With no sense of irony, Taizong declared that the style was too ostentatious and, anyway, the site was too hot in summer.

In 649 Taizong died and rule passed to his frail and naïve heir, Gaozong. After Gaozong took Wu Zetian for his consort, she quickly strengthened her position by suffocating his wife's new-born baby and pinning the crime on her. Now installed as empress, Wu Zetian was unstoppable. When Gaozong had a stroke, she assumed total control of China. The empire was expanded even further into Central Asia and in 651, she even received an Arab ambassador. Wu Zetian reigned through "puppet" heirs before eventually assuming total power in 690.

OVERT RUTHLESSNESS

The Empress Wu's treatment of her enemies was certainly sadistic. She had the arms and legs of the ex-empress Wang and a beautiful concubine called Xiao chopped off and threw them into a wine vat to die together. Their supporters fled or were killed and all Taizong's former advisers were removed. When rebel factions attempted a coup d'etat in 684 her response was to wipe out 12 branches of Taizong's family. Her secret service encouraged the denouncing of opponents and, in 697, this culminated in a purge of scholars and the nobility, who were killed or exiled.

Throughout all this Wu Zetian milked support from the masses by promoting Buddhism—unlike the Confucian

AD 618	626	641	705	751
Li Yuan replaces the Sui dynasty with his own T'ang dynasty	Li Yuan's second son, Li Shimin, forces his father to abdicate in a coup d'état	The influence of the T'ang dynasty spreads westward along the Silk Road	Empress Wu is deposed by her ministers and replaced by her son in a coup d'etat	Muslim armies defeat the T'ang at the battle of Talas; T'ang consequently lose control of central Asia

establishment it recognized the importance of women—and presenting herself as the nation's *Sage Mother*. In 685 she arranged for her lover, the Abbot of the White Horse Temple, to "discover" the *Great Cloud Sutra*, a text that predicted the imminent reincarnation of a female deity called Maitreya.

Unsurprisingly, the Empress Wu soon took the title Maitreya the Peerless, and later assumed the even more grandiose title of Holy and Divine Emperor. But her judgment was now failing. When, aged 72, she took two brothers as lovers, it signaled the end of her long reign. In 705, exasperated by the brothers' immoral and bullying tendencies, courtiers assassinated them. The empress abdicated the next day and died the same year.

T'ang China, 618–907 and (inset) China's "period of disunion" between the Han and Sui dynasties, 220–581. For 37 years prior to the T'ang dynasty, the short-lived Sui dynasty made many of the territorial gains shown in the main map.

The enhanced realism of the T'ang horses pictured above (center and right from the late 7th to early 8th centuries) is marked compared to that of the one on the left, dating from the turbulent post-Han mid-5th century.

T'ang China at height of power, c.750

- region under civil administration
- region under military government
- expansion during 7th century
- extent of Tibetan incursion, c.800

Inset map labels:
Dunhuang · Pingcheng (Wei north capital) · Wuwei · Ji'nan · Chang'an (Wei west capital) · Luoyang (Wei east capital) · **WEI** · Nanjing (Wu capital) · Chengdu (Shu capital) · **SHU** · **WU** · Guangzhou

After 220, China split into three rival states: Wei, Shu, and Wu

Border at collapse of Han dynasty, 220 AD

Main map labels:
Lake Balkhash · Damghan · Merv · Tashkent · Samarkand · Balkh · Herat · Kabul · Chinese protectorate 659–69 · Qiuici (Kucha) · Kashgar · Gilgit · Khotan · Karashahr · Turfan · Dunhuang · Chinese garrisons · *Taklimakan Desert* · *Gansu Corridor* · Lake Qinghai · Wuwei · Qin · Luoyang · Chang'an · Chegdu · Hong (Nanchang) · Jojun (Beijing) · *Yellow Sea* · Chinese protectorate 668–76 · P'yongyang · Nanhai · Guanzhou (Canton) · *South China*

The realism of figure modeling during the T'ang period also allowed for much whimsy, such as in this colorful *lokapala* or guardian beast, intended to keep evil spirits away from a noble's tomb.

755–63	818	829	863	878	c.875–907
Revolt by General An Lushan weakens dynastic power for decades	Strong centralized state control is re-established	T'ang forces fight off an invasion from Burma	T'ang armies again defeat the Burmese, this time at Hanoi	Chinese rebels kill 120,000 Christian, Muslim, Jewish, and Persian traders. Trade with West ends for a century	Famine and conflict destroys T'ang hold on power. End of dynasty triggers the Wars of the Five Dynasties

Scandal and Rebellion

The T'ang dynasty, like its Han predecessor, led a cultural and administrative renaissance in China. The capital city, Chang'an, was a bastion of religious tolerance; Buddhist sculpture and mural painting reached new heights of perfection. Porcelain—especially the famed "three-color glaze" wares—was prized throughout the ancient world. Poets flourished (almost all China's greatest were

ABOVE: Buddhism and Confucianism co-existed throughout the T'ang period, but Buddhism gave women greater recognition. Courtesans, like those pictured above, from the tomb of Princess Yung T'ai, came to have such power that it contributed to a male-dominated overthrow of the religion in the 9th century (see box, right). For wealthy T'ang officials, the extravagance of grave goods was paramount. In this collection from the tomb of Liu Tingxun, two officials, one civil, one military, are flanked by two guardians and two fabulous beasts. The figures, at 3¹/₂ feet high, are the tallest yet found. Liu Tingxun, a military commander, died in 728.

from the T'ang era), and the civil service system of public examinations was so well structured that key elements would survive into the 20th century.

By the reign of Xuanzong—Brilliant Emperor—(r.712–56), China had become the most powerful empire in the world. Enemies such as the Tibetans and the Asian Turks had suffered swingeing battlefield defeats, while at home grain reserves and treasury coffers bulged. Xuanzong purged the palace of the Empress Wu's advisers and ministers, blasted away a bloated bureaucracy, banned nepotism and profligacy at court, and restored central authority. Perhaps the effort of maintaining his glittering achievements eventually took its toll, or maybe he just became bored. Either way, by the early 740s he became obsessed with Yang Guifei, one of his sons' wives. It was a fatal weakness. Suddenly, her family—not the Emperor's talented advisers—took control and the public purse was ripped open. At one point 700 weavers were employed to boost Yang's collection of patterned silks and gauzes.

For Xuanzong's loyal followers, worse was to follow. Rumors swept the palace that Yang's friendship with a fat, uncouth Turkish general called An Lushan had blossomed into a steamy affair. In 751 she even adopted him as her son, allowing the savvy An to complete a breathtaking rise to power. When a chief minister died in 752, An launched a rebellion in the north, neatly timed to coincide with general unrest in the provinces. An massacred the townsfolk of Kaifeng and captured both Luoyang and Chang'an before declaring himself emperor. For Xuanzong an even greater anguish was to follow in the ignominy of exile. As he fled, his escort mutinied and demanded the death of Yang Guifei. Weeping, the pitiful ruler ordered his chief eunuch to strangle her with a silk cord. It was a murder later dubbed the "everlasting wrong" by a Chinese poet.

END OF T'ANG GREATNESS

The country's population plummeted from 53 million to 17 million during the An rebellion and it took more than a decade to restore peace. Even then the dynasty survived only through a patchwork alliance struck with central Asian tribes, and the old

authoritarian regime became a distant memory. Regional military governors grew in independence, openly withholding tax from their supposed masters, while a policy of clemency toward rebels allowed feuds to fester.

None of the 14 T'ang emperors after Xuanzong ruled with much stability—or even conviction—although there were some social and economic advances. Paper money changed hands for the first time and craft guilds increased the skills of the workforce. But such initiatives were rare in a dynasty that by the end of the ninth century had lost its way. In 907 the last T'ang emperor, the 15-year-old Aidi, was deposed by the military governor Zhu Wen and China entered 50 years of chaos known as the Five Dynasties period.

The Chinese characters on this coin say a lot about its history. The words read "Dali yuanbao." "Dali" is the name of the reigning emperor (r.766-79). "Yuanbao" means "coin." Coins of this kind were not made in the main Chinese homeland, and were more usually used in trading along the Silk Road in the northwest of Xinjiang province. It is thought that loyal Chinese officials, cut off in Qiuci (modern-day Kucha) from the homeland by Tibetan forces which had occupied the Gansu Corridor, had the coins minted after hearing that there had been a change of Emperor. The Dali yuanbao seen here and at lifesize is just under an inch in diameter.

CHAPTER FOUR

Empires of Faith

Mankind requires food, water, and shelter to survive. But in his darkest hours, companionship and faith sustain him too. Ancient empires used religion (organized faith) as a means of control, but for some faith was their main reason for existence.

The kingdom of Ethiopia was the first Christian country in Africa and for centuries the only independent nation on the continent. It is interesting to ponder the strength it gained as a nation from its faith. At Axum in Ethiopia the multi-storey buildings, funeral slabs, and coins that belonged to an empire that thrived between the second and seventh centuries are impressive. Its wealth was built on trade, particularly in ivory and skins.

FAITH FOSTERS CULTURE

In Asia the Abbasids were popular replacements to the Umayyads as the leaders of Islam, entirely because of the religious orthodoxy that they embraced. As descendants of Mohammed's uncle, they were imbued with an authority that few questioned. With the Abbasids, a golden age dawned: art, architecture, and literature benefited the whole world. At the end, military might defeated them rather than a reversal in their religious creed.

Similarly in Europe, under the Carolingians, dedicated Christians, learning and literacy increased dramatically. The continent enjoyed a brief renaissance during the era called the Dark Ages (because of its assumed lack of culture). Charlemagne was the charismatic leader who steered his people toward the Pope, with the combined might of the cross and the sword.

Carolingian knight and man-at-arms.

Islamic expansion relied on the strength of its cavalry.

In this chapter we focus on three very different empires founded on religious principles. All of them held such influence that despite the passing of many centuries their legacies are still with us today.

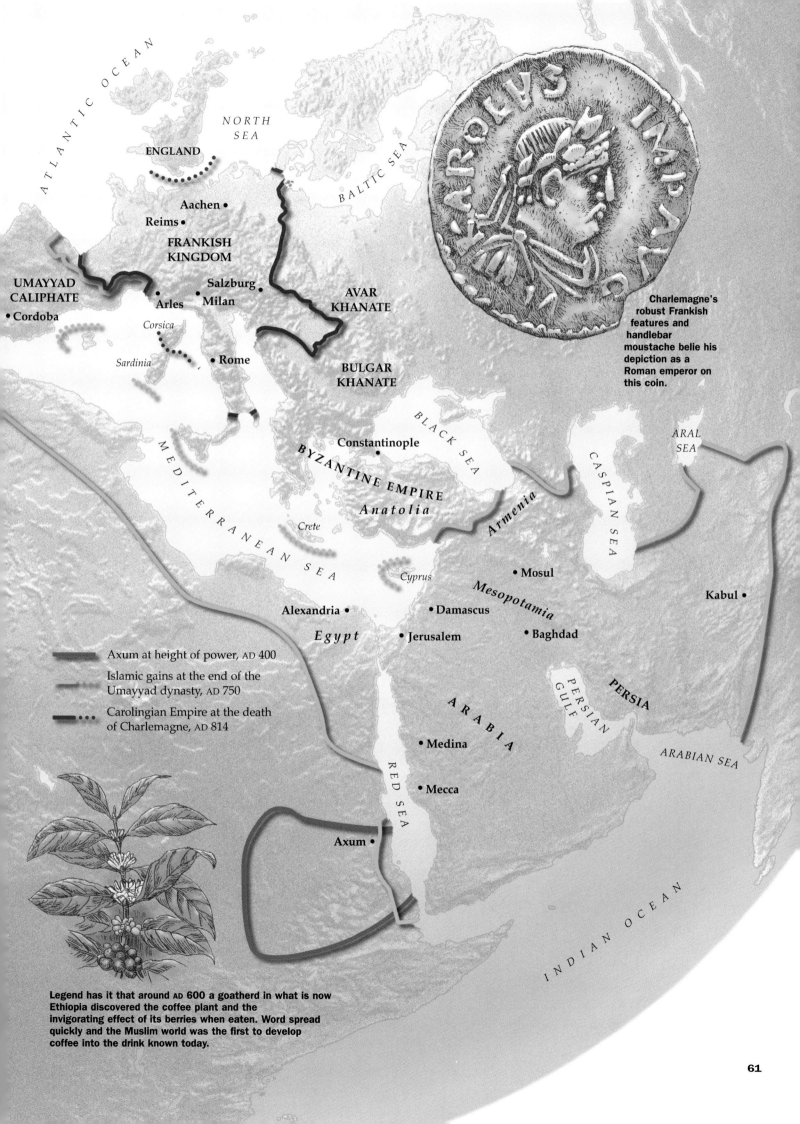

ATLANTIC OCEAN

NORTH SEA

ENGLAND

BALTIC SEA

Aachen •

Reims •

FRANKISH KINGDOM

UMAYYAD CALIPHATE

• Cordoba

Arles •

Salzburg •

Milan •

Corsica

Sardinia

• Rome

AVAR KHANATE

BULGAR KHANATE

Constantinople •

BYZANTINE EMPIRE

Anatolia

BLACK SEA

MEDITERRANEAN SEA

Crete

Cyprus

Armenia

CASPIAN SEA

ARAL SEA

• Mosul

Mesopotamia

Kabul •

Alexandria •

Egypt

• Damascus

• Jerusalem

• Baghdad

PERSIAN GULF

PERSIA

Axum at height of power, AD 400

Islamic gains at the end of the Umayyad dynasty, AD 750

Carolingian Empire at the death of Charlemagne, AD 814

A R A B I A

• Medina

RED SEA

• Mecca

ARABIAN SEA

Axum •

INDIAN OCEAN

Charlemagne's robust Frankish features and handlebar moustache belie his depiction as a Roman emperor on this coin.

Legend has it that around AD 600 a goatherd in what is now Ethiopia discovered the coffee plant and the invigorating effect of its berries when eaten. Word spread quickly and the Muslim world was the first to develop coffee into the drink known today.

Axum and the Ark

In a corner of East Africa, there lie the remains of a once-great empire with a convoluted, mythical, and mysterious past that still tantalizes researchers and archaeologists.

BELOW: The Chapel of the Tablet at Axum (Aksum), built by Emperor Haile Selassie in the last century, is said to house the Ark of the Covenant, containing the tablets of stone engraved with the Ten Commandments and given to Moses after the Exodus.

Axum was the center of an empire that dominated the region of modern Ethiopia and Yemen for more than three centuries, from the second to the fifth centuries AD. Axum replaced Da'amat, established since the seventh century BC in the northern highlands of Tigray, as the region's premier trading place. The Axum Empire remains shrouded in mystery, particularly due to its associations with the Queen of Sheba, Solomon, and the story of the Ark of the Covenant in the *Old Testament*. According to the Bible the Ten Commandments delivered to Moses on two tablets of stone were stored within a chest made of gilded acacia wood. Two cherubs stood at either end of a golden lid. The Ark measured 45 inches by 27 inches, and poles were attached to each side to enable porters to carry it. It is said that the Ark, built to Moses'

specification, was taken into battle during the time of King David and stored in a temple when Solomon was on the throne. After that, its whereabouts became shrouded in mystery. For years it was thought to have been destroyed in one of the campaigns against the Jews. A more recent theory says that the Ark was taken to Ethiopia and is, even now, stored in a monastery there, closely guarded by a monk. The Ark is said to be shielded from public view in the Chapel of the Tablet, built by Emperor Haile Selassie in the 1900s. Previously, it had been kept in the Church of Mary of Zion, Ethiopia's holiest shrine, in ancient Axum.

AXUM AND SOLOMON'S ISRAEL

A medieval account of the Ark's passage to Axum states: The Queen of Sheba—whose realm included Yemen and Ethiopia—visited King Solomon of Israel in pursuit of wisdom. By the time she returned to her capital Mahrib, the Queen was pregnant. The son she bore, Menelik, was anointed by Solomon as King of Ethiopia and went on to found a royal dynasty. According to one written account, when the elders of Israel sent their sons to visit him, they took the Ark with them. Other accounts claim that the Ark was taken from the Temple in Jerusalem

Map

Mediterranean Sea

Memphis •

- Roman Empire, 1 BC
- Meroë, 1 BC
- Axum, 1 BC
- Axum, AD 400
- Axum, AD 800
- border of modern Ethiopia

Thebes •

Mecca •

MEROE

Red Sea

HIMYARITE KINGDOM, AD 400

ABBASID CALIPHATE AD 800

Semitic people migrating from across the Red Sea probably mingled with the indigenous Kushite farmers in the Ethiopian lowlands to form the early Axumites.

Territory taken by Axum from Meroe

• Saana

• Adulis

Axum • (Aksum)

Lake T'ana

Lake Abaya

Lake Turkhana

c.1000 BC	c.550 BC	c.260 BC	AD 300–350	901	1220	1332	1441
Solomon and the Queen of Sheba are said to have founded Abyssinia (Ethiopia)	Arabs from Yemen cross the Red Sea to Ethiopia, intermarry with indigenous people, and found the kingdom of Axum	The port of Adulis on Ethiopia's Red Sea coast is one of the most important in the ancient world	Empire of Axum reaches its zenith	Christian Ethiopia signs trade pact with Muslim Yemen	Ethiopian Christians create churches hewn from rock	Ethiopian monastic movement is founded by Ewostatewos	Ethiopian Church signs accord with Roman Church

just before the Babylonians invaded Judah, taking its people into captivity. It went to the Upper Nile, where it was kept for years before being moved to Ethiopia.

Early assumptions held that the empire's founders were from Arabia, because their language, Ge'ez, is based on Arabic. Axum's sculpture and architecture were also seen to bear the hallmarks of the southern Arabs. It now seems more likely, however, that Axum's rulers were an indigenous people whose culture was strongly influenced by the Arabs from just across the Red Sea.

The first rulers were pagans. Under their leadership Axum grew into an important trading center. It dealt in goods like gold, ivory, animal pelts, incense, and slaves. Exports went out of the busy Red Sea port of Adulis at a time when Roman and Persian traders were vying for dominance. Merchants from Axum were frequent visitors to Egypt in the north, Somaliland in the East, and to the ports across the nearby Red Sea. Axum's land was fertile and productive. Axumite influence increased further when the Kushite kingdom of Meroe,

directly to the north, succumbed to invasion.

Little was known about Axum until the British Institute undertook excavations in 1973. Among the most impressive artifacts discovered so far are stelae—carved upright stones—of mighty proportions. There were tombs (previously visited by grave robbers) which contained glass items from Rome, precious stones, hunting weapons, and pottery. Minted coins have also been found. Work to reveal more about mysterious Axum continues.

ABOVE: An aerial view of the grouping of ancient stelae found at the edge of modern Axum.

BELOW: Ethiopia's most holy Christian shrine is the Church of Mary of Zion. Legend says the Ark of the Covenant was housed here until its removal to the Chapel of the Tablet.

1494
A Portuguese envoy is sent to Ethiopia, but detained by the Emperor

1509
Ethiopia sends an ambassador to Portugal

1529
Muslim forces attack from across the Red Sea, occupying the province of Shoa

1531
Portugal sends troops to assist Ethiopia against the Muslims

1632
Ethiopia frees itself from rule by Roman Church and returns to Coptic Christianity

19th and 20th centuries
European powers colonize the country

1936
Italian forces invade Addis Ababa; Emperor Haile Selassie flees into exile in London

1941
Following Italy's defeat in WWII, Emperor Haile Selassie is restored to the throne

Merchants and Muslims

Christianity came to Axum in the fourth century by a bizarre quirk of fate. A Christian philosopher by the name of Meropius, bound for India, was shipwrecked on the coast. Although he died, his two companions survived and when they began to spread the word of the gospels they found a receptive audience. Ultimately the fortunate Frumentius and Aedesius became valued members of the royal household. Frumentius even became regent for the young prince Ezana upon the death of the king. The relationship between the two was strong.

In maturity Ezana supported a move to make Axum a Christian nation. For his part, Frumentius was appointed the first *abuna* (bishop) by the Bishop of Alexandria. He became known as the Bishop of Peace and was later made a saint.

In the fifth century, nine monks arrived (from either Syria or Egypt) introducing the Axum church to monasticism. At this time

STOLEN GOODS

A bid for the return of a 75-foot high obelisk looted from Axum by Mussolini in 1938 after Italian troops overwhelmed the country continues. The obelisk is one of a group, to which the one pictured left also belongs. Ethiopians have sought the return of the object since 1945. An agreement to bring back the obelisk, which now stands in Rome, was struck in 1997 but it fell apart due to Italian concerns about its fate while Ethiopia was involved in a civil war. Ethiopia has also requested the return of a crown and a historic book taken by the British in 1868.

the Christian church was riven with debate about the nature and person of Christ. These newcomers were Monophysites—they believed that the divine and human natures of Jesus were the same. Many in the established church disagreed, and in 451 the Council of Chalcedon agreed with the establishment. The Monophysites were marginalized and retreated to cities on the edge of the known world—such as Axum.

The Ethiopian Church, along with the Coptic Church of Egypt and Christian churches in Syria, Turkey, and Armenia, thereafter operated in concert as a group, distinct from the rest of the Roman church. There was also an influx of Jews in the sixth century and some Ethiopians converted to Judaism. However, the empire remained predominantly Christian.

INVASIONS END AXUM'S ERA

At its peak, the Axum Empire incorporated Nubia and the Ethiopian highlands, and extended over the Red Sea to Yemen. However, decay set in during the last half of the sixth century. Long established trading routes shifted when the Byzantines, who were allies of Axum, went to war with the Sassanians—long-term foes of Axum. At this period Axum's southerly position meant that it had ceased to be the busy junction for merchants it had once been.

For years, Muslim forces had left the Axum Empire in peace because the prophet Mohammed taught that special favor should be shown to Ethiopians in return for the kindness offered to some of his companions. But relations finally deteriorated. The expansion first of the Sassanians and then of Islam drove Axum's people from the Yemen and even exiled them from the port of Adulis, which was crucial to its prosperity. Muslim unity further helped to isolate Ethiopians from their former Mediterranean allies, although Axum did maintain religious links with Egypt. Greek, the language of the Axum traders, became obsolete.

Many Ethiopians retreated to the hills to evade Islamic invasions and Axum appears to have been deserted by the end of the first millennium. Only with the rise of the Zagwe dynasty in the 12th century was the prestige of Ethiopia restored.

BELOW LEFT: A few Coptic icons exist of St. Frumentius, first bishop of Christian Axum, but no one can say what his true likeness was.

BELOW: This woven silk panel—probably a sleeve ornament—dates from the Coptic period, early 8th century. It was found in Upper Egypt, and is typical of the high quality of weaving and decoration that graced wealthy Coptic aristocracy in the region before the major Muslim thrust.

The Rise of Islam

Around the Mediterranean, Christianity had supplanted the pantheistic religions of most states, apart from the semitic races. Now, from this region, a new religious force emerged in the seventh century to form a new empire of faith.

Mohammed ascends to heaven on his horse. Artists depicted Mohammed's life but avoided the sacrilege of showing either his or his mother's face. Miniature of 14th century.

For centuries the Arab tribes were organized only into small nomadic bands, and skirmished among themselves and with their neighbors. Although feared and admired warriors, the prevailing Arab disunity weakened them. And then, with the birth of Islam, harmony and a sense of purpose arrived and transformed the Arabs into a major world force.

Islam, which means "submission" [to the word of God], evolved from the insights of Mohammed (c.570–632). He espoused the worship of a single god, Allah, and said he was Allah's messenger, the last in a long line of prophets that included Abraham, Moses, and Jesus. His revelations form the text of the *Koran*.

So striking was Mohammed's vision that within his lifetime his home of Mecca became a holy city devoted to the sole worship of Allah. It was in Mecca that Abraham had once built the Kaa'ba, a monument originally dedicated to numerous deities. Mohammed faced a great deal of opposition. Not only were colonies of Jews implacably opposed to his new religion, but so were fellow Arabs. The prophet was driven from Mecca and fled to Medina. There he gathered an army and ultimately returned to Mecca victorious.

Mohammed, who had a daughter named Fatima but no son, was succeeded on his death by Abu Bakr, his father-in-law. Abu Bakr instituted an agenda to spread Islam across the civilized world. The Islamic empire rapidly mushroomed, with the Arabian peninsular, North Africa, Spain, Mesopotamia, and Persia either converting or being annexed to the new credo within a century of the prophet's death. Few defeats befell Islam in battle, but one was at Poitiers in France in 733, against a Christian army mustered by Charles Martel. Trade was as important in spreading Islam as conquest. Trading routes that Arabs had sailed or caravanned for centuries became vectors of Mohammed's teaching.

SUNNI AND SHI'IA

Despite these astonishing successes there were difficulties over succession. The fourth caliph, Ali, (Mohammed's son-in-law)

AD 744	750	762	807	817	c.820	827	836
Revolt by the Abbasids in Persia leads to civil war in Arab Empire	The Abbasids gain power after overthrowing the Umayyad caliphate	Baghdad is chosen as the Abbasid capital	Harun al-Rashid grants the Franks a decree protecting Christian Holy sites in Jerusalem	The Aghlabids in Tunisia break free of the Abbasids to form their own Muslim dynasty	Reign of caliph Harun al-Rashid inspires writing of the Thousand and One Nights	Abbasid general Abdullah bin Tahir retakes Alexandria from Muslim pirates	Baghdad suffers from serious civil unrest between Arabs and their Turk mercenaries

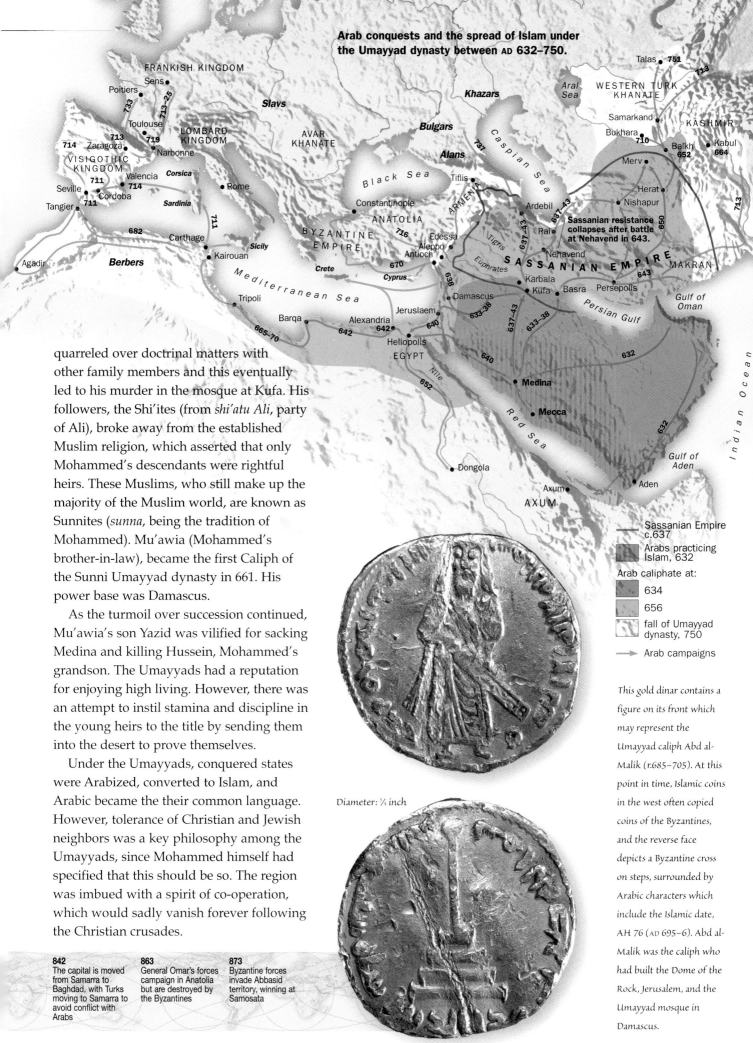

FRANKISH KINGDOM
Sens
Poitiers
733
Toulouse
713-25
713
LOMBARD
719
714 Zaragoza
KINGDOM
Narbonne
VISIGOTHIC
KINGDOM
Valencia Corsica
711 714
Seville
Cordoba
Tangier 711
682
Carthage
Sardinia
Rome
Agadir
Berbers
Mediterranean Sea
Tripoli
Barqa
665-70
Sicily
Kairouan
711
Crete
Cyprus
670
Slavs
AVAR
KHANATE
Black Sea
Constantinople
ANATOLIA
BYZANTINE
716
EMPIRE
Edessa
Aleppo
Antioch
Khazars
Bulgars
Alans
Tiflis
ARMENIA
Ardebil
Rai
637-43
Damascus
633-38
Jeruslaem
Alexandria
642
640
642
Heliopolis
EGYPT
640
652
Nile
Dongola
Red Sea
Medina
Mecca
Axum
Aden
AXUM
Aral
Sea
WESTERN TURK
KHANATE
Talas 751
713
Samarkand
Bukhara
710
KASHMIR
Balkh 652
Kabul 664
Merv
Herat
Nishapur
713
Caspian Sea
Sassanian resistance
collapses after battle
at Nehavend in 643.
650
Nehavend
SASSANIAN EMPIRE
MAKRAN
Karbala
Kufa Basra Persepolis
643
Euphrates
Tigris
Persian Gulf
Gulf of
Oman
632
632
Gulf of
Aden
Indian Ocean

quarreled over doctrinal matters with other family members and this eventually led to his murder in the mosque at Kufa. His followers, the Shi'ites (from *shi'atu Ali*, party of Ali), broke away from the established Muslim religion, which asserted that only Mohammed's descendants were rightful heirs. These Muslims, who still make up the majority of the Muslim world, are known as Sunnites (*sunna*, being the tradition of Mohammed). Mu'awia (Mohammed's brother-in-law), became the first Caliph of the Sunni Umayyad dynasty in 661. His power base was Damascus.

As the turmoil over succession continued, Mu'awia's son Yazid was vilified for sacking Medina and killing Hussein, Mohammed's grandson. The Umayyads had a reputation for enjoying high living. However, there was an attempt to instil stamina and discipline in the young heirs to the title by sending them into the desert to prove themselves.

Under the Umayyads, conquered states were Arabized, converted to Islam, and Arabic became the their common language. However, tolerance of Christian and Jewish neighbors was a key philosophy among the Umayyads, since Mohammed himself had specified that this should be so. The region was imbued with a spirit of co-operation, which would sadly vanish forever following the Christian crusades.

842
The capital is moved from Samarra to Baghdad, with Turks moving to Samarra to avoid conflict with Arabs

863
General Omar's forces campaign in Anatolia but are destroyed by the Byzantines

873
Byzantine forces invade Abbasid territory, winning at Samosata

Sassanian Empire c.637
Arabs practicing Islam, 632
Arab caliphate at:
634
656
fall of Umayyad dynasty, 750
→ Arab campaigns

Diameter: ¼ inch

This gold dinar contains a figure on its front which may represent the Umayyad caliph Abd al-Malik (r.685–705). At this point in time, Islamic coins in the west often copied coins of the Byzantines, and the reverse face depicts a Byzantine cross on steps, surrounded by Arabic characters which include the Islamic date, AH 76 (AD 695–6). Abd al-Malik was the caliph who had built the Dome of the Rock, Jerusalem, and the Umayyad mosque in Damascus.

67

Golden Age of the Abbasids

The infant religion was put in jeopardy by the continuing Shi'ite-Sunnite conflict. Discontent over taxation in subject states and breakaway movements eventually led to rebellion in Khorasan, where the rebels proclaimed Abu al-Abbas caliph in 749. (Al-Abbas was a descendant of an uncle of Mohammed who helped to run the Islamic empire following the prophet's death.)

Short-lived Umayyad resistance ended in 750 at the Battle of the Zab (in modern-day Azerbaijan). The new Abbasid dynasty based itself in Persia and Mesopotamia. They veered away from Syria and much of Arabia. Indeed, they isolated themselves from Arabian influences, which caused further resentment between the two forms of Islam.

Opportunists on the borders took advantage to set up independent caliphates. Yet despite these unpromising beginnings a golden age of Islam dawned.

The Umayyad family was slaughtered in the religious upheaval, although crucially Abd al-Rahman fled to establish a rival empire in Spain. By 929 there was even a competing emirate. For support they counted on the Berbers and other North African tribes and the result was that Moorish culture—vastly different from that flourishing in Persia—became prevalent in the western Mediterranean region.

The Shi'ite faction were among the supporters of the initial Abbasid uprising. However, links became severed and the Abbasids even reversed their views on Shi'ia beliefs. Conflict between both sides crystallized in a rebellion staged by the Shi'ites in Mecca in 786. After widespread killings, a minority of Shi'ites escaped and fled to West Africa to establish a realm of their own.

The city of Baghdad became the Abbasid capital from 762. According to records it took four years and 100,000 men to redesign the city. It proved well worth the effort. Baghdad became the intellectual center of the world. The first commentaries on the *Koran* were written there.

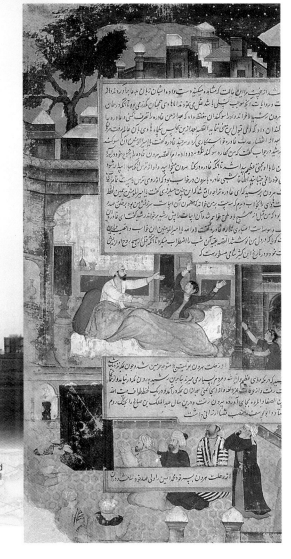

892	929	1055	1155–1194	1258
The capital is moved from Samarra back to Baghdad	Hamdanid dynasty takes advantage of now-weak Abbasid dynasty by taking over Syria and Kurdistan	The Seljuk Soghril-Beg enters Baghdad as a liberator and restores Abbasid faith to the Sunni form of Islam	The Abbasids regain control of Mesopotamia from the Seljuk Turks	End of the Abbasid dynasty as Mongol hordes sack Baghdad and slaughter its entire population

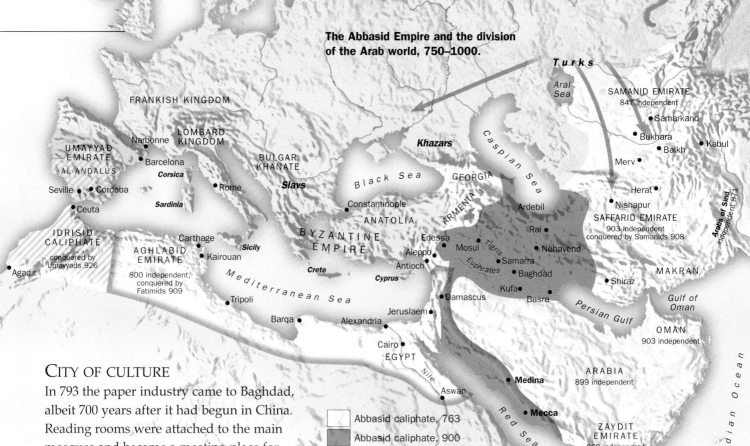

The Abbasid Empire and the division of the Arab world, 750–1000.

FRANKISH KINGDOM

LOMBARD KINGDOM

UMAYYAD EMIRATE
AL-ANDALUS

Narbonne
Barcelona
Corsica
Seville • Cordoba
Ceuta
Sardinia
• Rome
Slavs

IDRISID CALIPHATE
conquered by Umayyads 926
Agadir

Carthage
AGHLABID EMIRATE
800 independent, conquered by Fatimids 909
Kairouan
Sicily
Crete
Tripoli

Mediterranean Sea

Barqa
Alexandria
Cairo
EGYPT
Jeruslaem
Damascus
Nile
Aswan

BULGAR KHANATE
Khazars
Black Sea
Constantinople
ANATOLIA
BYZANTINE EMPIRE
Edessa
Aleppo
Antioch
Cyprus

GEORGIA
ARMENIA
Ardebil
Mosul
Tigris
Euphrates
Rai
Samarra
Baghdad
Kufa
Basra
Nehavend
Persian Gulf
Shiraz

Caspian Sea
Aral Sea
Turks

SAMANID EMIRATE
847 independent
• Samarkand
• Bukhara
• Balkh • Kabul
Merv •
Herat •
Nishapur •
SAFFARID EMIRATE
903 independent conquered by Samanids 908

Arabs of Sind independent 871

MAKRAN

Gulf of Oman

OMAN
903 independent

Medina
Red Sea
Mecca

ARABIA
899 independent

ZAYDIT EMIRATE
860 independent
San'a
Axum
AXUM
Aden

Gulf of Aden

Indian Ocean

□ Abbasid caliphate, 763
■ Abbasid caliphate, 900
□ Umayyad emirate, 763
▨ Umayyad caliphate, c.1000
□ Fatimid caliphate, c.990
➤ Turkish expansion, 990–1100

CITY OF CULTURE

In 793 the paper industry came to Baghdad, albeit 700 years after it had begun in China. Reading rooms were attached to the main mosques and became a meeting place for study and debate. For leisure, the board games chess and backgammon were popular. Religious occasions were keenly adhered to. One writer observed: "So faithful were they to the ordinances of their religion that if a man met his father's murderer unarmed in one of the sacred months he would not harm him."

One of the Abbasid caliphs was Harun al-Rashid (the upright), the grandson of Abu al-Abbas. Stories about his reign are the stuff of fables. At his son Mamoun's wedding ceremony pearls were used as confetti as the happy couple sat on a gold carpet inlaid with jewels. Guests were given slaves or land by their generous host. His cousin's wife Zubeidah is credited with beginning the fashion for jeweled shoes. It is said her palace boasted a golden tree adorned with golden mechanical birds, complete with a mechanism to make them chirp.

Markets in the Abbasid Empire were stocked with silks from China, spices from India, gems from Turkey, ivory, gold, weapons, and slaves from as far apart as Africa and Scandinavia. A post office existed, with services supplemented by carrier pigeon. Across the empire there were numerous hostels to provide shelter for weary travelers.

Harun al-Rashid expanded his empire's borders with the invasion of Cyprus and Rhodes. His clashes with the crumbling Byzantine Empire generally proved fruitful. Yet already there were rumblings of discontent through the Abbasid Empire that would soon threaten its very existence.

Dazzling in the sun, the geometric abstract decoration of Abbasid buildings graced even the far-flung outposts, such as the Shah-i-Zinda Mosque at Samarkand. This type of abstract Arabic decoration came to be known as "arabesque."

CHAPTER FOUR

RIGHT: The Mezquita (mosque) of Cordoba embodied the power of Islam in Spain. The original was built on foundations of a Visigothic church by caliph Abd al-Rahman I, starting in 785. Additions were made up to the end of the 10th century. After the fall of Islam in Spain, the Mezquita became a cathedral (the bell tower stands on the site of the original minaret. As in Cordoba, elsewhere Arab scholars set up academies to study the rediscovered sciences of geometry and astronomy, as below.

Philosophy and Failure

In literature and the arts Mamoun proved as sage as his father. One historian says: "[Mamoun] looked for knowledge where it was evident, and thanks to the breadth of his conceptions and the power of his intelligence he drew it from places where it was hidden. He entered into relations with the emperors of Byzantium, gave them rich gifts and asked them to give him books of philosophy, which they had in their possession. These emperors sent him those works of Plato, Aristotle, Hippocrates, Galen, Euclid, and Ptolemy... Mamoun then chose the most experienced translators and commissioned them to translate these works to the best of their ability. After the translating was done as perfectly as possible the caliph urged his subjects to read the translations and encouraged

them to study them. Consequently the scientific movement became strong under this prince's reign. Scholars held high rank and the caliph surrounded himself with learned men, legal experts, rationalist theologians, lexicographers, annalists, metricians, and genealogists. He then ordered instruments to be manufactured."

GLEANING WISDOM

Because the ancient Greeks were pagans, Christian monarchs had suppressed the "heretical" old Greek writings, which gathered dust in libraries throughout the Byzantine Empire, most notably in Alexandria, Egypt. As Islam swept through the region, Byzantine libraries fell into Muslim hands, and Arab scholars appreciated the knowledge of the ancient Greek thinkers contained in the books they found on dusty shelves. The result was an enormous leap forward in astronomy, mathematics, and medicine.

Descriptive geography and the art of cartography advanced tremendously. Mamoun founded the Academy of Wisdom in Baghdad, which became a major center for scientific study. Pioneering works on dictionaries and grammar were produced. Scholars from all over the world visited, in awe of the broad scope of literature.

A wide-ranging irrigation system was, among others, one technological advance under the Abbbasids that brought about a boom for agriculture. The destruction of this system in the Middle Ages by the Mongols

crippled the region.

The Baghdad caliphs attempted to impose their will on all their subjects, but in practice the majority of their people lived so far distant from the capital that the caliphs' whims were of very little consequence. In practical terms, the subject tribes and peoples had a great deal of independence—as long as they adhered to the Abbasid form of Islam.

The caliph's bodyguard was pride of the Abbasid army. Its main units comprised Turkik troops, who were both ferocious fighters and unswervingly loyal to Islam. Enemies faced a shower of fiery arrows from the experienced shots of the "flame-thrower" archers. However, changes in the military brought about by Mamoun after he seized the caliphate from his brother in 813 sparked fissures in the Abbasid Empire. In pursuit of a loyal troop, Mamoun gathered together a force of slaves and gave them unprecedented privilege. They were known as the Mamluks.

Hostility toward the caliphate was compounded with Mamoun's avowed aim to introduce Greek and Indian works alongside those of Islam. First Egypt then Persia declared themselves independent and the piecemeal disintegration proved impossible to stop. By the middle of the tenth century, the surviving Abbasid territories were taken over by the Buyid dynasty. The Abbasids retained a presence, but only as religious figureheads. The Abbasid dynasty in the east was ended in 1258 when Baghdad fell to the marauding and ruthless Mongols.

WHO HAS ALL THE BEST TUNES?

There was nothing to rival this cultural richness in the rest of Europe. The East stood head and shoulders above the West in terms of knowledge and sophistication. Nevertheless, when the Crusades got underway in 1096 to counter Islamic encroachment in the Holy Land, Muslims were depicted as ignorant infidels. In 1213 Pope Innocent III said: "The false prophet Mohammed… has seduced many men from the truth by worldly enticements and the pleasures of the flesh." The baseless propaganda worked well. Crusaders fought with gusto against Islam believing that they were on the side of the righteous.

The Wonders of Creation and the Oddities of Existence, written in 1270 by Zakariya Qazwini, a judge in Wasit, Iraq, remained popular science reading for centuries. In the illustrated compendium, Qazwini covered many topics including geography, natural history, astrology, astronomy, and angels. The archangel Gabriel, seen here, was important to both Muslims and Christians. Gabriel brought Mohammed the words of the Koran.

The Carolingian Empire

After the fall of the Western Roman Empire in the fifth century, there was a prolonged period of chaos as barbarian tribes flowed through the remnants of the empire. And then in the eighth century, a new unifying power emerged.

This mosaic depicts Saint Peter handing Charlemagne (right) the flag of Rome and Pope Leo III the holy stola—a symbol of the unity of Church and State. In reality, the deal that saw Charlemagne crowned Roman Emperor was a mutually advantageous one. In return for papal authority sanctifying the right of the monarch to rule, the papacy received the protection of a united Frankish Empire, which rivaled Byzantium. The papacy also enjoyed powerful support for its doctrine against bitter rivals the Byzantine Orthodox Church. It is unlikely that Charlemagne desired a wholesale fusion of Church and State in the way Leo and his successors clearly desired. The emperor later made a point of having his son crowned in his imperial city of Aachen rather than in Rome, and Pope Leo III was not invited.

Charlemagne (the name derives from *Carolus Magnus Rex,* meaning "Charles the Great King") came to power in AD 768 after the death of his father, Pepin. Pepin's Frankish kingdom was at first divided between Charles and his brother Carloman, but Charles took over both kingdoms when his brother died in 772. Ties between the Frankish kingdom and the Church in Rome had always been strong, but less than 30 years later, on Christmas Day 800, it would result in Charlemagne's coronation by Pope Leo III (p.795–816) as the effective political leader of western Europe—with the new title of *Imperator Augustus* (venerable emperor).

The full title was "Charles, most serene Augustus, crowned by God, great and pacific emperor, governing the Roman Empire." The events that led up to this dramatic coronation are well-documented. In 799 a revolt broke out in Rome, and Charlemagne marched south with his armies to restore Leo to papal power. Charlemagne's holy coronation as Roman Emperor was Leo's reward. The title really reflected the new political reality of Frankish power in Europe rather than any resurgence of the defunct Roman Empire.

At this time, the pagan Saxons posed a serious threat to the Franks. Charlemagne determined to incorporate their lands and convert them to Christianity. He waged a series of wars against them that lasted for 32 years. He dispersed some 10,000 people from the Saxon heartland to distant corners of the Carolingian domain to encourage their integration. In 782, he executed an estimated 4,500 rebellious Saxons. The cruelties on both sides were legendary.

History is kind to Charlemagne, however. The bloody battles, aggressive alliances, and devious diplomacy that helped to install him as undisputed king are often overlooked. His reputation derives from the sheer extent of his sovereignty and the cultural progress made under his leadership. He is sometimes referred to as the father of modern Europe, a reputation enhanced by the romantic epic poetry of Old French literature, which recalls his deeds and his chivalry. His title of Roman Emperor upheld the imperial image, since people longed for the halcyon days of the Roman Empire.

BRIEF PERIOD OF UNITY

At its peak, Charlemagne's empire encompassed the region that now comprises France, Switzerland, Belgium, the Netherlands, most of Italy, and sizeable chunks of Germany, Austria, and Spain.

AD 741–68	768	771	771	772	773	775	778
Reign of Pepin the Short	Charles and Carloman share control of the Frankish kingdom when their father, Pepin the Short, dies	Carloman dies and his family flees into exile in Lombardy	Charles takes full control of the Frankish kingdom and adopts the title Charlemagne (Charles the Great)	Charlemagne destroys the column of Irminsul at the River Weser, a tree worshipped by the pagan Saxons	Charlemagne conquers Lombardy and captures Carloman's family	War breaks out with the Saxons	Carolingian forces fight the Muslims in Spain

During his tenure he fought 53 campaigns to achieve this unification and freely confessed it would not have come about but for frequent use of the sword. He suffered some defeats, including one at the hands of Basques in Spain in 778, but these were rare.

Charlemagne led a strong, central government and where it ruled he was determined to inspire and innovate. As a student of language, astronomy, and the arts he sponsored the Carolingian Renaissance that centered on the study of the Latin classics. This went hand-in-hand with a program of education, assistance for farmers, and large building works—particularly churches. He founded a court library and an academy to support the education of his knights. Uppermost in his mind was the spread of Christianity. He was unceasingly generous to the Church and gave aid to the poor both at home and in his newly-conquered lands.

Innovative new laws recognized the rights of the different tribes that fell under his control. Despite his bloody war-waging he was undoubtedly an enlightened

monarch who genuinely cared about justice in his new lands, and he took considerable satisfaction in imposing order and fairness. An able administrator, Charlemagne kept ranks of clergymen at his side to act as civil servants. Chief among them was Alcuin, a monk originally from York.

Charlemagne's father, Pepin III—son of Charles Martel, who turned the Arab invasion back at Poitiers in 732—made an alliance with the papacy. In return, Pope Zacharias crowned him King of the Franks in 751, pictured above from a medieval French print.

Growth of the Carolingian Empire, 732–814.

Celts

NORTH SEA

Celts

Anglo-Saxons

Frisians

Elbe

ATLANTIC OCEAN

Celts

London

Utrecht

Saxons

SLAVIC PEOPLES

Frankish kingdom, 732

English Channel

Aix-la-Chapelle (Aachen)

Cologne

Rhine

THURINGIA

Frankish kingdom at accession of Charlemagne, 768

AUSTRASIA

Rouen

Reims

Bretons

Paris

Mainz

gains under Charlemagne, 768–814

Seine

NEUSTRIA

Loire

Rhine

ALEMANIA

Byzantine empire, 732

Poitiers

Salzburg

Umayyad caliphate, 732

BURGUNDY

BAVARIA

Charlemagne's throne, in Aachen.

Bay of Biscay

Bordeaux

Lyon

KINGDOM OF LOMBARDY

Danube

AVAR KHANATE

Sava

KINGDOM OF ASTURIAS

AQUITAINE

Rhone

Milan

Po

Venice

Croats

Serbs

Danube

UMAYYAD CALIPHATE

Narbonne

Arles

Marseilles

Ravenna

SLAVIC PEOPLES

BULGAR KHANATE

Zaragosa

By the 9th century, the Umayyad capital Cordoba was the largest city in western Europe.

Toledo

Barcelona

Corsica

Rome

Vlachs

Constantinople

Cordoba

Seville

Balearic Islands

Sardinia

Mediterranean Sea

In the "Patrimony of St. Peter," Charlemagne granted land to the Pope, which later became the Papal States.

Benevento

Naples

Palermo

Sicily

Syracuse

Order and Progress

Charlemagne made his headquarters at Aix-la-Chapelle, known today as Aachen. He chose the site for its thermal springs, which had baptismal significance for him and had been equally popular with the Romans four centuries earlier. Charlemagne would often make key decisions while bathing in the hot springs, either alone or with his advisors. Outside in the palace grounds roamed an elephant that had been a gift from the caliph of Baghdad, Haroun al-Rashid (*see pages 68–69*).

Charlemagne built a magnificent eight-sided church at Aix-la-Chapelle. It had marble columns, solid brass doors, silver and gold lamps, and antique Roman statues imported from Italy. The scholar Einhard recorded the key events of Charlemagne's life, in addition to much trivial but fascinating detail, in the biography *Vita Karoli Magni*. Einhard, who addressed Charlemagne as "my lord and foster father," accounted for his motivation in recording the life of Charlemagne by saying: "I would rather commit my story to writing… than to suffer the most glorious life of this most excellent king, the greatest of all the princes of his day, and his illustrious deeds, hard for men of later times to imitate, to be wrapped in the darkness of oblivion."

Einhard's devotion has furnished later generations with some fascinating insights. We know, for example, that Charlemagne was a sober person who abhorred drunkenness in others. He preferred a simple spit roast to any lavish banquet. He also delighted in reading, music, and examining a dissertation from a visiting scholar. Charlemagne was over six feet tall (measurement of his bones has subsequently verified this), so his physical presence must have been imposing in an age when the average height was several inches less than today's.

The Carolingian Empire, like most, was rooted in a personality cult. Charlemagne died on January 28, 814 at the age of 72, in the 47th year of his reign. A once-proud figure, he was by this time lame and frequently afflicted by fever. His son Louis had served as co-ruler in the last year of Charlemagne's life. Louis inherited from his father a passionate interest in the Church, and he established reforms in partnership with St. Benedict of Aniane. However, he was plagued by the increasing frequency of Viking raids that were threatening the very existence of the empire. Keeping Europe united became increasingly difficult. When control passed to Louis's sons, the empire's unity suffered still further while they squabbled over supremacy.

At this point, the empire was divided into

In this 14th-century manuscript illumination, Charlemagne is seen directing the building of his church at Aix-la-Chapelle (Aachen), pictured on the right today.

782	785	789	796	799	800	806	814
Thousands of Saxon prisoners are massacred and Charlemagne forces Saxony to accept Christianity	King Widukind of the Saxons finally surrenders to Charlemagne and converts to Christianity	Charlemagne issues the Admonitio Generalis, a decree to promote education	Charlemagne campaigns against his cousin, Duke Tassilo, and takes his land of Bavaria	Responding to a revolt in Rome, Charlemagne invades the city and restores Pope Leo III to power	As a reward for saving the Pope and Rome, Pope Leo crowns Charlemagne as Roman Emperor	Charlemagne makes provision for division of his empire to his sons after his death	Death of Charlemagne

rival domains: the West and East Frankish kingdoms or West and East Francia. Because East Francia (which became known as Germany, *see pages 128–129*) incorporated territories only recently captured from the pagan Slavs and Saxons, it was considered less civilized, and consequently evolved along completely different political and social lines from West Francia (which became known as France). The kingdom was divided into the semi-autonomous duchies of Swabia, Franconia, Bavaria, and Saxony. During the reign of the last Carolingian monarchs, these duchies became increasingly troublesome.

SURVIVOR AMONG EMPIRES

Despite the disunity, the Carolingian Empire survived for centuries under the name of Holy Roman Empire and witnessed a great deal of change. As time passed, however, the Church began to show increasing dissent over the fusion of spiritual

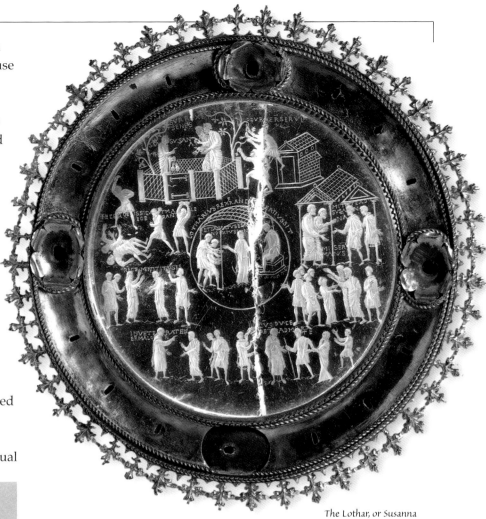

and temporal power. The unification of Church and State had worked well in Charlemagne's day because on the one hand the Church gained protection, and on the other the empire was given moral authority by the Church's sanction. By the 12th and 13th centuries, however, the need for this symbiotic relationship had long passed, and conflict between the papacy and secular leaders became endemic. Local rulers and warlords also increased their strength, further weakening central control.

By the time Rudolph of Habsburg became Holy Roman Emperor in 1273, the empire was a political union in name alone, with little or no military power at its disposal. Although it would remain on the European map until the early 19th century, the Holy Roman Empire was nothing more than a shadow of Charlemagne's creation.

Charlemagne's achievement of uniting so much of Europe for so long has often been praised since his death. More recent expansionist leaders, most notably Napoleon and Hitler, have based their own aspirations on those of Charlemagne. The "Great King" was canonized in 1165.

The Lothar, or Susanna Crystal, is a superb piece of Carolingian art, dating from between 855–869, from either Lotharingia (modern Lorraine) or Aachen. The energetic drawings are engraved on the rock crystal in the manner known as the Reims style. It shows the story of Susanna, who was falsely accused of adultery, as recorded in the Apochrypha. Susanna was found innocent after Daniel questioned the elders who convicted her and had them executed for bearing false witness. The large crystal (4¹/₂ inches in diameter) is framed in a 15th-century gilded copper frame.

CHAPTER FIVE

Steppe Empires

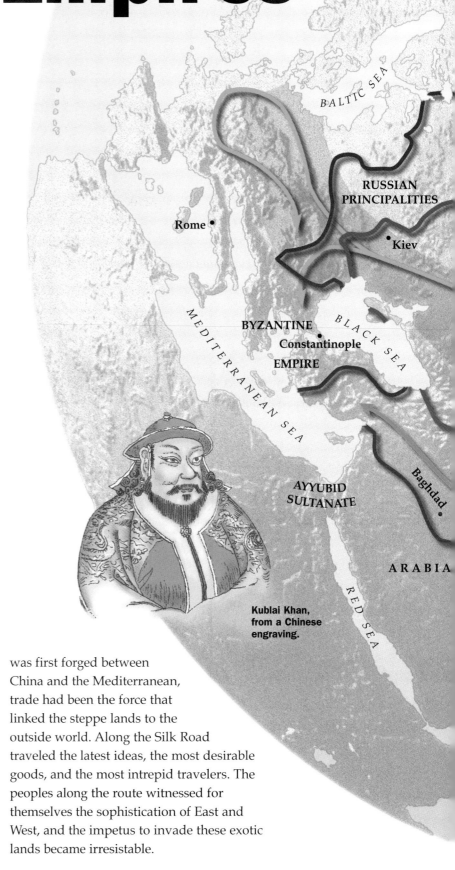

The vast Asian steppes form a monotonous, color-bled, seemingly endless landscape. Even today the region—which stretches from Europe to the Pacific Ocean—is home only to a relatively small population of hardy peoples. Throughout history the steppes have been considered foreboding and uncivilized—seemingly the last place on Earth capable of producing great empires. Yet from the disparate tribal peoples of this region came some of the most remarkable empire-builders the world has known.

Many and varied, some steppe empires lasted centuries; others barely spanned a generation. Terrorized Chinese and Europeans branded them barbarians. They feared the frequent waves of deadly invasion, which ranged from those of the brigand-raider Attila the Hun to Genghis Khan's true empire-building.

PLAYING ON WEAKNESS

Although the earlier eastern steppe tribes are generally referred to as Turko-Mongolian, the base Turkic peoples also carved out their own Asian empires, for example when the Seljuks held sway after capturing Baghdad under the leadership of Toghril Beg in 1055. But mostly the Turks served as soldiers in other peoples' armies, and consequently Turkish language and customs are still evident from Europe to the Far East.

The steppe empires relied not only on the strength of the Turks but on the weaknesses of the Chinese and European civilizations. When China periodically buckled under weak leadership the Mongol tribes took full advantage and invaded. Conversely, when Chinese leadership was strong the barbarian hordes were held at bay.

Since ancient times when the Silk Road was first forged between China and the Mediterranean, trade had been the force that linked the steppe lands to the outside world. Along the Silk Road traveled the latest ideas, the most desirable goods, and the most intrepid travelers. The peoples along the route witnessed for themselves the sophistication of East and West, and the impetus to invade these exotic lands became irresistable.

Kublai Khan, from a Chinese engraving.

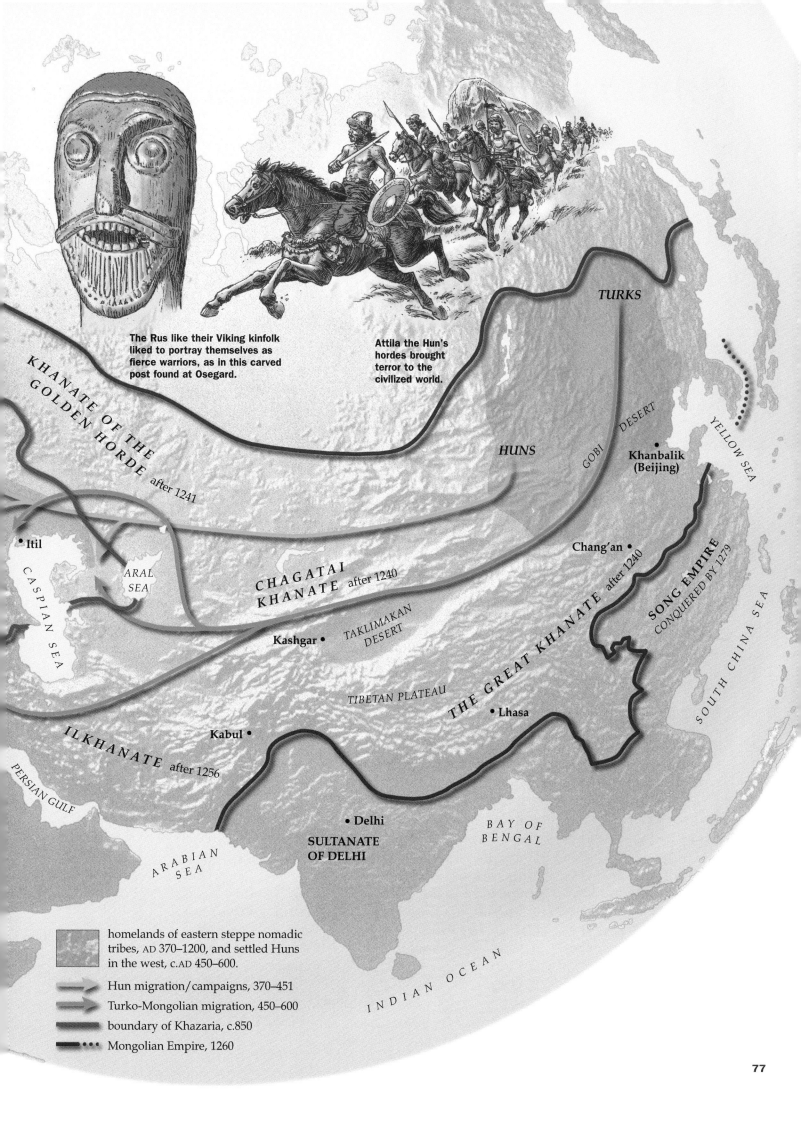

The Rus like their Viking kinfolk liked to portray themselves as fierce warriors, as in this carved post found at Osegard.

Attila the Hun's hordes brought terror to the civilized world.

KHANATE OF THE GOLDEN HORDE *after 1241*

TURKS

HUNS

GOBI DESERT

Khanbalik (Beijing)

YELLOW SEA

• Itil

CASPIAN SEA

ARAL SEA

CHAGATAI KHANATE *after 1240*

Chang'an •

SONG EMPIRE CONQUERED BY 1279

Kashgar •   TAKLIMAKAN DESERT

THE GREAT KHANATE *after 1240*

SOUTH CHINA SEA

TIBETAN PLATEAU

Lhasa •

ILKHANATE *after 1256*

Kabul •

PERSIAN GULF

• Delhi

BAY OF BENGAL

SULTANATE OF DELHI

ARABIAN SEA

homelands of eastern steppe nomadic tribes, AD 370–1200, and settled Huns in the west, c.AD 450–600.

Hun migration/campaigns, 370–451

Turko-Mongolian migration, 450–600

boundary of Khazaria, c.850

Mongolian Empire, 1260

INDIAN OCEAN

Raiders from the Steppes

At the start of the fifth century AD, Rome was under continual migratory pressure from barbarian Germanic tribes across the Rhine. It was less a desire to be a part of Rome than a fear of what loomed over the eastern horizon.

Farmers tend to their crops near the ruined walls of Constantinople (modern-day Istanbul). The huge walls were begun during the 5th century by the Roman emperor Theodosius II (r.408–450) to keep out the army of Attila the Hun. Theodosius used Visigoths and Viking mercenaries in the guard. Disaster befell the project when an earthquake demolished most of the wall in 447. Construction began again immediately, before the Huns could attack.

For the Roman world, the ravages of the Huns were the first encounters with a savage nomadic people from the mythical East. But in fact, the Huns were only a part of a continually evolving history of rising and falling Turko-Mongol empires. The Huns were not the first of their kind, but they were the first of a seemingly endless line that would fall on the remnants of the Roman Empire.

The Huns were descended from the Hsiung-nu (*see page 49*). The Turkic-speaking Hsiung-nu drove other steppe tribes westward, including the Kushans (who then built an empire extending from the Aral Sea to the Indian Ocean by AD 50). Before their Mongolian empire collapsed in AD 48, the Hsiung-nu plagued the Han Chinese for several centuries. For centuries after the Hsiung-nu faded, no single power in the region filled the vacuum. By about 370, the Huns began organizing and migrating

westward, crossing the Ural Mountains and entering eastern Europe. Here, they encountered Slavic and Germanic tribes clustering around the edges of the Roman Empire. The Huns reached the height of the powers under Attila (r.434–53). At this crucial point, internal strife and conflicting politics had almost brought the Roman Empire in the west to its knees. Attila seized the advantage, and his effect on European civilization was devastating.

RUTHLESS TIMES

The nomads of Central Asia were fierce fighters and Attila's reputation for savagery is based in fact. It is known that he razed cities, including Belgrade and Sofia, in his first campaign against the Eastern Romans, which began in AD 441. At the conclusion, he demanded some 2,100 pounds of gold each year by way of tribute from Constantinople. There followed a short spell of peace, marred by Attila killing his brother and co-ruler Bleda. Afterward, he renewed his attack on Eastern Roman territory, devastating everything that stood between the Mediterranean and the Black Sea.

c.300 BC	c.200 BC	AD 48	370	451	683	850	912–965
Turko-Mongols adopt horse-riding and become a fully mobile nomadic race	Stirrups are invented in northern China or the eastern steppes	The Hsiung-nu fade from power, splitting into several groups. The Chinese settle the southern group in northern China	The Huns begin migration toward Europe	Attila the Hun is defeated during invasion of Gaul	Western Gök Turks and eastern T'u Chueh empires unite under the khagan Elterish	The free Jewish state of Khazaria spans between the Caucasus and Kiev, and the Black and Caspian Seas	The Viking Rus crush Khazarian power.

In the west, he fared less well, not because initial Roman responses were better organized, but because the Germanic tribes trapped against the Rhine hindered the Huns' progress. Later, determined Roman resistance, as well as co-operative opposition from the Visigoths, thwarted Attila's ambitions in Gaul. On the retreat to Hungary, he threatened major Italian cities— even Rome. Only personal mediation by Pope Leo I prevented the city's destruction. Because they lacked the written word and built little of permanence, the Huns' legacy is sparse. An important source of information about Attila are the writings of the Roman diplomat Priscus of Panium, who

DIFFERENT KINDS OF HUNS

Attila's Huns are sometimes referred to as the Black Huns to distinguish them from the Ephthalites, or Hunas, who are referred to also as the White Huns (*see pages 53, 55*). The White Huns' westward migration ran further south than the Black Huns, and for some 400 years they paused in the region north of the Taklimakan Desert. Splitting up, some White Huns attacked the Persian Empire, while others turned south to bring down the Indian Gupta dynasty.

helped to negotiate a fragile peace settlement.

Despite the destructive power they wrought right across Europe and Asia, the Huns were prone to the internal strife typical of nomadic warrior people. Attila's dominion ranged from the Rhine to the frontiers of China. However, on his death in 453 the empire disintegrated. It is important to note that the Huns were not a single tribe but a combination of many that came together under Attila's banner, including peoples he had previously overwhelmed.

In Mongolia, a new power called the Juan-Juan eventually filled the vacuum after the Hsiung-nu's fall. In turn this regime collapsed during an uprising c.550 by people known to the Chinese as the T'u-chueh.

The Huns held a major advantage over the Roman cavalry in the first engagements—the stirrup. Invented c.AD 200 in the eastern steppes, a rider equipped with stirrups could maneuver his mount with greater flexibility than a stirrup-less opponent. Because the Romans had never developed this simple device, the Huns outrode them. More importantly, because stirrups allowed them to control the horse with only their legs, both hands were free to devastate Roman ranks with accurate arrow fire. The Mongolian stirrup pictured here is modern; ancient ones used a toe cap, rather than a flat, suspended platform.

	Hsiung-nu empire, c.175 BC
	Kushan empire, c.AD 50
.....	civilized borders
	Black Hun migration and campaigns
	Ephthalite migration
	Huns, AD 450

This fanciful 16th-century medallion found at Pavia, Italy, depicts Attila the Hun with horns, equating the barbarian invader with the Devil.

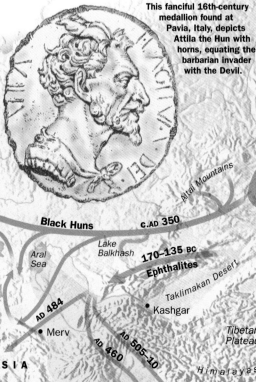

Catalaunian Plains 451
After the indecisive battle, Attila besieged the town of Orléans, the furthest west the Huns reached, but failed to take it. In the same year they retreated south and east.

Orléans

Rome

434   C.AD 400

Constantinople

Mediterranean Sea

Black Sea

ANATOLIA

Caspian Sea

Aral Sea

Black Huns   C.AD 350

Lake Balkhash   170–135 BC

Ephthalites

AD 484

Merv

AD 460   AD 505–10

PERSIA

Taklimakan Desert

Kashgar

Altai Mountains

Lake Baikal

Following the Huns, the Avars migrated west in 553, fleeing from the T'u-chueh. In 562, they arrived in Europe, allied themselves with the Sassanians and carved out their own empire— the Avar Khanate in the lands of the settled Huns.

Tibetan Plateau

Himalayas

CHINA

Luoyang

Yellow Sea

INDIA

The region surrounding the Altai Mountains had long been home to nomadic races such as the Scythians and Sarmatians. These people developed highly skilled metal-working abilities, which passed on to their descendants, such as the T'u Chueh. Pictured here is a saddle decoration of rams' heads from the c.5th century BC.

T'u Chueh Turn to the West

Also of Turko-Mongol stock, the T'u Chueh originated from the Huns' earlier homeland, the Altai Mountains. They were skilled ironworkers, perhaps inheriting the talents of the Scythians who flourished in the region some thousand years before them. The key to their success was to create unity among the diverse communities on the steppes.

A leader named Bumin founded the new Turkic order, although an untimely death cut short his reign. The rambling territory was split between his son Muhan, ruling in the east, and his brother Ishtemi in the west. Westerners knew them as Gök Turks or the Blue (Celestial) Turks. In an era of confusion and chaos, with the great civilizations of East and West in a weakened state, coalitions of tribes such as the Turks were able to conquer new lands for themselves in a way that would not have been possible in the heydays of ancient Rome and China.

Pressures mounted on the twin empires, particularly in the east, where the Chinese intensified attacks. Indeed, for a while the T'u Chueh were overwhelmed by the Chinese, who penetrated as far west as Samarkand. The Turks in the west had a volatile relationship with the Sassanians of Persia, sometimes as allies against the

Chinese, and at other times as enemies squabbling over mutually desired territory.

In 683 the two Turkic empires united under the *khagan* (leader) Elterish (r.683–92). with Mongolia as the heart of the empire. Under his successor, Kapghan (r.692–716), the Turks thrived. However, only one other khagan was installed—Bilgä (r.716–734)— before the empire disintegrated.

The Turks developed a fine military tradition that inspired fear and respect in equal measure. Their great success in battle was thanks in part to the accuracy of their horse-mounted archers. Those skilled at shooting backward as well as forward were permitted to wear white falcon feathers in their helmets. Highly disciplined and clad in metal or hardened leather armor, they attacked in an arrow formation. Mercenaries drawn from neighboring lands were included in the ranks.

THE GÖKS

The Gök Turk Empire extended from the Black Sea to China, embracing not only steppe but also desert. To overcome the difficulties of hostile terrain the army used two-humped Bactrian camels. There was a great deal of ceremony in the process of going to war and the steppe tribes wielded a psychological advantage with their use of drums. The stretched animal skin that covered their drums was replaced before each battle to ensure that the drums retained their loud and threatening sound.

At the head of Turkish society was a khagan with more power than the T'u Chueh's leader; a demi-god to his people who believed in the mystical power of Shamans, the most ancient of priests. The khagan's tent was made of red silk lavishly decorated with threads and supported by ornate poles. His gilt throne sat upon four carved peacocks. Revealing a further inclination toward vivid color, warriors often braided their long hair in the bright hues of silk ribbons. As a sign of submission, those in the lesser military ranks shaved the fronts of their heads. In the summer the khagan and his court moved north to rich grazing lands. When the weather worsened they retreated south in search of food, in the time-honored nomadic way.

The successors to the Gök Turks were the Uighurs who assumed power following a Gök revolt. Like the Gök Turks they were in effect the leaders of a federation. In fact, Uighur government differed to that of the other steppe tribes by the fact that there was a khagan from one sub-tribe and a prime minister from another, so diminishing the dictatorial nature of rule. All the Turkish steppe tribes shared a similar language, and thus a fraternal bond between the Turks of the region was maintained and continued in the face of considerable political upheaval. However, the Uighurs were more supportive of their Chinese neighbors. They also departed from nomadic tradition by founding a capital city.

Another Turkic people, the Kyrgyz, were the next in line for power. Little is known of them, although they distinguished themselves by evading Mongol domination in the 13th century. The Uighurs were held back on the Chinese border, where they flourished for some four centuries until the Mongol invasions.

Wild Bactrian camels cross a river at the edge of the Mongolian steppes, with the rugged foothills of the Altai Mountains in the background. Distinguished by its two humps from the Egyptian single-humped dromedary camel, the Bactrian became the main form of transport for both traders and Turkish soldiers in the hostile terrain of steppe, desert, and mountain range encountered right across the wide empire.

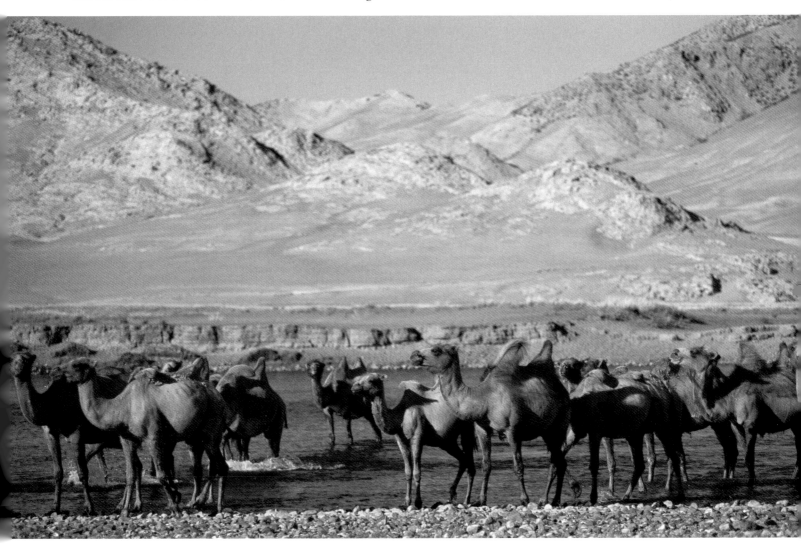

Khazaria

In the seventh century, in the region between the Black and Caspian Seas, a free Jewish state emerged. Its people were an amalgamation of Khazar Turks—part of the Gök Turkic migration, Bulgars (western Huns), and Caucasians.

The story of the obscure Jewish Empire of Khazaria, which flourished in Asia in the eighth and ninth centuries, is at once intriguing and astonishing. Legend has it that the Jewish faith was adopted in this infant empire after the Khazari khagan Bulan heard in detail from an Arab mullah, a Christian priest, and a Jewish rabbi on the merits of each religion. After deliberation, he chose Judaism, making it the official creed of his subjects. The date of this event is still in question and may have been as early as 740 or as late as 861.

Nowhere else, before or since, has a non-Jewish nation undergone such a conversion. Bulan faced the strength of expansionist Islamic Arabs to the south and equally expansionist Christians to the west. By adopting Judaism, he of course incurred the wrath of both, providing in effect a bulwark to both religions' spread across Asia. A series of wars between Khazaria and the Arabs

At the eastern edge of Khazaria, near the Aral Sea, the steppes stretch away, back toward the Turkic homeland beyond the Ural Mountains and across the desert wastes.

prevented Islam from spreading across the whole of eastern Europe at a time when it was rapidly gaining converts. It also became a refuge for Jews, who were subjected to persecution in virtually every other contemporary civilization. Nowhere else in the early medieval world were Jews in charge of their own fate as in Khazaria.

The roots of Khazarian power emerged about AD 650, when this Turkic kingdom formed following the break-up of the western arm of the Gök Turks and the collapse of the rival Avars. Initially, the Khazar regime was almost identical to that run by the Göks, with a khagan and a prime minister. Like other Turkish groups of the period, the Khazars used a runic script that originated from Mongolia.

EMISSARY BRINGS FAITH

Arab scholars of the time provide the modern world with most of the information we have concerning the Khazars. Writing in the 11th century, a Muslim chronicler elaborated on the man who brought the Jewish faith to Khazaria, although details surrounding his identity remain sketchy:

"One of the Jews undertook the conversion of the Khazars, who are composed of many peoples and they were converted by him and joined his religion… for this was a man who came single-handedly to a king of great rank and to a very spirited people, and they were converted by him without any recourse to violence and the sword."

He went on to discuss how the Khazars had adopted associated practices, including circumcision, the observance of Jewish feast days, and abstention from eating certain animals. One of Bulan's descendants, Obadiah, consolidated the newly-established religion with the construction of synagogues. He invited Jewish intellectuals to Khazaria to convince doubters among the aristocracy.

Crucially, it was not only the nobles and the military elite who were converted. The common people embraced the new religion too, although there remained a degree of tolerance to older practices. Pagan shamanism—the Khazar's original religion—remained in place, and Islam and Christianity were also tolerated to some extent. Incredibly, a seven-strong Supreme Court with representatives of all the faiths (Judaism, Islam, Christianity, and Slavic Pagan) was established to ensure a fair

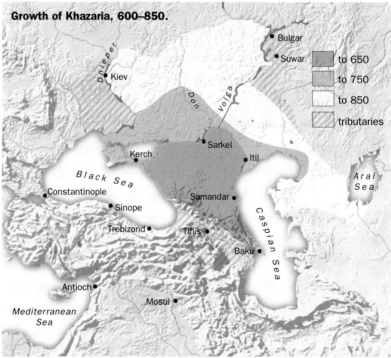

hearing for people of all persuasions. Such religious tolerance was unheard of in most parts of the world, and it reflects the fact that the Khazar lands were on a crossroads of cultures. An attempt by St. Cyril to convert the Khazars to Christianity failed, although his expedition from Byzantium in 860 did recruit numerous Slav converts.

By the tenth century, the use of Hebrew and Aramaic script among Khazars was commonplace. Archaeologists have uncovered vessels from the region of the Don river bearing the word "Israel" in Hebrew.

Peace on the Steppe

Although the Khazars hailed from nomadic stock it is clear that after their conversion to Judaism they quickly opted for a more settled existence. Farming, trading, and the production of goods quickly took root, and these advances brought prosperity to the new Khazarian civilization.

Although it was sufficiently wealthy to finance a standing army complete with cavalry and mercenaries this was not an empire that thrived on hostilities. Khazaria did play a role in the defeat of Persia in the seventh century, allying itself with fellow Turks and the Byzantines to do so. There were also a series of wars in the eighth century against the Arabs that established the southern boundary of Khazaria as the Caucasus Mountains.

However, the Khazars are more commonly associated with a period of peace on the steppe—a "pax khazarica," as they were people more concerned with commerce than conquest. With peace came greater opportunities to trade and an influx of wealth. Some of the empire's wealth was founded on the tributes paid by subservient tribes, including Slavs, Magyars, Huns, and Pechenegs. The main source of income that kept the empire buoyant for some five centuries was trade between East and West. Goods that were bought and sold included silks from China, furs from the Scandinavia, candlewax, honey, silver, and spices. They traded with Arabs, Byzantines, Vikings, the Chinese and many others, and founded new cities, although traditional tents were still more commonplace than permanent dwellings.

A semi-nomadic people, the Khazars found horses were a vital asset, even after they began to settle in the lands north of the Caucasus Mountains. Their riding equipment was more advanced than any in western Europe at the time. This two-piece bridle-bit is made from iron but decorated with inlaid silver and scrollwork. Slots on the long S-shaped cheek pieces were attached to the bridle itself. It was made some time between the 9th and 10th centuries, and found in the Perm region of Russia. Found with it were a pair of iron stirrups and a silver-inlaid ax-hammer, the usual equipment of a Khazar mounted warrior.

Rus warrior chasing after a Khazar warrior with braided hair (Turkic warriors often used colored ribbons in their hair); from a fragment of a drinking horn found in Chernigov.

A RESPECTED POWER

Such was the level of co-operation between the Khazars and their neighbors that Byzantine engineers built a fortress on the Don River at Sarkel for them. Byzantine emperors Justinian II and Constantine V both took a Khazar wife. Khazaria became a beacon for Jews from both Islamic and Christian countries. Consequently many emigrated to Asia in search of religious freedom, bringing with them the latest arts

and technologies from other parts of Europe and Asia. All this helped to strengthen Khazaria and made it into a cosmopolitan and progressive civilization.

At its greatest extent in about 850, Khazaria stretched between the Black and Caspian Seas and straddled the Volga and Dnieper rivers. The waterways, like the Silk Road, were vital trading links. The Khazars built the Ukrainian city of Kiev—later it became capital of the first Russian state, Kievan Rus, and grew to be a serious rival. The most enduring of the Khazar regional capitals was Itil (now Astrakhan) at the mouth of the Volga. An administrative center, trading post, and religious heartland for Jews, it also had a mosque to serve its Muslim population.

Ultimately Khazar power was crushed in a campaign by Svyatoslav, the ruler of Kiev. Khazaria was then picked over by the neighboring Pechenegs, Oghuz, and Byzantine peoples. Khazar traders existed under increasingly difficult circumstances until at least the 12th century, but after that all mention of them ends. The region was all the poorer for the passing of the Khazars. The Pechenegs who largely took over Khazar lands were much less progressive and their presence did much to upset the carefully cultivated flow of trade in eastern Europe.

END OF JEWISH FREEDOM

When the Khazarian Empire collapsed the Jewish population is thought to have gone to Eastern European countries like Hungary and Bulgaria. There is also speculation that the Mountain Jews in the Eastern Caucasus are descendants of the Khazars. It is probable that many of the Jews living in the region were compelled to adopt Islam when they fell under new Islamic leaderships.

A road runs through cultivated fields in Kazakhstan. Like all Turko-Mongolians, the Khazars were highly mobile, but settling on the steppes of what would become south Russia, many took to stock rearing and arable farming.

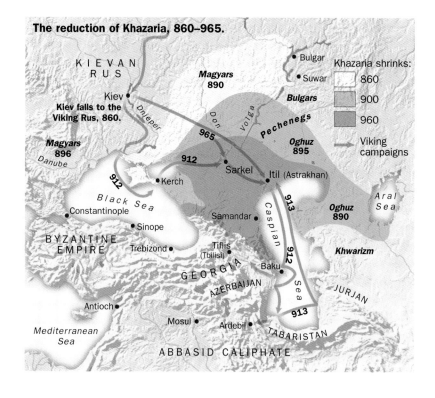

The reduction of Khazaria, 860–965.

KIEVAN RUS

Bulgar
Suwar

Magyars 890

Bulgars

Kiev
Kiev falls to the Viking Rus, 860.

Pechenegs

Magyars 896

Oghuz 895

Danube

965
912

Kerch

Sarkel
Itil (Astrakhan)

Aral Sea

Black Sea
Constantinople

Samandar

Oghuz 890

Sinope

Caspian Sea

913

BYZANTINE EMPIRE

Trebizond

Tiflis (Tbilisi)

912

Khwarizm

GEORGIA

Baku

AZERBAIJAN

913

Antioch

JURJAN

Mosul

Ardebil

913

Mediterranean Sea

TABARISTAN

ABBASID CALIPHATE

Khazaria shrinks:
860
900
960

Viking campaigns

The Mongol Khans

The wild steppes of Mongolia had already produced several nations of raiders to terrify Europe and the Middle East. During the 13th century the greatest and most terrible power of all prepared to fall on both East and West.

According to one Islamic scholar: "In the Muslim countries devastated by Genghis Khan not one in a thousand inhabitants survived." The name of Genghis Khan is synonymous with massacres and mayhem, sadism and savagery. Yet in forging his enormous empire across Asia Genghis Khan speeded the advance of Chinese technology to the west, including the arts of printing and explosives manufacture, which would be vital catalysts for Europe's development. In doing so he unified and arguably civilized the disparate people of the steppes, and ironically instituted a period of peace.

In addition he inaugurated a relay system for communications, a legal framework, and a written language. Certainly, he was guilty of some appallingly barbarous behavior—but he was a man of his time. He knew that without ruthless elimination of his enemies he would not achieve his goals.

It is difficult to distinguish myth from fact in the tales circulating about his early years. Born in about 1165, he was the eldest son of a Mongol chief and was named Temüjin, for a Tatar chief recently slain by his father. According to the somewhat fanciful *Secret History of the Mongols*, apparently written soon after his death as a chronicle of his life and times, he was born with a blood clot in his hand, denoting greatness. One of his ancestors was said to be a gray wolf of divine origin.

GENGHIS'S BAPTISM OF FIRE

When Temüjin was nine, the Tatars—neighbors and enemies of the Mongols—poisoned his father and, together with his mother and siblings, he was cast out of the clan into exile. Food was scarce and comforts were fewer still. His mother Höelün gave him sound advice: "Remember, you have no companions but your shadow." Clearly it all helped to harden the resolve of the adolescent Temüjin, not only to survive but also to succeed as no other Mongol before him. The *Secret History* testifies that Temüjin, with his spellbinding eyes, had considerable personal charisma, even as a boy, and this kept others in his thrall. Already his ruthless

Passersby drop pebbles on this stone sculpture of a turtle to bring them good luck. It marks the site of Karakorum, Mongolia, Genghis Khan's capital city.

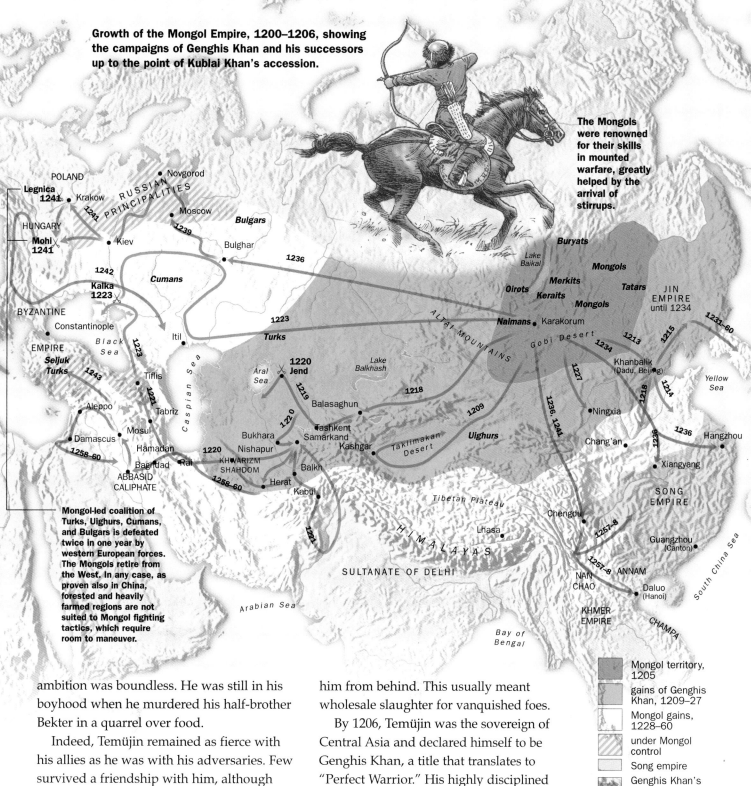

Growth of the Mongol Empire, 1200–1206, showing the campaigns of Genghis Khan and his successors up to the point of Kublai Khan's accession.

The Mongols were renowned for their skills in mounted warfare, greatly helped by the arrival of stirrups.

Mongol-led coalition of Turks, Uighurs, Cumans, and Bulgars is defeated twice in one year by western European forces. The Mongols retire from the West. In any case, as proven also in China, forested and heavily farmed regions are not suited to Mongol fighting tactics, which require room to maneuver.

POLAND
Novgorod
Legnica 1241
Krakow
RUSSIAN PRINCIPALITIES
1241
Moscow
Bulgars
HUNGARY
Mohi 1241
Kiev
1239
Bulghar
1236
Buryats
1242
Cumans
Kalka 1223
1223
Mongols
Merkits
Tatars
JIN EMPIRE until 1234
BYZANTINE
Constantinople
Black Sea
Itil
1223
Turks
Oirots
Keraits
Mongols
1231–60
1215
EMPIRE
Seljuk Turks
1243
Tiflis
1221
Tabriz
Aral Sea
1220 Jend
Lake Balkhash
Naimans
Karakorum
Gobi Desert
1213
1234
Khanbalik (Dadu, Beijing)
Yellow Sea
Aleppo
Mosul
1219
Balasaghun
1218
1209
1227
1218
1214
Ningxia
Damascus
Hamadan
1220
Bukhara
Tashkent
Samarkand
Kashgar
Taklimakan Desert
Uighurs
1236, 1241
Chang'an
1236
1236
Hangzhou
1258–60
Baghdad
Rai
Nishapur
KHWARIZM SHAHDOM
Balkh
Xiangyang
ABBASID CALIPHATE
1258–60
Herat
Kabul
Tibetan Plateau
SONG EMPIRE
1221
HIMALAYAS
Lhasa
Chengdu
1257–8
Guangzhou (Canton)
South China Sea
SULTANATE OF DELHI
NAN CHAO
1257–8
ANNAM
Daluo (Hanoi)
Arabian Sea
KHMER EMPIRE
CHAMPA
Bay of Bengal

Mongol territory, 1205
gains of Genghis Khan, 1209–27
Mongol gains, 1228–60
under Mongol control
Song empire
Genghis Khan's campaigns
Mongol campaigns

ambition was boundless. He was still in his boyhood when he murdered his half-brother Bekter in a quarrel over food.

Indeed, Temüjin remained as fierce with his allies as he was with his adversaries. Few survived a friendship with him, although this may have been as much the fault of their vacillating loyalty as of his ruthlessness. The first targets of his conquests were other steppe tribes, including Tatars—who were virtually wiped out—and the various Turkish enclaves. He operated under the auspices of the Kerait tribe, then broke faith with them. His final Mongol targets were the Naimans, destroyed in a bitter battle. His war plans were awesomely straightforward. He never left an army intact, for fear it would attack

him from behind. This usually meant wholesale slaughter for vanquished foes.

By 1206, Temüjin was the sovereign of Central Asia and declared himself to be Genghis Khan, a title that translates to "Perfect Warrior." His highly disciplined army was in magnificent form, with skilled horsemen and expert bowmen. The survivors of each conquered tribe were few in number, and those who did survive could only do so through unquestionable loyalty to Genghis. However, Genghis knew that if his armies were left idle for long his authority would soon be undermined, so he embarked on continuous conquest throughout his lifetime. First he targeted the Chin State of northern China in the east, and then the Islamic states that lay to the west.

A portrait of the older Genghis Khan, painted by a Chinese artist.

Descendants of Genghis Khan's Mongols still herd their cattle on the steppes of Mongolia (right). A group of horsemen ride their horses at a gallop across dusty grasslands, past horse herds in corrals

Savagery and Succession

When the Mongol armies invaded the Islamic nations of Afghanistan and Persia, their conduct was one of unmitigated brutality and primitive, pitiless atrocities. Enemy soldiers were butchered—including those who surrendered. Civic and religious leaders were executed, women and children put to the sword and cities ransacked. The only human beings Genghis spared were skilled laborers, who were relocated to the Mongol heartland to make weaponry for his army. The Khwarezm-Shah Empire, previously larger and more powerful than that of the Mongols, was entirely erased from the stage of history.

After they sacked the prestigious city of Urganj, the Mongols diverted the Syr Darya river so that it flooded the ruins, taking the city off the map. At Bamyan even the livestock was slaughtered as a reprisal for

the killing of Genghis Khan's grandson during the fighting. When the city of Herat in northern India rebelled there was a six-month siege followed by relentless slaughter in which an estimated 1.6 million people were killed. Irrigation works that had maintained a fragile system of agriculture in the region were destroyed. It has been suggested that Genghis wanted to protect the southern flank of his empire by creating a broad swathe of uninhabited land as a buffer zone against his enemies.

However, even when the battles were won and the Mongols were returning to their homelands in the winter of 1222, the killings continued. Only when the armies were back in Mongolia did a five-year spell of peace ensue. Genghis died quite suddenly on August 18, 1227, probably as a result of a fall from his horse during a hunting expedition. His final wish for the invasion of the His-Hsia (Xixia) kingdom of western China was carried out. With due ceremony, his body was carried to a secret location in the Kentei Mountains where he was buried with some 40 young women, horses, and other treasures. At the time of his death his empire stretched from the Caspian to the Pacific, and from Siberia in the north to the Pamirs and Tibet in the south.

Genghis reaped the rewards of his ruthless military strategy. Despite his penchant for cold-blooded killing he was capable of taking advice, particularly from his wife Borte. It seems he also learned of the benefits of literature and science during his murderous campaign in Persia. A spiritual man, Genghis Khan prayed to Tangri, God of the Eternal Blue Sky. Yet he was not above murdering a tribal shaman who he considered to have assumed too much power.

c.AD 1165	1174	1180	1183	1200	1206	1208	1209
Temujin (Genghis Khan) is born	Temujin's father is murdered	Temujin kills his half brother	Borte, Temujin's wife, is kidnapped	Temujin emerges as a local warlord	Temujin is enthroned as Genghis Khan	Genghis Khan defeats his last Mongol rivals, the Naiman	Genghis wages his first foreign campaign

FOLLOWING THE GREAT KHAN

The question of survival of his massive empire troubled him. He once confided: "After us the people of our race will wear garments of gold, eat sweet, greasy food, ride decorated horses, hold the loveliest of women and will forget the things they owe to us." His chosen successor was his son Ogotai, whose alcoholism brought about his early death in 1241. Genghis's other three sons were given spheres of the empire to rule, although ultimate power lay with Ogotai. Ogotai, who may in fact have been conceived when his mother Borte was kidnapped by a rival tribe early in Genghis Khan's reign, operated in the west in present-day Russia. Chagatai went to rule in northern Iran while Tolui ruled eastern Mongolia. They all made fruitful efforts to further expand the Mongol Empire. The descendants of the Mongols in Russia became known as the Khans of the Golden Horde, and they terrorized the region for years. Respect for the memory of Genghis Khan, and perhaps a genuine fraternity, maintained a high degree of co-operation between the regional empires.

However, upon the death of Ogotai, the different branches of the family began to jostle for premier position. There were wars

ARTS FLOURISH DESPITE MONGOL VIOLENCE

Despite turmoil under the Mongols, many traditional Chinese arts, including ceramics, flourished under the Yuan dynasty and formed the basis for the next great artistic flowering under the Ming dynasty. Chinese potters developed underglaze red decoration during the Mongol Yuan dynasty, similar to the patterning seen on this jar (from Jiangxi province, southern China, 14th century). Under the Mongols, Islamic preference for the color meant that blue underglaze pottery dominated the industry, which delivered its wares along the Silk Road, when conditions permitted.

to exert supremacy and the entire empire lay exposed while the feuding continued. However, the situation was saved largely with the emergence of a notable leader, a grandson of the great Genghis. His name was Kublai Khan.

1215	1215	1218	1220	1221	1222	1222	1223
Genghis destroys Zhongdu (Beijing)	Kublai Khan is born	Insults draw Genghis westward	Genghis takes Samarkand and Bukhara	Armenia, Azerbaijan, and finally Georgia are subdued	Ukraine falls	Genghis searches for immortality	The Prince of Kiev's army is utterly destroyed by the Mongols

The Enlightened Khan

Remembered more for his luxurious lifestyle than for wars or brutality, the western view of Kublai Khan is fashioned very much by the words of Marco Polo, the Venetian traveler. *"[Kublai Khan] is the most powerful of men in subjects, lands, and treasures, that there is on earth or ever was, from the time of our first father Adam to this day."*

Polo described the halls and chambers of the Khan's palace in Shang–tu as being all gilded and the whole building was marvelously embellished and richly adorned. In its grounds, he claimed, there were game animals, harts, and stags, which provided food for his beloved falcons. He hunted on horseback with a leopard lying across his saddle that was used to bring down the prey. There was also a cane-built palace in the park: *"It is reared on gilt and varnished pillars, on each of which stands a dragon entwining the pillar with his tail and supporting the roof on his outstretched limbs. The roof was also made of canes, so well-varnished that it is quite waterproof. And the Great Khan has had it designed that it can be moved whenever he fancies, for it is held in place by more than 200 cords of silk."*

At the time of his return to Venice, many found Polo's exotic descriptions risible. Modern historians have also cast doubt on the authenticity of his claims. Glaring omissions in the accounts of his travels—which were dictated to a writer much later while Polo languished in jail—include the Great Wall of China, which existed at the time, and the practice of feet-binding among women. There is no mention of Polo in eastern records but this may be because he was known by another name. Skepticism about his adventures dogged him for the rest of his days. On his deathbed a friar urged him to confess that the stories were false. Polo replied: "I did not write half of what I saw."

MONGOL AND CHINESE FUSION

Kublai had a much more progressive agenda than his grandfather. It was his dream to unite China under Mongol rule, to which end he began the Yuan dynasty in 1272. Educated by a Chinese scholar, Kublai did not embark on military campaigns until he was 36 years old. His career was distinguished by a cautious approach involving heavy investment in planning. He inclined toward mercy rather than massacre. While he and his armies overwhelmed Korea and southern China he suffered his two most notable defeats, both against Japan. He also encountered hostility from a cousin, the somewhat uncultured Khaidu,

| 1226 Genghis wages his last campaign | 1227 Death of Genghis | 1231 Mongol forces conquer Korea | 1239 Tibet is overrun | 1241 The Punjab is raided, but not entirely subdued for decades | 1241 Death of Ogotai Khan, third son of Genghis | 1241 After Ogotai's death, Mongol armies return to Karakorum to select a new khan, saving Europe from full invasion | 1260 Kublai Khan becomes emperor of China |

Kublai Khan gives his emissaries the golden tablet which is their passport. This illumination from a 15th-century manuscript depicts the moment when the long-absent father and uncle of Marco Polo take their leave of the (fancifully drawn) Khan to return to Venice. Kublai charges the Polos to return to him with some Christian monks to enlighten him about the teachings of Christ. The monks never materialized, but Marco Polo did make the journey.

and Kublai's forces were often engaged in suppressing unrest in southeast Asia, which he had taken for the empire. His capital was first situated at Cambaluc, but later at Beijing, and his detractors were quick to accuse him of abandoning traditional Mongol ways in favor of the Chinese. A Buddhist by faith, he had genuine affection for his millions of subjects and ensured there was education and famine relief for the poor as well as transport and trading opportunities for the rich.

Following the death of his wife and favorite son, Kublai retreated from public life, to over-indulge in food and drink. He died in 1294 after 34 years in power, and was buried alongside his grandfather.

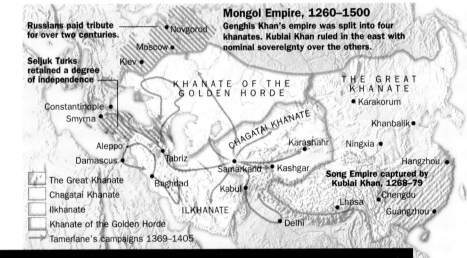

Mongol Empire, 1260–1500
Genghis Khan's empire was split into four khanates. Kublai Khan ruled in the east with nominal sovereignty over the others.

Russians paid tribute for over two centuries.

Seljuk Turks retained a degree of independence

THE GREAT KHANATE

KHANATE OF THE GOLDEN HORDE

CHAGATAI KHANATE

ILKHANATE

Song Empire captured by Kublai Khan, 1268–79

Novgorod
Moscow
Kiev
Constantinople
Smyrna
Aleppo
Damascus
Tabriz
Baghdad
Samarkand
Kashgar
Kabul
Delhi
Karakorum
Khanbalik
Karashahr
Ningxia
Hangzhou
Lhasa
Chengdu
Guangzhou

The Great Khanate
Chagatai Khanate
Ilkhanate
Khanate of the Golden Horde
Tamerlane's campaigns 1369–1405

THE LAST MONGOL CONQUEROR

The Mongol leader Timur "the lame" or Tamerlane (r.1361–1405) was also a noted empire-builder. Claiming descent from Genghis Khan, the Muslim Timur was born in a Tatar settlement near Samarkand, the city on the Silk Road that would one day be his capital. He swept through Mongolia, Turkey, Russia, and India but failed to consolidate his gains. His untimely death occurred when he was poised to invade China. Timur was brutal but nevertheless a noted supporter of the arts. His sarcophagus lies in Gur-i-Amur mausoleum, Samarkand, in modern Uzbekistan.

1274	1280	1281	1292–3	1294	1344	1355	1368
Unsuccessful attempt to invade Japan	Tibetan scholar Phags-Pa devises a script for the Mongolian language	A second attempt to invade Japan ends in disaster when a storm wrecks the Mongol invasion fleet	Unsuccessful attempt to invade Java	Death of Kublai Khan	The Hungarians successfully repel the Mongols	There is a popular revolt against Mongol rule in China	The Mongols are successfully expelled from China

To the Edge of the World

The years between the sixth and sixteenth centuries AD saw the creation of powerful new empires far beyond the traditional realms of the Old World. Burgeoning business between China and India brought the marine equivalent of the Silk Road—a fast sea route through Southeast Asian waters—which in turn nourished the maritime state of Srivijaya. This Sumatra-based trading empire aggressively protected its status as the arbiter of Far Eastern sea-trade, and in the process of conducting oceanic trade, it substantially advanced sailing technology.

In North Africa trans-Saharan trade handsomely sustained the Berber peoples, particularly given the influence that came with their control of West African gold mines. With one eye on this market, a group of Berber warriors known as the Almoravids established themselves in Morocco, where they founded great Mediterranean entrepôts such as Marrakesh. In the 11th century, Almoravid forces pushed south toward the Gold Coast (Ghana) and north into Spain. In Spain they successfully countered Christian resistance, but their eventual downfall came at the hands of Muslims elsewhere whom they had sought to dominate.

AWAITING DISCOVERY

At about the same, in what is now central Mexico—on a continent still unknown to the peoples of the Old World—a mysterious military empire was taking control. As with most empires, in Toltec civilization the binding force was religion, driven in this case by a warrior elite. Elaborate rituals and human sacrifice were employed as overt tools of oppression. The notorious Ball Game re-enacted mythological battles while divining the future but often ended in the sacrifice of those on the losing side.

Finally this chapter considers one of the shortest-lived yet most fascinating of all world empires, that of the Inca. The speed with which this small mountain chiefdom expanded was astonishing. So was its development of advanced engineering techniques, speedy communications, and efficient food distribution systems that were more advanced in many ways than those existing in contemporary Europe. Yet when the Spanish came the Inca demise was surprisingly swift. Their ruler, revered and obeyed as a god, was rendered powerless within weeks by a double-dealing Spanish adventurer and his 180 soldiers.

The demise of the Inca is an object lesson in how even the most successful of empires can have fatal flaws. The Inca were a military society and possessed the toughest of warriors, yet their reliance on the wisdom of their ruler and their inability to grasp the deadly threat posed by the Spanish brought about their downfall seemingly in the blink of an eye. The historian Edward Hyams summed up their plight in his book *The Last of the Incas*, comparing their civilization to a dance in which daily and seasonal patterns were ceaselessly repeated: "The great dance had been their reality," he wrote. "They awoke into the nightmare of chaos."

PACIFIC OCEAN

Santiago

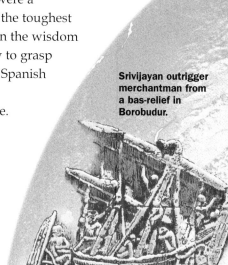

Srivijayan outrigger merchantman from a bas-relief in Borobudur.

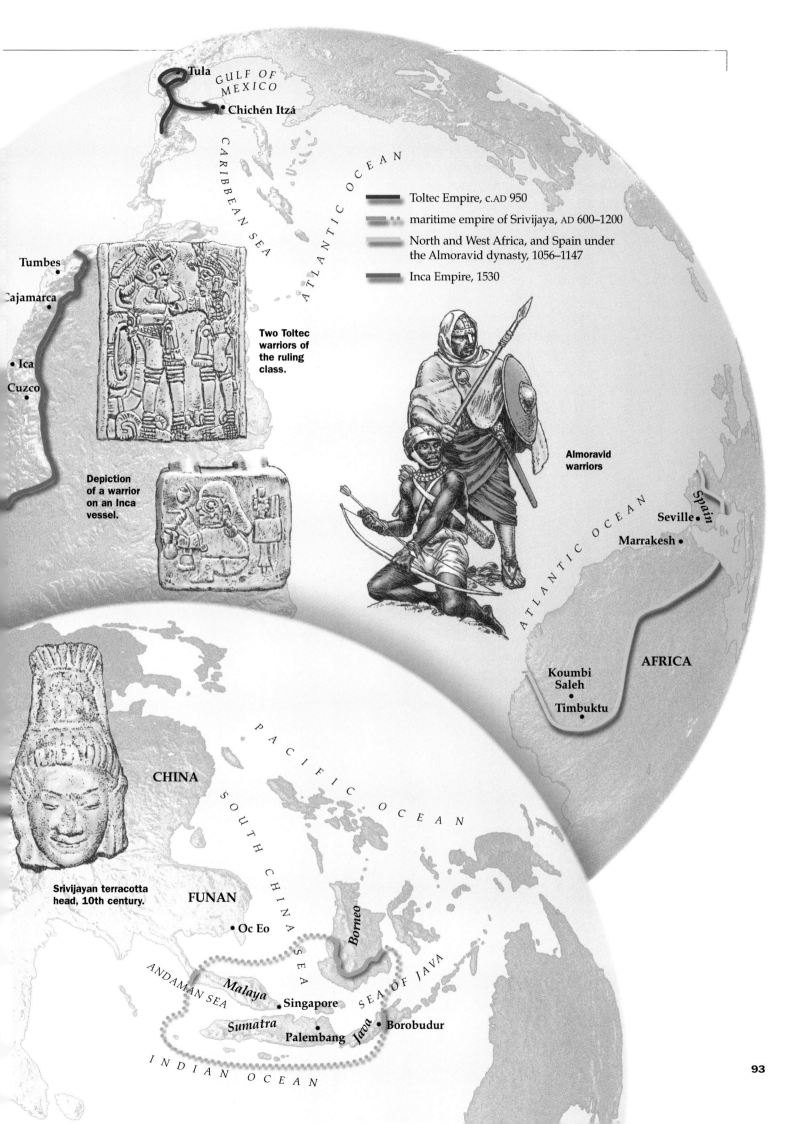

Tula

GULF OF MEXICO

Chichén Itzá

CARIBBEAN SEA

ATLANTIC OCEAN

Tumbes

Cajamarca

Ica

Cuzco

Toltec Empire, c.AD 950

maritime empire of Srivijaya, AD 600–1200

North and West Africa, and Spain under
the Almoravid dynasty, 1056–1147

Inca Empire, 1530

Two Toltec
warriors of
the ruling
class.

Depiction
of a warrior
on an Inca
vessel.

Almoravid
warriors

Spain

Seville

Marrakesh

ATLANTIC OCEAN

AFRICA

Koumbi
Saleh

Timbuktu

Srivijayan terracotta
head, 10th century.

CHINA

PACIFIC OCEAN

SOUTH CHINA SEA

FUNAN

Oc Eo

Borneo

ANDAMAN SEA

Malaya

Singapore

SEA OF JAVA

Sumatra

Palembang

Java

Borobudur

INDIAN OCEAN

93

The Militaristic Toltec Empire

The city-state of Teotihuacán dominated the Valley of Mexico for more than 400 years, until its mysterious decline in the eighth century AD. Into the vacuum migrated people from the north, who built the first Mesomaerican empire.

At Teotihuacán, the Feathered Serpent Quetzalcóatl dominates many structures. Here, the sides of steps leading to one of numerous platforms lining the Avenue of the Dead are decorated with heads of the god, showing off the feathered neck ruff.

The classical era of Central American (Mesoamerican) history begins with one of the ancient world's most mysterious cities. No written records are known to exist from Teotihuacán but the archaeology suggests it rose to prominence around AD 100 as the capital of a state that strictly enforced control over its population through a powerful priesthood and military. Burial pits at the site have revealed the remains of some 120 people, mostly clad in warrior uniforms and wearing necklaces of shells carved to resemble human teeth. Their hands were tied behind their backs—grisly evidence that they had been sacrificed.

The extent of Teotihuacán's influence can be seen in its enduring ideology. The city's principal god—the ubiquitous Quetzalcóatl (Feathered Serpent)—crops up in various forms within the Toltec, Aztec, and Maya civilizations, and 500 years later Aztec rulers were still making pilgrimages to see the capital they believed to have been built by gods. At its height, Teotihuacán's population may have reached 250,000, a staggering size for the time, and its empire was probably larger even than that of the Aztec.

The reasons for the city's decline around 750 are unknown, although one strong theory suggests the environment, and consequently the economy, were devastated by deforestation of the surrounding highlands. Certainly the vast quantities of lime plaster used for internal decoration would have required the burning of hundreds of thousands of trees. What is clear is that by the ninth century there was a mass migration from the north of modern-day Mexico toward Lake Texcoco, the heart of Teotihuacán territory (and now all but filled in with Mexico City). Among these migrants were the Toltec (the name has many interpretations including "craftsmen" and "master builders") and they rapidly ensconced themselves as the new warrior elite.

Early in the tenth century, Toltec armies plundered and destroyed Teotihuacán under the leadership—according to tradition—of Mixcóatl (Cloud Serpent). His son Ce Acatl Topiltzin subsequently unified several distinct tribes into an empire. This leader-deity also supposedly discovered corn, invented the calendar, and promoted science. He later took the title Quetzalcóatl. History and legend tend to merge with his story and

c.350–300 BC	100 BC–AD 100	AD 36	200	c.300–600	534	c.850	c.900
The earliest Mayan city-states appear	Surge in Teotihuacán's population; expansion continues until the 7th century	The first Maya calendrical inscriptions are made	The Pyramids of the Sun and the Moon are constructed at Teotihuacán	Teotihuacán becomes an influence on the Maya	Teotihuacán's abandonment begins	Toltecs led by Mixcoatl establish military supremacy in central Mexico	Chichén Itzá becomes a dominant Mayan center

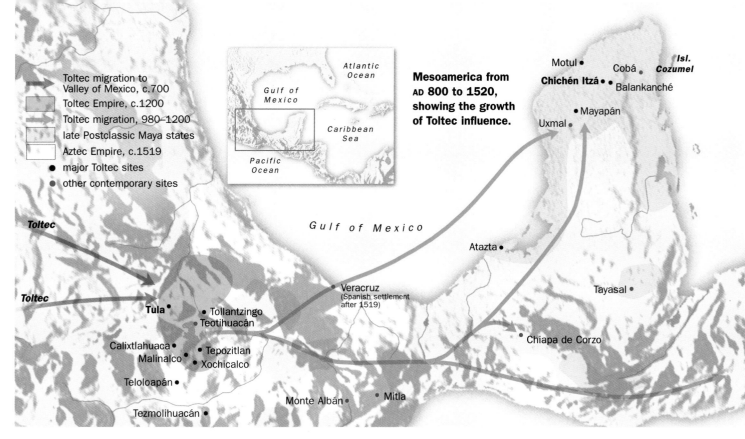

Mesoamerica from AD 800 to 1520, showing the growth of Toltec influence.

Legend:
- Toltec migration to Valley of Mexico, c.700
- Toltec Empire, c.1200
- Toltec migration, 980–1200
- late Postclassic Maya states
- Aztec Empire, c.1519
- ● major Toltec sites
- ● other contemporary sites

it is unclear whether Ce Acatl Topiltzin adopted the name of an established deity, or was endowed with godly status in later years.

TOLTEC EXPORT INFLUENCE

Of the many epic legends about Quetzalcóatl, the most famous concerns his expulsion from Tula, the Toltec capital. The god was apparently deceived by his arch-enemy Tezcatlipoca, driven from the city, and left to wander through wasteland for years until he reached his homeland on the east coast. There he was swallowed by a sacred fire, his ashes turned into birds, and his heart rose as the morning star.

Some accounts claim he sailed to a mythical land, promising to return one day. This is apparently the version preferred by the later Aztec leader Moctezuma II. When he met the invading Spanish in 1519, he greeted the conquistadors with treasure, convinced that they were the returned armies of Quetzalcóatl.

As well as the Feathered Serpent, Toltec people revered animal images such as jaguars, coyotes, and eagles. These began as the symbols of military units but later appeared as far away as Chichén Itzá and

Mayapán, cities of the Maya in the Yucatán, further evidence of the all-embracing web of Toltec culture. Tula became a center of excellence for metalwork (particularly gold and copper), architecture (including gigantic statues, porticoes, and serpent-like columns) and pyramid-building. Trade routes developed quickly, extending from Costa Rica to what is now the southern border of California.

Detail of a fresco painting from a palace wall in Teotihuacán. Depicted is a warrior-priest, dressed in the plumed feather headdress that denotes his status as an Eagle Warrior, one of the warrior castes that would dominate Mesoamerican culture.

950	950	928	987	1156	1187	1524	1546
The Toltec capital city of Tula is built	Toltec influence has spread throughout Mesoamerica	The classical period of Maya civilization comes to an end	Toltec forces seize Chichén Itzá and begin to dominate the Puuc-Maya in the Yucatán	Last Toltec king, Heumac, flees the destruction of Tula	Mayan leader Hunac Ceel expels the Toltec from Chichén Itzá and establishes a new Mayan capital at Mayapán	Spanish conquest of the Maya	Spanish occupying forces put down a Mayan insurrection

Tula's Temple of Quetzalcóatl is topped by huge basalt columns, each depicting a Toltec warrior bearing arms and in full military dress. Their chests bear the firebird symbol, emblem of the Tula ruling elite. Toltec warriors conquered all of central Mexico and virtually depopulated the Yucatán countryside, concentrating the Mayan nobility as hostages in the city of Chichén Itzá.

City of Conquest—Chichén Itzá

The Toltec capital, Tula, is located some 50 miles north of modern-day Mexico City. It is mentioned in several written sources (both in Spanish and in indigenous Mesoamerican hieroglyphics) and was dominated by a religious complex that included the Temple of the Warriors (*Tlahuizcalpantecuhtli*), dedicated to Quetzalcóatl. This 40-foot-high stepped structure is topped by grim-faced, carved stone warriors some 15 feet tall. These basalt giants formed the roof supports for a temple. Beneath them are stone reliefs of jaguars, coyotes, and eagles eating hearts, all symbols of the empire's military orders. The northern base of the pyramid faces a freestanding Serpent Wall. This bears various repetitive mythological designs, one of which involves serpents consuming human skeletons, and was perhaps a concealed ritual area. Among Tula's other distinctive architectural features is a low stone platform called a *tzompantli* (an Aztec word, meaning "wall of skulls") on which the decapitated heads of human sacrificial victims were displayed.

THE BALL GAME YOU REALLY NEEDED TO WIN

The Toltec are credited with inventing *tlatchli*, the Ball Game, a little-understood spectacle played on a large stone court with a hard rubber ball. The game was a re-enactment of epic battles between the gods, so it was neither an athletic contest nor an entertainment. The ball courts had stone rings set into the center of the walls. One objective of the game was to drive the ball through the ring to win. Players had a major incentive to perform well. If they lost, they were sacrificed. This relief from Chichén Itzá depicts the ritual sacrifice at the end of a game, where the captain of the losing side is decapitated.

NEW TOLTEC ORDER

The puzzling thing about this early classic Toltec-Maya period is that there are virtually no other important sites. Apart from the Balankanché cave near Chichén Itzá, which contains a ritual chamber dedicated to the rain god Tlaloc (Chac in Maya), the Puuc culture seems to have been wiped from the face of the earth by the invaders. One explanation is that the Toltec herded all the northern Maya close to their new capital as a means of stifling rebellion and inculcating new military and religious values. The depopulated countryside resulted in few archaeological sites.

At Chichén Itzá the Tula-style *tzompantli*, jaguar thrones, and sinister Chac Mool figures make the cultural links to Tula obvious. In many ways Chichén Itzá was Tula on a grander scale. Its Temple of the Warriors and ball court are far larger than anything at Tula and the Chac Mools are gigantic by comparison. Toltec ritual slaughter was carried out at the Well of Sacrifice (a natural cenote or limestone sinkhole), down which human remains have been found. This sacred well also contained thousands of artifacts in the form of jade, pottery, and metal discs depicting Toltec-Maya wars.

The oldest Puuc-style buildings are concentrated in the south of Chichén Itzá and pre-date "purer" Toltec designs in the northern sectors by several centuries. The city's most imposing structure however is the pyramid of Kukulcan (the Mayan version of Quetzalcóatl), a four-sided temple pyramid linked to Feathered Serpent worship. There is nothing quite like this at Tula; it is more likely that the inspiration came from other Mayan pyramids further south at Tikal and Copán.

By the 12th century, Toltec civilization was in rapid decline. A new, nomadic people, the Chichimecs, invaded the Valley of Mexico, sacked Tula, and embarked on lengthy warfare. Within a hundred years the region was falling under the sway of a new military empire—the Aztec.

The prime purpose of Toltec art and architecture was to inspire fear and servitude, in contrast to the uplifting aesthetics of Teotihuacán. The reclining Chac Mool figures are particularly sinister. They are thought by many archaeologists to be sacrificial altars. Six of these figures were recovered during initial excavations at Tula, all of them mutilated.

The Toltec legend of Quetzalcóatl's exile from Tula by Tezcatlipoca mentioned on the the previous pages may be a fictional version of real-life events, given that Toltec culture apparently split into two distinct branches in about AD 1000. One theory is that half the civilization persisted in following an aggressive, warrior cult while the rest sought a more peaceful civilian existence. The politics and chronology will probably never be certain but there is strong artistic evidence that a Toltec faction moved south and west and conquered the Puuc-Mayan city of Chichén Itzá. From this strategic point at the center of the Yucatán peninsula, the Toltec founded a new militaristic state.

This Chac Mool is one of the gigantic stone figures at Chichén Itzá. It sits on the top platform at the front of the Temple of Warriors, head turned from the camera, as though staring out at the Pyramid of Kukulcan in the distance beyond. All Chac Mools conform to a standard: reclining on their backs, heels tucked in and knees up, head turned (perhaps to intimidate spectators at a sacrifice), both arms at the sides holding a flat plate on the figure's stomach. Modern Maya translate the name Chac Mool to mean "Red Hand," and believe the plate was to catch the sacrificial victim's blood, or carry the excised heart. Archaeologists are unsure about this, and the real meaning of Chac Mool still eludes us.

Srivijaya and the Trade Winds

At times when the Silk Road fell prey to marauding armies, the sea trading route prospered. As sailing vessels improved, so did the prospects of Southeast Asian states.

FACING: The sweeping eaves of a traditional Batak house in northern Sumatra jut out like the prow of a sailing ship. The design is said to recall the nation's maritime heritage, but is also said to resemble, from the side, a figure kneeling in prayer. The house, constructed on a base of pillars, is built with fitted dowels and rope, entirely without nails

The Cambodian maritime state of Funan was destined for prosperity. Occupying the tip of the Indo-Chinese peninsula near the present Vietnamese border, this loose alliance of ports was perfectly positioned to service the sea trade between India and China. Between the third and sixth centuries AD, its ships provided an efficient alternative to the trans-Asian Silk Road caravans—especially in times of civil unrest. But just as the Silk Road was superseded by Funan, so Funan's days were numbered by the rising power of Srivijaya.

Funan's strategic importance lay in the vulnerability of sailing vessels of the day and their need to hug coastlines to avoid open-sea weather. They also needed regular, easy access to ports to resupply. Ships from Chinese ports rounded southern Vietnam to moor-up in ports such as Oc Eo, a settlement

Sculptured head of Kirti Mukka, a deity of coastal Funan dated to the 6th century AD. The ceramic piece was excavated from the site of Oc Eo, one of the major sea trading ports until the Srivijayans began to dominate.

far enough inland to offer a sheltered haven and close enough to rice fields to take on provisions. Replenished, the ships crossed

the Gulf of Thailand to unload at the Isthmus of Kra. From here, the cargo went overland to ports on the Andaman Sea, ready for the journey northwest to India. The system worked well for centuries until the arrival of new marine technology in the Indonesian archipelago.

This came in the form of fast, sturdy ships and better use of sail. The new craft were crewed by Malay seamen who visited Funan with their own highly-prized cargoes of aromatic resins, such as sandalwood, and spices. Soon they were tapping directly into Chinese and Indian markets using a route through the Malaccan Straits. Merchants recognized that they were a fast and reliable means of conducting long-distance trade. By the sixth century AD, the cumbersome journey via Oc Eo and the Isthmus of Kra had become economically unviable. There was now a dominant player in Southeast Asian maritime affairs—Srivijaya.

The existence of this state was recorded by Chinese historians, but only in the last hundred years or so has archaeological evidence pinned its central hub to south Sumatra. Palembang has emerged as one of several cities (the Srivijayan Empire was not organized on territorial lines but on a network of key ports and cities) and stone inscriptions found there have identified some of its rulers. More recent excavations uncovered high quality Chinese porcelain from the T'ang period (seventh to ninth centuries AD), several large Buddhas, and a superb tenth-century statue of Ganesh, the Hindu elephant-god.

MARITIME MONOPOLY

Like Funan, Srivijaya's great advantage was its location. Alternating monsoon winds meant there was never enough time to sail uninterrupted from China to India via the Malaccan Straits, and ships needed a safe

c.AD 700	c.1000	1016–17	1025	1377	1404
The kingdom of Srivijaya becomes dominant on the island of Sumatra	East Java's King Dharmauamsa unsuccessfully attacks the Srivijayans	Srivijayans attack and destroy the kingdom of East Java	Rajendra I of Chola attacks Srivijaya, takes Palembang and key ports, and reopens Indian trade routes to China	Islamic Empire of Java conquers Hindu Sumatra	Chinese admiral Cheng Ho subdues Sumatra

haven—sometimes for several months—to await the right trade winds. Palembang had a large sheltered harbor on the Musi river and could supply enough food for its visitors' needs. Just as important, Srivijayan kings had a shrewd grasp of their customers' requirements. They deployed so-called "sea-nomads"—the Orang Laut people—to police the Straits and see-off pirates. Orang Laut boats also drummed up business by forcibly directing passing vessels to Palembang, enforcing dominance over rival harbors in the region.

Buddhism was another key component in Srivijaya's success. Here was a religion that actively sought to spread its teachings, and the flotilla of boats between India, China, and Southeast Asia afforded priests every opportunity to undertake missions in the Indonesian archipelago. The seventh-century Chinese pilgrim I Ching spoke of Srivijaya's king as a patron of Buddhism and recommended Palembang as a seat of learning:

"In the fortified city of Fo-shih [Palembang]," he wrote, *"there are more than a thousand Buddhist priests whose minds are bent on study and good works… if a Chinese priest wishes to go to the West to understand and read [original Buddhist scripts] there, he would be wise to spend a year or two in Fo-shih and practice the proper rules there; he might then go on to central India."*

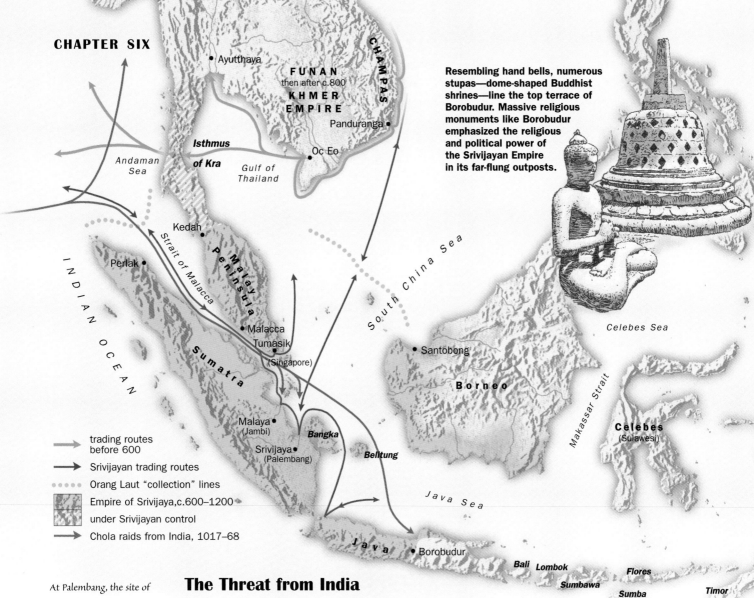

• Ayutthaya

FUNAN
then after c.800

KHMER EMPIRE

CHAMPAS

Panduranga •

Andaman Sea

Isthmus of Kra

Gulf of Thailand

• Oc Eo

Kedah •

Perlak •

Strait of Malacca

Malay Peninsula

South China Sea

I N D I A N O C E A N

Sumatra

• Malacca
Tumasik
(Singapore)

• Santobong

Celebes Sea

B o r n e o

Malaya • (Jambi)

Bangka

Makassar Strait

Celebes
(Sulawesi)

Srivijaya • (Palembang)

Belitung

trading routes before 600

Srivijayan trading routes

Orang Laut "collection" lines

Empire of Srivijaya, c.600–1200

under Srivijayan control

Chola raids from India, 1017–68

J a v a S e a

J a v a

• Borobudur

Bali *Lombok*

Flores

Sumbawa

Sumba

Timor

Resembling hand bells, numerous stupas—dome-shaped Buddhist shrines—line the top terrace of Borobudur. Massive religious monuments like Borobudur emphasized the religious and political power of the Srivijayan Empire in its far-flung outposts.

At Palembang, the site of the palaces of the kings of Srivijaya, the River Musi still acts as a maritime highway and a water home for thousands of Sumatrans.

The Threat from India

According to Arab texts written in the tenth century, the kings of Srivijaya held a curious daily ritual that graphically demonstrated their wealth. This involved casting a bar of gold into the sea with the words: "Look, there lies my treasure." As a public relations exercise this achieved two key objectives. First, it reminded potential rivals of the immense wealth and power of the Srivijayans. Second, it helped promote the ruler as a man with heightened spiritual awareness; a leader bestowed with quasi-mystical powers.

This was particularly important for a trading polity that needed to keep distant outposts in line. While Palembang was governed personally by the king and his senior staff, other ports were left in the care of local chiefs rather than royal employees. Still, if necessary the king had blunt tools at his disposal. He commanded loyalty through threat and reward—and his underlings were kept in line.

Religious ceremonies

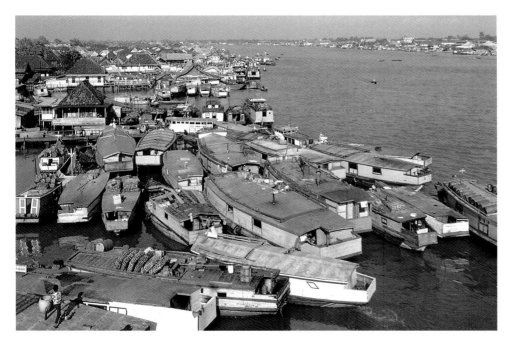

during which oaths of allegiance were sworn helped to bind the empire. The seventh-century Telaga Batu stone, found at Sabukingking, near Palembang, has the longest inscription yet attributed to Srivijaya. Its curved top bears the carving of a seven-headed snake—a symbol of water and fertility—and beneath the writing is a stone likeness of a *yoni* (vagina). The idea was to pour water over the stone during ceremonies of allegiance, and oath-takers would drink from the *yoni*. The stone, measuring four feet in height, lists officials of the empire, all of whom were required to say the following:

"All of you, as many as you are—sons of kings… chiefs, military commanders, confidants of the king, judges, surveyors of groups of laborers, surveyors of low castes, cutlers, clerks, sculptors, sea captains, merchants… and you—washermen of the king and slaves of the king, all of you will be killed by the curse of this imprecation if you are not faithful to me…. However, if you are submissive, faithful and straight to me and do not commit these crimes… you will not be swallowed with your children and wives… Eternal peace will be the fruit produced by this spell which is drunk by you…"

MYSTERIOUS EMPIRE-BUILDERS

Historical knowledge about the deeds of Srivijayan rulers remains patchy. Sanskrit inscriptions talk of an early king, probably Jayanasa, who in c.AD 684 took to the sea with 20,000 men to acquire "magic power" and bring victory, power, and riches to the empire. Two years later these forces attacked Java. By AD 775, Srivijaya had extended its rule as far as Kedah, in northwest Malaya. An inscription recording this accomplishment mentions a king called Sri Maharaja, a descendant of the Sailendra dynasty and "destroyer of his enemies." The Sailendras or "Lords of the Mountains" are thought to have once ruled Funan, later re-establishing their regime in central Java and Palembang. They were the builders of the extraordinary Hindu-Buddhist monument at Borobudur.

Around 990 Srivijaya was attacked by the rival neighboring kingdom of Java, forcing it to appeal for Chinese help. The tables were turned 16 years later when Srivijaya sacked its enemy's capital and executed the king. Yet by now the empire was in terminal decline. In 1025 the Chola ruler of Coromandel, on India's southwest coast (where Srivijaya had once built Buddhist temples for its commercial agents), launched a massive raid on Palembang and the colonies. Though the regime survived, it never regained its former maritime greatness and regional power passed to the Javan states of Majapahit and Singosari during the 12th and 13th centuries.

Seen from below, the 9th-century terraces of Borobudur march into the sky like the peaks of the Himalayas. The fusion of Indian Hindu culture with Indian and Chinese Buddhism resulted in a wealth of sculpture and bas-reliefs in both religious idioms. The circular top terrace is a parade of Buddhist stupas, containing statues of the Buddha. Borobudur is in central Java, a few miles from the old Javanese capital of Yogyakarta.

The Almoravid Gold Road

A new Islamic force grew rich on gold during the 11th century and forged an empire that ran from Spain in the north to the west coast of Africa in the south.

An aerial view of modern-day Marrakesh reveals the heart of a north African trading city that has changed little in appearance since the first days under its Almoravid founders. The minaret of the Koutoubia mosque, built in the first years of the Almohad dynasty, can be seen at the very top center of the picture.

Gold has built and broken empires. As the most indisputable guarantee of purchasing power it remains of vital importance for nations even today in times of war or political uncertainty. In North Africa its strategic importance was once overwhelming. During classical and medieval times, whoever controlled the gold routes from Ghana in West Africa controlled international trade across the Mediterranean.

The existence of West African gold had been known to explorers such as the Phoenicians since before 500 BC. The Romans were certainly aware of its potential, but because the Sahara proved a barrier to conquest, they avoided direct interference with the supply routes operated by nomadic desert tribes. However, the decline of the Roman Empire reduced the status of the

denarius aureus (gold dinar), and Islamic dinars minted by the caliphs of Cordoba, Damascus, and Baghdad became the standard European currency. These were used as far away as the Anglo-Saxon kingdom of Offa, on the Welsh borderlands, although by the ninth century AD, supplies of gold in Europe were difficult to find.

In 969 the scenario changed. The Fatimids, a dynasty of Tunisian and Algerian Muslim rulers who claimed direct descent from the Prophet Mohammed's daughter, seized control in Egypt and rotated trade links away from the Persian Gulf toward the Mediterranean and northern Africa. Their prosperity hinged on the discovery of new gold supplies in Ghana, and the Fatimid dinar was soon regarded as an international currency, much like the U.S. dollar is today. The Fatimids flourished for well over a century until they yielded to an aggressive new internal force—the *Al-murabitum*, the Almoravids.

A NEW FUNDAMENTALISM

This Berber-speaking people rose to prominence in the 11th century on a wave of puritanical Muslim sentiment. The traditional account is that a desert Sanhaja tribal leader went on pilgrimage to Mecca, where he saw the extent to which his own peoples' observance of Islamic law had been eroded. He returned with a cleric called Ibn Yasin, urging him to lead a campaign of Muslim fundamentalism throughout the Maghrib region of northwest Africa.

At first Ibn Yasin's condemnation of rich and decadent Berber lifestyles was not greeted well by the Sanhaja and their tribal allies the Tuareg. It was only after Ibn Yasin had trained a religious military elite to enforce his doctrine that the new values became adopted. The reformers were called the *Al-murabitum*, literally meaning "people

AD 1054	1070	1075–77	1076	1076	1085	108	1102
Berber chieftan Abu Bakr establishes the Almoravid dynasty in North Africa	Abu Bakr founds the city of Marrakesh in Morocco	Almoravids conquer northern Morocco and western Algeria	City of Kumbi, capital of Ghana is sacked	Almoravid armies invade southern Spain	After fall of Muslim Toledo, the Almoravids are asked to aid all Muslim states in Spain	Death of Abu Bakr, Almoravid dynasty founder	Valencia is put under siege

of the *ribat*" (a monastic garrison in which pious Muslim recruits are trained in military and religious disciplines). The meaning of the word has been disputed, however, since it implies that Ibn Yasin's warriors occupied a particular *ribat*. In fact its physical existence is considered unlikely and the meaning of *Al-murabitum* was probably something like "the men committed to the cause of defending true Islam."

After their subjugation of Sanhaja

African gold and was brought to the northern coast in the time-honored manner, by desert caravan. Such seemingly inexhaustible wealth—equaling hundreds of millions of dollars by current values—strengthened the Almoravids' hand militarily. During the late 11th century, trading ports flourished along the North African coast. Inland at the edge of the Sahara, great trading depots sprang up and while the greatest of these, Sijilmasa, is now long gone, Marrakesh remains a testament to Almoravid enterprise.

In a period spanning less than a hundred years, the Almoravids left behind few enduring public buildings (although they began many for the succeeding Almohads to finish), but the simple, elegant shrine at Koubba el Baadiyin is one such.

tribesmen, the Almoravids became a force to be reckoned with. They rapidly established control of the Saharan trade routes and, by the mid-11th century, advanced into Morocco. On Ibn Yasin's death, however, the empire split into two. Yusuf Ibn Tashfin controlled the whole of Northern Morocco, while his brother, Abu Bakr, ruled the South. Both later extended their spheres of influence with the justification of enforcing the tennets of pure Islam.

Whatever public reasons were put forward, the Almoravids also gained control of the gold trade. Now there was a new gold standard, the Almoravid dinar or *marabotin*. It relied on the same high-quality West

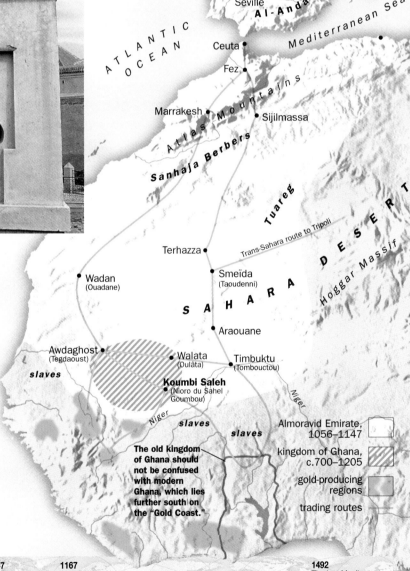

Extent of the Almoravid Emirate between 1056 and 1147.

Cordoba
Seville
Al-Andalus
ATLANTIC OCEAN
Mediterranean Sea
Ceuta
Fez
Atlas Mountains
Marrakesh
Sijilmassa
Sanhaja Berbers
Tuareg
SAHARA DESERT
Hoggar Massif
Terhazza
Trans-Sahara route to Tripoli
Smeïda (Taoudenni)
Wadan (Ouadane)
Araouane
Awdaghost (Tegdaoust)
Walata (Oulâta)
Timbuktu (Tombouctou)
slaves
Niger
Koumbi Saleh (Nioro du Sahel Goumbou)
Niger
slaves
slaves

The old kingdom of Ghana should not be confused with modern Ghana, which lies further south on the "Gold Coast."

Almoravid Emirate, 1056–1147
kingdom of Ghana, c.700–1205
gold-producing regions
trading routes

1118	c.1120	1139	1143–47	1167	1203	1212	1492
Saragossa is lost to the Christians in the Almoravids' first serious reversal	Ibn-Tumart founds the Berber Almohad dynasty	Afonso of Portugal beats the Almoravids and becomes king of Portugal	Almohad dynasty overthrows the Almoravids	Almohads push Normans out of Tunisia and take North Africa	Almohads conquer the Balearic archipeligo	Large swathes of Almohad Spain are taken by Christians in the reconquista	The last Muslims are expelled from Spain at Granada by Christian forces

ABOVE: Ruins of the old
trading city of Wadan
(Ouadane). During the
11th century, many towns
near to the old kingdoms
of Ghana and Mali grew
wealthy on the trade of
gold and slaves from the
more southerly regions of
West Africa.

FACING TOP: The minaret
of Seville Cathedral, once a
mosque, is graced with
simple arabesques. Begun
at the very end of the
Almoravid period, it was
completed by Almohads,
who confirmed Seville as
the new capital of Spain.

RIGHT: Detail from the
mantle of the Almoravid
"king" of Seville. The
Andalusian Moors
requested aid from the
Almoravids, but their
Islamic cousins wrested
control from Cordoba, and
made their base in Seville.

Masters of Marrakesh

Devotion to Islam provided the spur for
Almoravid conquest, and an empire was
quickly created. Consolidating and retaining
this empire proved more difficult, however.
The Sanhaja and Tuareg chiefs had suffered
an invasion of their southern territories
during the 11th century by nomadic Zenata
people, who disrupted desert trade routes to
the north coast. Meanwhile a strengthening
Ghanaian kingdom had taken control of a
southern trading outpost, Awdaghost.
Consequently there were sound reasons to
impose greater authority on the region, and
religious fanaticism again provided the
impetus. Soon the Almoravids were
portraying themselves as the scourge of the
Zenata intruders, tax liberators (particularly
taxes unsanctioned by the Koran), and
champions of anti-corruption. Their rough,
puritanical reputation made them an enemy
to be feared.

The death of the empire's founding father,
Ibn Yasin, in c.1059 brought the brothers
Abu Bakr and Yusuf ibn Tashfin to power.
Some three years after this, Abu moved
against the Ghanaian regime in what became
a debilitating and bloody *jihad* (holy war)
against a brave and determined opposition.
It was not until 1076 that Abu's Almoravids

eventually won the day, sacking the
Ghanaian capital and taking control of the
kingdom's vast natural wealth. However,
this proved to be something of a Pyrrhic
victory. The victorious forces soon squabbled
over the spoils of war and there was a total
absence of strong central leadership. For
more than 150 years Ghana reverted to tribal
hierarchy.

TIME RUNS OUT

Further north, Yusuf fared rather better.
After conquering Morocco and Algeria, and
founding Marrakesh, he turned his attention
to the Moorish provinces of southern Spain.
Here there was growing unrest among

THE WARRIOR SLAVES

Black slaves were first used as soldiers in
northern Africa in the ninth century AD by
the Aghlabid regime of Tunisia. They won
a reputation for bravery and loyalty and
were often hand-picked as members of a
royal bodyguard—not least because they
were considered unlikely assassins. The
Almoravids used them in wars against
Christian Spain, and they were well
represented in later Almohad armies.

Muslims at the rise of a powerful new Christian ruler—King Alfonso VI, Spanish monarch of Leon and Castile, who was determined to reconquer Spain for Christianity. He encouraged Christians to migrate north, away from Muslim territory, so that he could send his armies south to devastate the region. When his forces took the strategically important city of Toledo in 1085, and regrouped near the Tagus, the Moors pleaded with the Almoravids to come to their aid. Yusuf duly obliged. He entered Andalusia in 1086 and defeated Alfonso. But if Spanish Muslims thought stability was assured they were hopelessly wrong. Almoravid commanders were scathing of their cousins' luxurious palaces and contemptuous of their tolerant brand of Islam. It was an uneasy alliance that would last barely half a century.

The problem now for the Almoravids lay in maintaining popular support. Their empire positively dripped with wealth from

gold and trade interests, while Marrakesh stood out as the glorious embodiment of their prosperity. This was all very well but it led to great resentment, especially among the Berber-speaking Masmuda tribes of the Atlas Mountains. These people complained that the Almoravids had lost their way. They saw Marrakesh growing fat on wealth and regarded its occupants as bigots; not saviors.

When, in c.1125, a young revolutionary preacher called Ibn Tumart established a *ribat* opposed to the regime, he became a natural leader for both the Masmuda tribes and the Zenata desert nomads who had been so hounded in the early years of Almoravid supremacy. This new movement, the Almohad (literally "the monotheists"), established itself with astonishing speed. By 1147, Ibn Tumart's successor, Abd al-Mumin, was master of Marrakesh and Caliph of all Morocco. Soon the Moors of Spain also bowed to his supremacy and by 1174 the Almoravid Empire was finished.

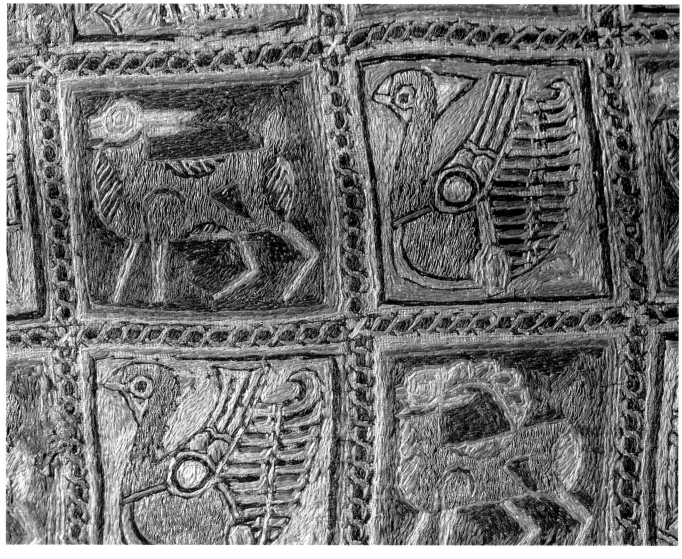

The Inca State Machine

While Spanish conquistadors were bringing to an end the empire of the Aztec in Mesoamerica, a few hundred miles to the south another great pre-Columban American empire had reached its zenith... but the Spanish would soon arrive.

Sitting at cloud level on a peak in the Peruvian Andes, the city of Machu Picchu was discovered by American explorer Hiram Bingham in 1911. The complex had lain undisturbed since the Inca abandoned it after the invasion of Pizarro. However, the Spaniards never found the city.

The rise and fall of the Inca Empire is probably the most dramatic in history. From an insular mountain heartland in southern Peru, Inca warriors struck out to dominate an area stretching 2,175 miles from north to south, and 500 miles wide, subjugating up to 16 million people in the process. Yet, incredibly, the empire lasted less than a century—destroyed in a matter of years by a handful of audacious (and rapacious) Spanish conquistadors.

The term "Inca" originally described a supreme ruler, an earthly incarnation of the sun, although the term came to be synonymous with all members of this Quechua-speaking people. Expansion first began in about 1437, when the Inca ruler Viracocha extended the boundaries of Cuzco, his city fortress, to cover a radius of about 25 miles. Inspired by this, over the following decades his son Pachacuti, grandson Topa Inca Yupanqui, and great-grandson Huayna Capac embarked on a series of conquests in an area stretching from northern Chile and Argentina, through Ecuador, Peru, and Bolivia, and deep into the southern reaches of Colombia.

That they maintained hegemony over such a vast area of mountain country and tropical rainforest is hard to imagine. Yet the Inca managed it by enforcing an efficient regime of food production, state taxes, a devolved regional government (the empire was actually called *Tahuantinsuyu*, Land of the Four Quarters), and an advanced command and control network based on stone roads linking the realm's military strongholds.

UNPARALLELED EFFICIENCY

There were up to 25,000 miles of roads, with the main links running across the Andes from Cuzco to Quito and south into present-day Chile and Argentina. They could be used only on imperial orders—typically to facilitate troop movements or llama trains carrying goods—but were also manned by athletes carrying messages in relay. Great numbers of these state-trained sprinters working together were probably capable of covering 250 miles in a single day.

Supreme power was held by the Inca himself; the living god whose word was law. These rulers commissioned great public buildings, and the mortarless stonework of Inca temples, palaces, and fortresses—typified by Cuzco and Pachacuti's mountain retreat at Machu Picchu—is legendary. According to one Spanish chronicler, Pedro de Ondegardo, it must have taken 20 men an entire year to dress some of the larger stone blocks.

Feeding the masses was a priority and

c.AD 400	c.1200–1230	1470
Moche culture extends from the Andes to the Pacific	Manco Capac founds the Inca state at Cuzco	The Inca conquer the Chimú Empire in coastal Peru

religion was therefore heavily geared to promoting agricultural success. The principal spiritual deity was Viracocha—creator of the world—but there were also gods of the weather, sun, and stars, and goddesses of the moon, earth, and sea. Live animals, and occasionally people, were sacrificed at the more important ceremonies, one of which involved the ruling Inca casting the first seeds of the planting season.

Maize and potatoes were the most important crops. Government officials supervised everything from seed selection to irrigation. These supervisors could also bring in outside labor where necessary; a useful way of damping down potential flashpoints in the empire. If a far-flung tribe started making trouble, its warriors were resettled nearer to a garrison to quell potential rebellion. In Cuzco such groups were known as *mitmac* labor and were allowed to live in allocated areas among others of their home culture.

Taxes were heavy and based on food production. Generally, a harvest was split three ways—between the laborer, the state, and the gods. Since religion and state were of course intertwined, ruling Inca profited greatly. However there was also a recognition that food reserves for distribution in times of hardship were vital to maintain control.

Pizarro and his force of conquistadors arrived under sail from Panama in 1530–1. His arrival in Tumbes went unopposed. Massively outnumbered, Pizarro captured the Inca ruler Atahualpa in a daring raid on Cajamarca. Atahualpa—invariably shown in heroic pose, as in this 18th-century engraving—was executed by Pizarro a year later.

The skill of Inca masons is never better shown than at the fortress of Sacsahuaman (pictured below), guarding Cuzco. The stones all interlock with hairline seams without use of mortar. The fortress did not hold back Pizarro when he attacked in 1536.

Quito
Ambato
Riobamba
ANDES
Tumbes
Saraguro
Sullana
1532
Cajamarca
Chan Chan
Huaraz
Huánco
Tarma
1532
Jauja
Pachacmac
Ayacucho
Huaytará
Machu Picchu
Pisac
Ica
Cuzco
Andahuaylas
1536
Nazca
Ayaviri
Lake Titicaca
Atico
Chuquito
Tiwanacu
La Paz
Cochabamba
Paria
Lake Poopó
Pica
Tupiza
Tilcara
La Playa
Chilechito
ANDES
ANDES
Santiago

PACIFIC
OCEAN

Inca territory, c.1400
Inca territory, 1525
Inca highways
Pizarro's invasion, 1532–33

1524	1525	1527	1529	1532	1533	1535–6	1537
A Spanish expedition from Panama, led by Pizarro, explores Peru	Death of Huayna Capac at height of Inca Empire	Atahualpa becomes ruler of the Inca Empire, succeeding Huayna Capac	Pizarro's forces invade	Atahualpa seized by Pizarro, held for ransom, but eventually murdered	Pizarro's forces move on Cuzco, ultimately taking the city and the Inca Empire	Inca revolt in Peru is defeated by Spanish occupation forces	Manco Capac II recaptures Cuzco and establishes a new Inca state at Vilcabamba

FACING TOP: At Pisac, near Cuzco, the masonry of the fortress is more regular than at Sacsahuaman. Also visible at Pisac are terraces cut into the mountainside, by which means the Inca increased the area of available farmland.

CENTER: More elaborate in decoration than work from Chimú (conquered by the Inca in 1470, but from whom the Inca borrowed much), this ceremonial Sun knife represents exactly the wealth Pizarro was after. In the end, European disease proved as effective against an indigenous population with no resistance to it as European weaponry in exterminating the Inca. This Inca clay figure is covered in pustules which indicate syphilis. Smallpox also wiped out thousands.

Spaniards dupe Atahualpa

The fall of the Inca Empire is a story of cruelty, greed, and religious zealotry; a historical tragedy in which an invading power used its might against bewildered natives. It also highlights the vulnerability of a theocracy—rulers feted as gods—and the speed with which a highly-disciplined society can disintegrate into chaos.

By 1525, the empire had reached its zenith. However the death of the Inca Huayna Capac that year exposed a crisis of succession in which one son, Huascar, was pitted against his half-brother Atahualpa. In the ensuing civil war Atahualpa was victorious and he imprisoned his rival. At this point the Spanish explorer Francisco Pizarro and his band of 180 fortune-seeking adventurers marched into the cauldron of Inca internecine hostilities.

Pizarro had risen from poverty to play a leading role in the Spanish exploration of the Pacific. In 1524 he teamed up with the military commander Diego de Almagro and the priest Hernando de Luque to conquer and Christianize Peru for the Spanish crown. More importantly from Pizarro's point of view, this provided the possibility to get rich quick. Spanish rumors had been rife that there was an exotic civilization to the south whose gold they could plunder.

Contemporary reports suggest that when the Inca first set eyes on the Spaniards they believed the fair-skinned strangers were gods returning home. Pizarro may also have convinced them that he was returning religious artifacts. Certainly his first encounters involved cordial exchanges with the natives and it was not until 1531 that he landed an attacking force of 180 men.

During the march inland Pizarro learned of the Inca civil war and recruited defeated Huascar loyalists. Then he presented Atahualpa with an ultimatum: unless the emperor converted to Christianity he would be regarded as an enemy of the Church and Spain. Atahualpa's refusal was the excuse

Pizarro needed to legitimize his attack. The Inca force was quickly overwhelmed. Ironically, the only Spanish casualty was Pizarro himself—injured as he prevented his men from killing Atahualpa. He knew the captured ruler would be needed to front a puppet state.

MACHIAVELLIAN TACTICS

At first Atahualpa was treated with respect and encouraged to communicate with his people. Indoctrinated by the notion that their Inca's word was law, the masses obligingly carried on their daily business apparently untroubled by the presence of occupying Spanish soldiers. Atahualpa meanwhile struck a deal with Pizzaro to

1541	1572	1591	1783	1821
Pizarro is assassinated in Lima	Tupac Amaru, the last independent Inca ruler, is executed	Spain passes a law integrating the former Inca Empire into the Spanish Empire	Tupac Amaru II and his family are tortured and executed by the Spanish	Peru declares its independence from Spain

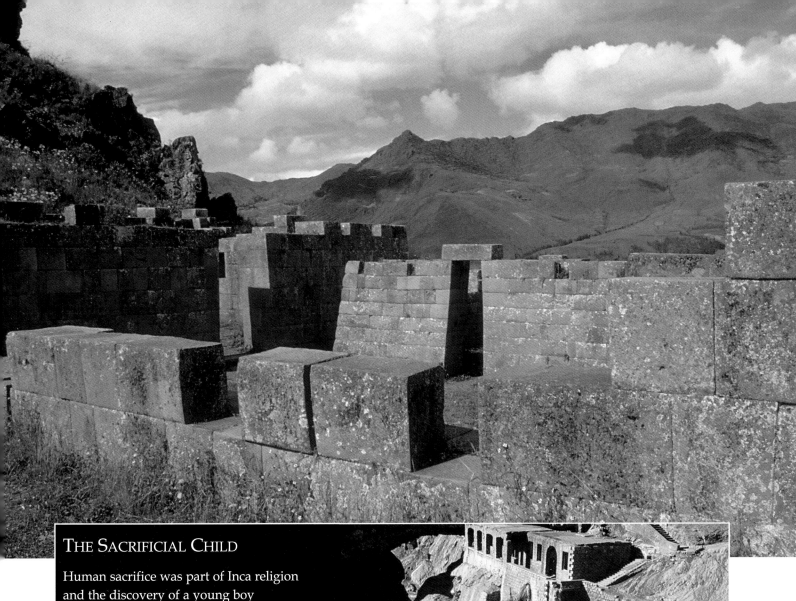

THE SACRIFICIAL CHILD

Human sacrifice was part of Inca religion and the discovery of a young boy mummified by ice 17,500 feet up Mount Aconcagua on the Argentine-Chilean border has given archaeologists a tantalizing glimpse of this ritual. The boy— a "messenger to the gods" according to Inca tradition—was wearing fine clothes and carried gold and shell figurines along with a bag of coca leaves. It is thought he was killed late in the Inca era, although the precise method of sacrifice is unclear.

buy freedom by handing over a room full of gold and silver. Even so, the Inca leader was suspicious. He rightly feared his position would be hopeless if Huascar was seen as the more malleable puppet ruler. Quietly, he gave the order to execute his half-brother.

It made no difference. With his strongroom now full of treasure the duplicitous Pizarro put Atahualpa on trial for murder, insurrection, and idolatry. The Inca was found guilty and garroted the same

night—even as he embraced Christianity and pleaded for his life.

The ensuing years proved disastrous both for the Inca and their conquerors. Puppet rulers were unable to quell revolts across the empire, land was neglected, famine killed thousands, and European diseases proved devastating. In 1537 Pizarro and Almagro quarreled over territory and fought a civil war. This ended the following year with the execution of Almagro, and in 1541 a rump of his supporters assassinated Pizarro.

Like the Romans in Europe, the Inca controlled a vast empire thanks to their amazing highway construction program. Pictured above, an Inca bridge spans a torrent on Mount Aconcagua, an Inca religious center (see box). The highway system required many such engineering feats.

Iceland

ATLANTIC OCEAN

Christiania •
• Edinburgh   Stockholm •
NORTH SEA   Kalmar
Dublin • York   Copenhagen •   BALTIC SEA
England   Hamburg •   Lübeck •
London •

Orléans •
France
ALPS
Bordeaux •
Venice •
Spain   Italy
Corsica   • Rome
• Cordoba   Balearic   Sardinia
Islands

Carthage •
AFRICA
MEDITERRANEAN SEA
Crete
Cyprus

Alexandria •
Jerusalem •

KHAZARIA
CASPIAN SEA
CAUCASUS
BLACK SEA
Adrianople • • Constantinople
ANATOLIA
Antioch •
ARABIA
RED SEA

Byzantine Empire, 565
Byzantine Empire, 1204
Angevin Empire, 1180
Union of Kalmar, 1397

Two sufferers of the bubonic
plague, from the 15th century
Toggenberg Bible. The Black
Death devastated Europe in
the 1340s.

Byzantine cavalry
and foot soldiers,
11th to 12th centuries.

The seal of
Richard I the
Lionheart, Angevin
king of England, and
famed hero of
the Third
Crusade.

The Medieval World

When the Western Roman Empire disintegrated in the fifth century AD, emperors in the east managed to stave off the tribes of barbarians that overran western Europe. The Eastern Roman Empire became known as the Byzantine Empire and, with the superbly fortified city of Constantinople as its capital, it survived for a millennium until 1453, when it was finally captured by the Islamic Ottoman Turks. Indeed, it is possible to argue that the Eastern Roman Empire lasted almost until the end of the medieval era, although in reality the Byzantine Empire became increasingly Greek in culture as the centuries passed, and bore very little resemblance to its Latin forebear.

Throughout its existence the Byzantine Empire was threatened by the tribes and nations that surrounded it. Its survival is mainly due to the fortifications that protected Constantinople. The city lies at the end of a peninsula. Across this peninsula were elaborately constructed defenses that were four and a half miles long, with a moat and three walls, and a sea wall. Approximately 400 towers augmented these barriers, and for centuries they proved impossible to breach. A soldier on the Fourth Crusade stated: "Those who had never seen Constantinople before gazed very intently at the city, having never imagined there could be so fine a place in all the world." Under Byzantine leadership, Christianity flourished and the Orthodox Church was born and prospered.

In western Europe, England and France during medieval times were a patchwork of warring regions, with large swathes of territory under the leadership of royal dynasties such as the Angevins. Through the reign of Henry II, England became a well-administered and efficient kingdom, but his successors failed to build on his achievements.

NEW BEGINNINGS

This was the Crusading era in Europe, and Henry's son Richard the Lionheart made his name fighting Saladin and his Muslim armies in the Holy Land. But Richard did not only have the forces of Islam to fight—he and his Angevin family were perpetually feuding, and his brother John made an unsuccessful attempt to take the throne while Richard was in France. After Richard's death John finally became king, but he ruled so weakly that his barons eventually forced him to sign away much of his power in the now famous document, the *Magna Carta*.

In the 1340s the whole of Europe was cast into despair at the onset of the Black Death—bubonic and pneumonic plague. This dreadful disease devastated all the European countries, but especially nations with small populations such as Norway. Out of the devastation wrought by the Black Death, Norway eventually rose and formed a union with Sweden and Denmark. Together they created a force to be reckoned with in the north, and a major rival to the German Hanseatic League that dominated trade in the Baltic Sea at this time. Throughout western Europe, empires were being formed and coming of age as never before.

The Byzantine Empire

Classical Rome died in 470, the recognized date of the fall of the Roman Empire in the west. The legacy of over 1,200 years went to the eastern Roman Empire, or Byzantium.

The see-saw fortunes of the Byzantine Empire have left it with a tarnished image, yet this was an empire that endured for more than a millennium. Its astonishing longevity, vast wealth, and far-reaching influence place it squarely in the elite of empires—the worthy successor of the Roman Empire from which it was born. However, its vital geographical position on the crossroads between Europe and Asia proved to be both blessing and tragedy—catalyst for downfall.

According to one story, in 658 BC Greek colonists traveling from Megara reached the Bosphorus and settled there. They named the settlement after their leader, Byzas. Even in AD 73 when Vespasian incorporated the busy trading town into the Roman Empire, it was still only modestly sized.

By the mid-third century, in the face of increasing turbulence internally and pressure on every border, Diocletian (r.284–305) decreed that the empire should be split. In 286, he appointed Maximian co-emperor to rule the west, while he concentrated on the east. This state of affairs changed after Constantine (r.306–37) became emperor in the west after Diocletian's abdication in 305 (*see page 41*). Relations between the western and eastern arms of the empire became critical and civil war broke out. In 324 at Adrianople near Byzantium, Constantine emerged the victor and sole emperor of the Roman Empire. He commanded his "New Rome" to be built on the site of old Byzantium. Although the new city soon renamed itself Constantinople after its founder, its culture retained the name Byzantium and the imperial court was

known as the Byzantine court. Constantine's enthusiasm for the city meant that in just a few years the extensive building works he had ordered were completed. Monuments from all over Asia and Greece were either imported or seized to embellish its buildings and open spaces.

According to tradition, Constantine became convinced of Christian virtues in 312 when he saw a cross in the sky and the words *In hoc signo vinces* (In this sign thou shall be victorious) just before his victory in battle at the Milvian Bridge, near Rome. Although only baptized on his death bed, Constantine had already paved the way for Christianity to become the state religion. Despite the fusion of Hellenistic (pagan) and Christian beliefs, the new faith remained important to Constantinople even when Julian "the Apostate" came to power for four years in 360. He chose the old pagan ways above Christianity and suppressed Christians where he could. Soon after his death, the Roman Empire split once more, with Valens in power in the east and his brother Valentinian in the west.

CHRISTIANITY IS ASSURED

Now the spread of Christianity increased. Over-zealous Christians ripped down pagan temples all over the empire. In Alexandria the ancient Temple of Serapis and the library attached to it—reputedly containing 700,000 volumes—were entirely destroyed. Such was the force of feeling that in 393 the Olympic Games, held every four years since 776 BC, were ended because of an ancient connection with the Zeus cult.

Perhaps the most lauded of the early Byzantine emperors was Justinian I (r.527–65). The historian Procopius recorded some of the emperor's accounts even though he confessed to hating Justinian because he believed he was in league with the devil.

Aurelius Valerius Diocletian was born in 245 in the Roman province of Dalmatia. He rose to be a general during a time of turbulence in the empire. In 284 his soldiers pronounced him emperor. He managed to restore much of Rome's glory In short order through a program of reforms. It was the norm for emperors to die in power; unusually, Diocletian abdicated in 305 to become an ordinary Roman citizen.

AD 324	470	527	536	552	673–78	697	812
Emperor Constantine founds Constantinople at the site of the Greek city Byzantium	Fall of Western Roman Empire	Byzantine Empire formed under Roman emperor Justinian in Constantinople	Byzantine general Belisarius captures Rome	Byzantines gain control of southern Spain from Visigoths	Constantinople besieged by Arabs	Byzantine Carthage destroyed by Arabs	Byzantium recognizes Charlemagne and the Holy Roman Empire in the west

MAXIMIANVS

Justinian appears in this mosaic from Ravenna supported by religious and military orders. His most inspired military appointment was that of Belisarius, his general who swept the Vandals from North Africa and the Ostrogoths from Italy. The gold solidus of Justinian, pictured below, was widely minted throughout the empire. Justinian's reform of Roman law left a legacy of law codes that influenced Europe until after the Middle Ages.

Nevertheless, Justinian appears to have been a respected, responsible leader. He codified Roman law and began the great Hagia Sophia church in Constantinople, which stands where the original Byzantium was founded (*see page 117*). Outraged that lands once part of the Roman Empire—including most of Italy—were now in barbarian hands, Justinian organized a large army of re-conquest. Against expectations, his commander, Belisarius, was successful in regaining the kingdoms of the Vandals in North Africa and Ostrogoths in Italy.

The Byzantine Empire, 480–540, and the campaigns of Justinian and Belisarius.

Southern Spain was reconquered in 554 after civil war in the Visigothic kingdom.

Ravenna, capital of the Ostrogoths, was captured by Belisarius in 540.

FRANKISH KINGDOM

ALPS

Lombards

CARPATHIANS

Bulgars

Dnieper

Don

Huns

Crimea

Alans

VISIGOTHIC KINGDOM

Danube

• Milan

Ravenna

ADRIATIC SEA

Danube

Naissus •

• Cherson

BLACK SEA

Corsica

• Rome

TYRRHENIAN SEA

Adrianople •

• Constantinople

Sardinia

Thessalonika •

ANATOLIA

• Carthago Nova

ATLAS

• Carthage

Sicily

• Syracuse

Malta

Athens •

Rhodes

Cyprus

• Antioch

SASSANIAN EMPIRE

MEDITERRANEAN SEA

Crete

Damascus •

• Leptis Magna

Jerusalem •

Alexandria •

Nile

eastern Roman Empire, 480
Byzantine Empire, 565
kingdom of Ostrogoths, 520
kingdom of Vandals, 520
campaigns of Belisarius:
533–34
535–40

For centuries, the massive and imposing walls of Constantinople protected the bustling imperial city within. The Seven Towers Fortress pictured here was one of several strongholds, built as part of the outer wall ring.

Triumph and Tragedy

The Byzantine Empire had some long-term allies and a number of time-honored foes. Friends of the empire included Ethiopia (*see pages 62–65*), Khazaria and, until the 11th century, Rome. Among the enemies were tribes like the fearsome Avars (*see page 79*), who also allied themselves with the Persian Sassanian Empire. In the 590s the emperor Maurice went to war after the Avars seized Sirmium, a Byzantine frontier town in the Balkans. The Avars were so successful that they marched to the walls of Constantinople. The dispute then became bitter and long-running. It is remembered mostly for the Avars' execution of 12,000 Byzantine prisoners of war in a bid to force the emperor's hand.

In 602 Byzantine soldiers mutinied. The hapless Maurice was murdered by Phocas, who then emerged as a terrible despot. The armies that now threatened Byzantium—

ostensibly to avenge the death of Maurice but in reality to carve up his territory—included the Sassanians and once again the Avars. The Persian army took possession of Egypt, the Holy Land, and eastern Anatolia between 607–628.

The Byzantine Empire was in grave danger of obliteration. However, in 610 Heraclius, the son of the Roman governor in Africa, responded to desperate Byzantine appeals. He sailed from Carthage to Constantinople, overthrew Phocas, and made himself emperor. Once in power he made substantial changes to the army, local government, and state finances that helped put the empire back onto a firm footing and kept enemies at bay. Land concessions made to men eligible for military service helped to create a well-motivated, loyal army. Greek became the Byzantine Empire's official language instead of Latin.

In 627 Heraclius was ready to take the

823	867	961	974	1052	1064	1071	1081
Arabs take Sicily from the Byzantines	Macedonian dynasty is founded as Basil I becomes emperor	Crete is recaptured from the Arabs	Byzantine Empire controls northern Palestine and Syria	Normans control Byzantine southern Italy	Armenia becomes part of the Byzantine Empire	Byzantines lose control of Anatolia at the Battle of Manzikert	Trade agreement established between Venice and the Byzantines

initiative. With funds from his newly buoyant economy, he paid the Avars a sizeable sum to withdraw. This enabled him to move his army out of Armenia to attack the Sassanians. Heraclius won the key battle at Nineveh decisively and then moved rapidly to Jerusalem. Here, he retrieved and resurrected the Calvary cross which had been seized by the Persians.

ISLAM THREATENS

Despite foreign victories, there was unrest at home that centered on Christian dogma. Heraclius could not find a path through the theological controversy surrounding the nature of Christ. Dissent over the difficult issue of whether Christ was divine or human ripped the Church apart. Eventually the eastern, or Orthodox Church under its Patriarch, split from the earlier Roman Church under the Pope.

Even as Heraclius wrestled with this thorny problem, a new crisis arose in the east. Arab armies teeming out of Arabia, spreading the word of Islam, rapidly

overwhelmed the Sassanian Empire, then seized the regions that the Byzantine Empire had just recovered. Exhausted, the Byzantine army proved unable to stem the Muslim tide. When Heraclius died in 641, it once again seemed that the Byzantine Empire was on a precipice, ready to tumble into oblivion.

Heraclius's epileptic son, Constantine III, died within months of his father. His half-brother and mother were then butchered. Their successor, Constans II, was the young son of Constantine III and one of the least likely candidates to save the Byzantine Empire. Yet once again fate was kind. Arab dominance faltered in the face of internal bickering (*see pages 66–67*). Constantinople held firm in the face of fragmented opposition.

From 633 onward, the Byzantine Empire faced an onrush of Arab campaigns. Not every encounter with Muslim forces was a Byzantine disaster, however, and one such victory was celebrated in the Synopsis Historion, *a manuscript by John Skylitzes, written at the end of the 11th century. Called the Victory of Petronas, it shows Byzantine cavalry bloodily trampling on fallen Arabs.*

1099	1118	1137	1183	1204	1261	1280	1326
Crusaders defend Constantinople from the Muslims	Byzantine Empire empowered by new emperor, John II Comnenus	Antioch ceded to the Byzantines	Reform under Emperor Andronicus I	Constantinople captured and sacked by Crusaders	Byzantines recapture Constantinople	The Bulgarian States collapse, divided between Serbs and Byzantines	Ottoman Turks begin to seize Byzantine territory

The Decline of Byzantium

Losses continued: North Africa and Sicily to the Muslims, the Balkans to the Bulgars, and Genoa and Ravenna to the Lombards. Despite these setbacks the fortified city of Constantinople—that most resilient of capitals—remained secure. This time a dynasty of Macedonian emperors (r.867–1059) were the heroes. Again, it was not only inner strength but also external trade and the consequent loss of revenue also contributed to the weakening of the empire. Hopes for a revival came with the accession of Alexius I Comnenus in 1081, yet he would also bring a hitherto unknown horror to bear on Byzantium. Alexius appealed to his fellow Christians in the Roman Church for help against the Seljuk Turks, a new threat expanding from Anatolia. His call to the Pope for help resulted in the First Crusade.

weaknesses that helped the Byzantines to victory, including the disintegration of Arab unity and the pressure exerted on the Bulgars by the rival Magyars.

By the time of the "Bulgar-slayer" Basil II (r.976–1025) the Byzantines were the dominant force in eastern Europe. Missionaries, led by brothers Cyril and Methodius from Thessalonika, had been busy converting the Slavs to Orthodox Christianity and extending their influence into Russia. By 1018 Bulgaria had been incorporated into the empire and the eastern frontier extended to Armenia.

The momentum was lost within 20 years of Basil II's death as a succession of lackluster rulers came to the throne. Links between Roman and Orthodox Christianity grew ever more tenuous. The Italian states of Genoa and Venice proved robust rivals for

A FATAL INVITATION

Relations between Roman and Orthodox Christians were strained, as they had always been. The Pope in Rome claimed direct descent from Saint Peter and therefore primacy over all Christianity. Popes tried to enforce their supremacy over the Patriarch of the Orthodox Church in Constantinople. In 1054 the Pope excommunicated the Patriarch for allegedly refuting his authority. It is a measure of Alexius's desperation that he called on Rome at all.

A few Crusaders were chivalrous and pious pilgrims intent on winning back the Holy Land. Most were merely interested in the spoils of war and were as happy to plunder the Byzantines as the Muslims. Eventually, in 1204, Christian Crusaders sacked Christian Constantinople. Emperor Michael VIII Palaeologus recaptured the city

1337	1341–47	1356	1361	1372	1391–98	1396	1453
Byzantine presence in Asia Minor eradicated as Ottoman Turks take Nicaea	Civil war	The Ottoman Turks gain control of the Dardanelles	With the loss of Adrianople, the Byzantine Empire only has Constantinople	Ottoman Turks conquer Bulgaria	Constantinople sieged by Turks, who are paid tribute	Hungarian Sigismund fails to break through the Turks' blockade (Battle of Nicopolis)	End of the Byzantine Empire as Constantinople falls to the Turks

from the occupying forces in 1261 but Constantinople never again knew the splendors of its past.

Constantine XI was on the throne when on May 29, 1453 the next wave of Turks, the Ottomans, succeeded where so many armies had failed, and breached the massive defenses of Constantinople. Prudent in victory, the Ottomans permitted the Patriarch to remain in a city that boasted religious tolerance. Constantinople remained largely Christian and Greek-speaking until the 20th century.

Byzantine Empire at:
628
867
1025
1204

One of the greatest legacies of the Byzantine Empire is its art, which was conservative, highly stylized, and invariably religious in theme. This art survived the age of iconoclasm between 717–867 during which the worship of icons—now firmly associated with the Orthodox Church—was prohibited. The Byzantines also developed the Cyrillic alphabet. In the empire's final gasp, many Byzantine scholars left Constantinople for Italy when the Ottomans invaded, and their skills contributed greatly during the flowering of the Renaissance.

The Angevin Dynasty

An argumentative, often brutally vicious family from the Loire Valley in France contended for the English throne in the mid-twelfth century, and created an empire stretching from Scotland to the Pyrenees.

This 14th-century manuscript illumination shows Henry II, seated, discoursing the relationship of Church and State with Archbishop Thomas à Becket. A deceptively serene scene, in fact the knights in the background represent those who will shortly murder Becket.

In an abbey in Fontevrault, southwest France, the tombs of Henry II (r.1154–89), his queen Eleanor of Aquitaine, and their son Richard the Lionheart lie side-by-side. This tranquility belies the truth of their tempestuous relationship. Henry imprisoned his wife for 15 years for supporting their rebellious sons against him. His initial refusal to recognize Richard as his heir led the prince to plot Henry's downfall with the king of France. Only in death were the three reconciled, and their conflict was characteristic of the power struggles in this mighty family dynasty.

Henry II's empire stretched from the Scottish borders to the Spanish Pyrenees.

He was not the first Angevin (which means, "of Anjou") but he was arguably the most successful. The dynasty started in the tenth century with the obscure Ingelger. His successors added further French territories to Anjou until one, Fulk V, married his son Geoffrey Plantagenet to Matilda, the daughter of Henry I and widow of Holy Roman Emperor Henry V. Anjou and England—and therefore Normandy—were united.

This was Henry II's inheritance, but marriage to Eleanor of Aquitaine made it substantially larger. The largest province of France, dwarfing the French king's own territories, it also came accompanied by Gascony, Poitou, and Auvergne. Still not content, Henry annexed Ireland in 1170 and also Brittany, where he installed his brother Geoffrey as Duke. Scotland conceded to him after he defeated its king, William I.

KINGS HUMBLED AND RANSOMED

Although Henry II was a generally just ruler, he surrendered to bureaucracy in dealing with the large realm. This led to his clash with the Church and the infamous murder of Thomas à Becket, Archbishop of Canterbury. Henry's attempts to increase his control over Church appointments was opposed by Becket, determined to prevent erosion of ecclesiastical power. Becket fled to France's safety, but was given permission to return to Canterbury in 1170. However, his continued obduracy led to the king's fury erupting. "What a parcel of fools and dastards have I nourished in my house," he cried, "that not one of them will avenge me of one upstart clerk?"

His outburst cued four knights to decisive action. They sailed for England and, on December 29, 1170, confronted Becket in Canterbury Cathedral and slew him. A horrified Henry repented the murder. On

1129	1135	1152	1153	1154	1192–94	1204–05	1215
Geoffrey of Anjou marries Matilda, widow of Henry V	Rivalry between Matilda and Stephen of Blois causes English civil war	Henry of Anjou marries Eleanor of Aquitaine when her marriage with Louis VII is annulled	Henry invades England and forces Stephen to make him heir to the throne	Plantagenet dynasty is established as Henry II is made King of England	Richard I becomes a prisoner of Emperor Henry VI	King John at war with Philip II	King John signs the *Magna Carta*

July 7, 1171, he presented himself as a humble pilgrim to be chastized by the monks of Canterbury Cathedral before spending the night in pennance at Becket's shrine.

During a 34-year reign, Henry spent only 13 in England, preferring his more culturally advanced French possessions. When he died at the age of 56, the extent of his empire and the strides he had made in judicial reform provided cold comfort for a man beset by the rift between himself, his wife, and his sons. Indeed, Richard I (r.1189–99) reached the throne by chance. William, his eldest brother, died in infancy, while the next in succession, Henry, Duke of Normandy, died in 1183. Although schooled in the arts, Richard distinguished himself as a soldier and it was the army life that he loved. In the Third Crusade (1189–92), he campaigned against Saladin in the Holy Land, and experienced mixed fortunes. Returning home overland, he was captured in Austria by the forces of Holy Roman Emperor Henry VI and kept hostage for over a year. Eventually, a ransom of 150,000 silver marks freed him.

On his return he found his young brother John plotting to seize the throne. Indeed, it had only been skilful work by Richard's representatives in England that held John at bay for so long. After conducting a second coronation at Winchester on April 17, 1194, Richard departed the next month to quell uprisings in the French provinces. He would never return to English shores, since he was killed by an arrow wound while laying siege to a castle. In his ten-year reign Richard spent only six months in England.

ANGEVIN OR PLANTAGENET?

The dynasty's name is taken from the place of origin, but the son of Fulk V, Geoffrey Count of Anjou (1113–51), also called Plantagenet, always wore a branch of broom in his cap. Thus his surname was derived from the Latin *planta* (sprig) and *genista* (broom plant). When Henry of Anjou came to the English throne after forcing King Stephen of England to name him as the heir, the Angevin dynasty was thenceforth also referred to as Plantagenet.

Angevin Empire, 1180

under Angevin control, 1180

French royal demesne, 1180

1242 England invades France

1278 England under Edward I conquers Wales

1296 Edward invades Scotland to quash rebellion

1297 Edward invades France to support Flanders, occupied by Philip IV

1325 Edward II abdicates under pressure from estranged Queen Isabella and her lover Roger Mortimer

1356 Edward the Black Prince captures John II of France

1360 Edward III accepts sovereignty of southwest France, repeals claim on French throne

1399 Henry Bolingbroke overthrows Richard II, ends the Angevin-Plantagenet dynasty and starts Lancastrian House.

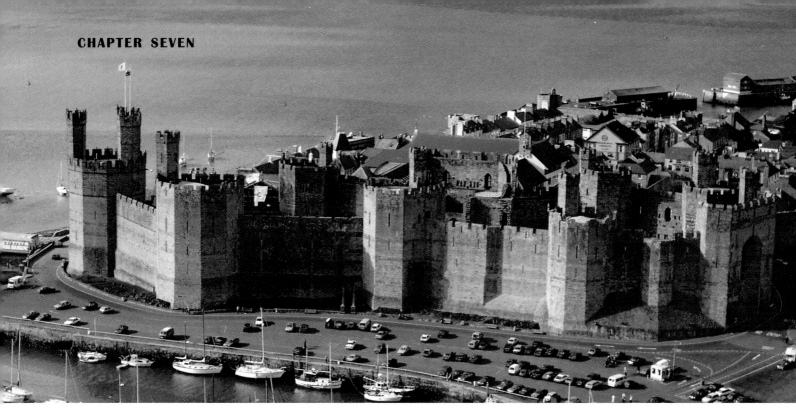

ABOVE: Edward I intended the Welsh to know they had been permanently defeated by building large castles at key sites, such as Caernarfon, started in 1283.

BELOW: At the Battle of Poitiers (1356), Edward III's son, the Black Prince, captured the French king.

Impetuosity and Impotence

One unsympathetic historian states of Richard: "[He was] a bad son, a bad brother, a bad husband, and a bad king." Yet he was imbued with nobility—with his dying breath he ordered that the archer who fired the shot that fatally wounded him be spared (the order was ignored and the archer was executed). John (r.1199–1216) succeeded Richard and did little to recommend himself as a monarch. Weak, lazy, and mean, he was

every inch the villain depicted in the *Robin Hood* tales. But he was also an able administrator—his only redeeming feature.

Henry and Richard had enjoyed the strength of character that kept their nobles disciplined, but John found this a difficult task. At first, the Norman and English barons were content for John to rule as he liked. However, those in Anjou, Maine, and Touraine sought his replacement by his nephew Arthur. John managed a temporary respite by arresting and eventually executing Arthur. But John then mismanaged his French barons who were inflamed at the brutal murder. With collapsed morale and help refused, the provinces of Normandy and Anjou fell to the king of France. John withdrew to England.

HEMMING IN A KING

In England, John's wayward behavior and typically paranoid attitude to the nobility were especially unwelcome. More trouble brewed when a disputed election to the important post of Archbishop of Canterbury led to a split with Rome. In 1209, the Pope excommunicated John and all England. John responded by confiscating Church estates. The move was ill-timed. King Philip of France was poised to invade (with the Pope's blessing), and the excommunicated barons and commoners of England were rumbling with discontent.

John was forced to make his peace with

Rome, but it was insufficient to appease his opposition. On June 15, 1215, the monarch was forced to sign the *Magna Carta*. A charter designed to curtail abuse of power by the reigning monarch, *Magna Carta*'s reforms ensured fair terms for the Church and nobility and laid the foundations for trial by jury and equitable taxation for all. At the time, it was a symbol of baronial power against a despised monarch. First Henry II's godlike right to absolute power had been challenged by the Church, now his son's had been brought to book by his own barons. The monarch was obliged to accept rule by the consent of a parliament of barons—at least to some degree. For the first time since ancient Greece and Rome, hints of democracy were showing.

Quarrels between John and the barons continued, to the point when Prince Louis of France was invited by the rebels to take the throne. Civil war ensued, during which time Louis entered London and John ravaged the lands of east England, particularly targeting Church property. John died at Newark in 1216 of dysentery, apparently caused by excessive feasting.

John's son Henry III (r.1216–76) proved to be as weak as his father, and when he attempted to repudiate the terms of the *Magna Carta*, he was captured in 1258 by rebels under Simon de Montfort's leadership. Dissension between the rebels allowed Henry's son Edward to defeat them in battle. Edward I (r.1272–1307) was the first Angevin since Henry II to show qualities as both a soldier and a statesman. Through continuous campaigning, he kept his nobles busy… and under control. During his reign, he expanded the empire in Britain by conquering and enforcing English rule of Wales and the re-conquest of lowland Scotland. Fierce Scottish resistance kept the Angevins from a complete takeover, and Edward's less able soldier son, Edward II (r.1307–27), lost much ground.

Under Edward III (r.1327–77), military campaigns moved back to French soil, as king and son, the Black Prince, tried to regain lost Angevin territory. The ruinous war was to drag on for almost a hundred years, during which period, English holdings on the Continent shriveled.

Edward III was succeeded by his infant grandson, Richard II (r.1377–99). A baronial regency, set up to manage the empire's affairs, only created further unrest among other barons and the peasants, who revolted in 1381. After coming of age, Richard II proved to be a vain and tyrannous king, who tried to reduce parliament's control. Lacking support at all levels, Richard made an ill-fated foray against rebellious Ireland. In 1399, Henry Bolingbroke of the House of Lancaster landed from France, aroused the country, and declared himself King of England as the legitimate heir of Henry III. By right of conquest, he claimed the throne and was crowned Henry IV of Lancaster. The Angevin dynasty was finished.

The mournful face of King Richard II suits a monarch at the end of a dynasty. This gilt-bronze tomb effigy in Westminster Abbey was made after his wife, Queen Anne of Bohemia, died in 1395. Richard married Sabella of France in the following year. After being deposed by Henry IV in 1399, Richard retired to Pontefract Castle, where he died in 1400.

The Union of Kalmar

At the top of Europe, three nations linked by the Baltic Sea formed an empire to dominate trade in the region. But it was the strength of inividuals that made it work, and the power of commercial opposition that caused it to fail.

FACING: Architect of the union between Norway, Denmark, and Sweden, Queen Margaret I combined ruthless political skills with military determination.

Along the Silk Road from east to west came silks, spices, and oriental ideas, and Europe prospered. However, along that same route came the Black Death, carried by fleas on the backs of rats. This dreadful disease first emerged in 1347 in an epidemic that lasted for four years. Thereafter, it returned in deadly waves engulfing cities, towns, and villages until the 15th century when outbreaks were curtailed. Few parts of the continent escaped unscathed. Nations with small populations suffered the worst.

Although 13 million died from the plague in China, an equal number survived, and the Chinese recovered more rapidly than small European kingdoms like Norway. When the Black Death reached Norway at the end of

1349, the population numbered about 400,000. Two-thirds died, leaving farms untended, reducing noblemen to peasants, depriving the government of administrators, and driving the Scandinavian country to the brink of extinction. It took three centuries for Norway to recover.

Norway had been home to the Vikings, the raiders and traders of the ninth and tenth centuries. Much of western Europe including Ireland, Scotland, England, France, Iceland, and Greenland, as well as swathes of Russia had been settled by Vikings. Since these seafaring people had no central government, their endeavors could not be described as an empire. Nevertheless, the era gave rise to kings like Harald Fairhair, the first king of Norway, his son Erik I Bloodax (notorious for killing seven of his eight brothers), and Olav I Tryggvason, who was baptized in England and worked to Christianize his kingdom.

Shortly after the Viking period, Norway became united as a pagan kingdom. At the beginning of the 11th century, King Olav I became Norway's first Christian monarch, and in 1030, Christianized the country. This stone cross he erected stands overlooking the sea at Stavanger.

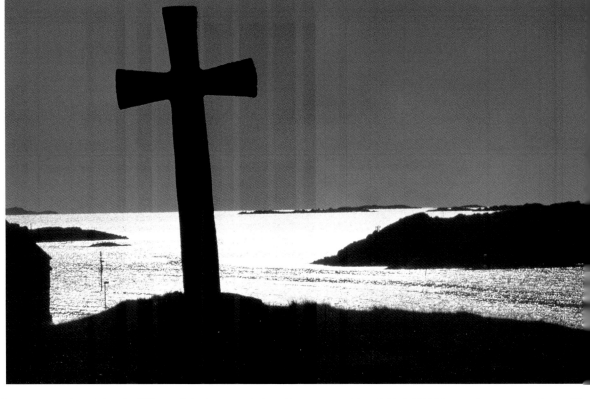

c.900	982	c.1000	1028	1066	1184	1319	1365
Harald Fairhair unites Norway's princedoms and becomes the country's first king	Greenland discovered by Norwegian explorers; Erik the Red establishes a colony in 986	North America is reached by Norwegian explorers	Led by King Canute, Denmark conquers Norway	Harald Hardrada, the last Viking king, is killed at Stamford Bridge	Sverre beats Magnus V's claim to the throne	Norway and Sweden are ruled by Magnus VII	Magnus VII retires to Norway when nephew Albert of Mecklenburg becomes king of Sweden

By the Middle Ages the Viking era already belonged to the past. The kingdom attempted to re-invent itself by creating a union with Sweden, when the daughter of the king of Norway married the son of the king of Sweden. Their son, Magnus VII Eriksson, inherited both thrones. Turbulent family rifts coupled with the effects of the plague left Norway and Sweden in difficulties, but out of these uncertain times came a united Scandinavia and a world-class empire. The architect of this new empire was Margaret I (r.1375–1412).

Margaret cements unity

Margaret was the youngest daughter of King Waldemar IV Atterdag of Denmark and, as a child, she was betrothed to Haakon VI, son of Magnus VIII Eriksson of Sweden, already king of Norway. Despite old rivalries between their fathers, which continued to rear up, Margaret and Haakon were married in 1363 in Copenhagen when she was just ten years old.

Her adolescence was spent in Norway, where the daughter of Sweden's St. Bridget tutored her. At the age of 17 she bore her only child, Olaf. Margaret saw her husband lose Sweden to a rival claimant, his cousin Albert of Mecklenburg, who also had designs on the Danish throne. She was determined to preserve her family's power and ensured that, on the death of her father in 1375, her son Olaf inherited the crown. He was only five years old at the time, so she ruled in his name.

Margaret turned her attention to Sweden, still in Albert's hands. She was preparing for war with Sweden when Olaf suddenly died in 1387 at the age of just 17. To fill the void Margaret looked to her sister's grandson, Eric of Pomerania, who was at the time just six years old. She adopted him as an heir to safeguard the family line and continued her campaign for Sweden, which then included the territory of today's Finland.

The Swedish nobles were dissatisfied with their king and were, by 1388, willing to proclaim Margaret as Sweden's rightful ruler. With her support they staged an uprising. Margaret finally confronted Albert in 1389 in battle, took him prisoner, and released him only when peace was guaranteed, some six years later.

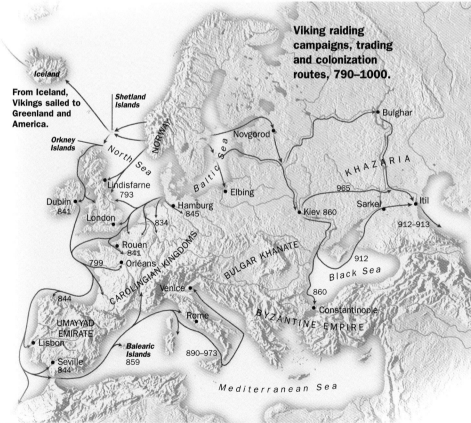

Viking raiding campaigns, trading and colonization routes, 790–1000.

1397	1435	1450	1457	1481	1497	1523	1532
Norway, Denmark, and Sweden are united by the Union of Kalmar	Eric of Scandinavia ends wars with the Hansa, who were drawn into a dispute over Schleswig	Danish King Christian I unites Norway and Denmark	Christian becomes king of Sweden	Christian I's reign over Norway ends	Norway, Denmark, and Sweden are ruled by King John of Denmark after he conquers Sweden	The Union of Kalmar dissolves after King Gustav makes Sweden independent	Christian II of Denmark fails to conquer Norway and is taken prisoner

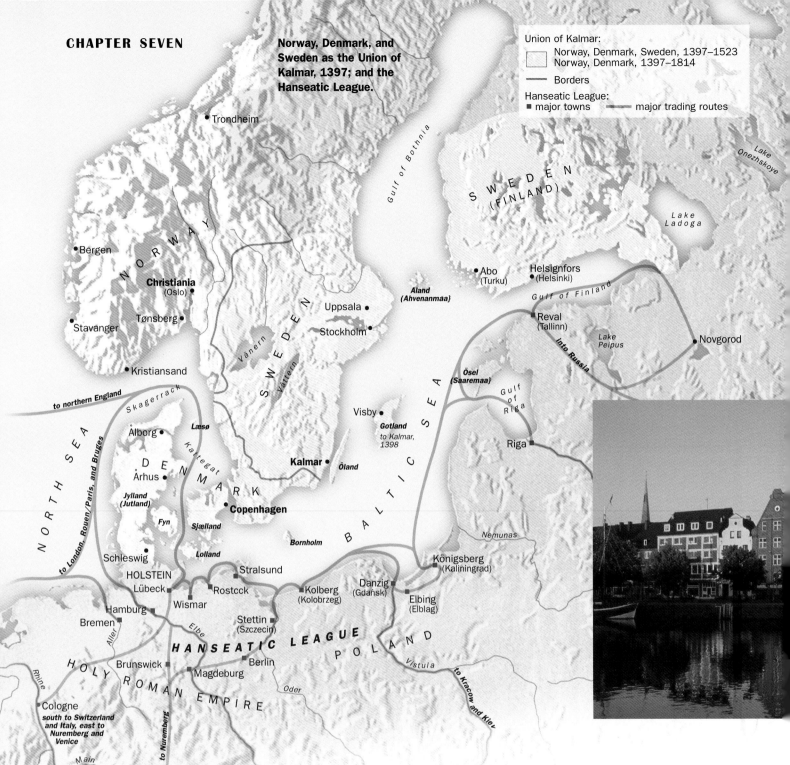

Norway, Denmark, and
Sweden as the Union of
Kalmar, 1397; and the
Hanseatic League.

Union of Kalmar:
Norway, Denmark, Sweden, 1397–1523
Norway, Denmark, 1397–1814
— Borders
Hanseatic League:
■ major towns   — major trading routes

Trondheim

S W E D E N
(FINLAND)

Lake
Onezhskoye

Gulf of Bothnia

Lake
Ladoga

N
O
R
W
A
Y

Bergen

Christiania
(Oslo)

Tønsberg

Stavanger

Kristiansand

Uppsala

Stockholm

Åland
(Ahvenanmaa}

Abo
(Turku)

Helsignfors
(Helsinki)

Gulf of Finland

Reval
(Tallinn)

into Russia

Lake
Peipus

Novgorod

to northern England

Skagerrack

S
W
E
D
E
N

Vänern

Vättern

Ösel
(Saaremaa}

Gulf
of
Riga

Ålborg

Læsø

Kattegat

Visby

Gotland
to Kalmar,
1398

B
A
L
T
I
C

S
E
A

Riga

to London, Rouen/Paris, and Bruges

D
E
N
M
A
R
K

Århus

Jylland
(Jutland)

Fyn

Kalmar   Öland

Copenhagen

Sjælland

Bornholm

N
O
R
T
H

S
E
A

Lolland

Schleswig

HOLSTEIN

Lübeck

Stralsund

Rostcck

Kolberg
(Kolobrzeg)

Danzig
(Gdańsk)

Königsberg
(Kaliningrad)

Nemunas

Hamburg

Wismar

Elbing
(Elblag)

Bremen

Elbe

Stettin
(Szczecin)

Aller

H A N S E A T I C   L E A G U E

P
O
L
A
N
D

H
O
L
Y

Rhine

Brunswick

Magdeburg

Berlin

Oder

Vistula

to Kracow and Kiev

R
O
M
A
N

E
M
P
I
R
E

Cologne

south to Switzerland
and Italy, east to
Nuremberg and
Venice

Main

to Nuremberg

Unity and Power

By the time young Eric was crowned king of
Sweden he already had the lands of Denmark
and Norway firmly under his control. But
although he was ostensibly the three-way
ruler of Scandinavia, in reality Margaret kept
a firm grip on the reigns of power. Eric's
coronation took place in June 1397 in Kalmar
in southern Sweden. It was here that a
congress formalized the union of the three
countries, which until then had maintained
their own individual governments. Even
now it would take another year before
Margaret had control of Stockholm, at that
time held by Albert's remaining supporters.

If Margaret had hoped that the Congress
of Kalmar would smooth the way to absolute
power for the monarchy everywhere within
the realm, she was mistaken. Many Swedish
nobles were concerned about the power
Margaret had accrued for herself and her
descendants. This faction preferred the way
things were handled in the Holy Roman
Empire at the time, where a form of election
selected the most able man or woman for the
task. With sly diplomacy, Margaret installed
royal sheriffs loyal to her throughout the
empire to monitor opposition. She favored
high taxation and even confiscated church
estates to bolster the treasury.

LAND PURCHASES GROW EMPIRE

Her main problem was the defense of the southern borders against Holstein, a traditional foe, and the Hanseatic League, or Hansa as it was also known. The Hansa, formed in 1350, was an association of 150 north German towns including Bremen, Hamburg, and Lübeck, that dominated trade in the Baltic. Undoubtedly the Hansa wielded more economic muscle than Margaret's empire and they were always ready to take up arms against any rival, but she nevertheless succeeded in holding them at bay. Because of the difficulties of defending Denmark, it took up most of her attention.

In comparison to the rest of Scandinavia, Norway was a backward country at this time. Not only was its population sparse but its soil was notoriously poor and landowners were unable to exploit the region (only after 1550 were the natural resources of timber, iron ore, copper, and bountiful fish exploited). The constant skirmishing between Sweden and Denmark, both of which occupied strategic positions in the Baltic, also overshadowed Norway. Margaret reclaimed areas pawned previously for cash to increase the size of her domain. She bought Gotland from the Teutonic Knights, who had occupied the island since 1398.

Before her death in 1412 she arranged for her successor Eric to marry Princess Philippa, the daughter of Henry IV of England. Eric proved unable to hold the empire together and all Margaret's gains were lost within a generation. He was deposed in all three kingdoms between 1438 and 1442. His nephew, Christopher of Bavaria, became the Danish king and was accepted in both Sweden and Norway after pledging to administer the three countries separately. The Union of Kalmar lasted until 1523 when Sweden broke away. Denmark and Norway remained united by the Union until 1814 when Norway was united once more with Sweden following the Napoleonic Wars.

Although Margaret's dreams of building a powerful, enduring political entity were never fully realized, her empire succeeded in giving three countries with small populations a major voice in northern Europe.

ABOVE: The original castle at Kalmar was built in the late 12th century to counter attacks by heathen pirates. Kalmar, called the "Key to Sweden," was largely rebuilt at the end of the 13th century and then heavily modified in the 16th. It remained one of Sweden's most important strongholds throughout the period of the Union.

LEFT: Houses lining a canal in Lübeck testify to the wealth of the Hanseatic League's major city. Powerful sea and overland traders, the Hanseatic League opposed any threat to their monopoly of Baltic trade from the Union of Kalmar.

CHAPTER EIGHT

The Age of Discovery

The nature of empires was about to change. Until the end of the medieval era, European empires had existed by controlling vassal states—neighbors who were allowed varying levels of autonomy in return for trade and military concessions. When the Portuguese and Spanish started to navigate the oceans, this limited world of feudalism quickly came to an end, as small European nations sought to acquire territories in newly-discovered parts of the world.

At least, this was true of the countries on the Atlantic fringe of Europe—Spain, Portugal, England, and France. The main continental power, the Holy Roman Empire, was destined by geography to lose out on the colonial era and instead became embroiled in the religious strife of the Protestant Reformation more deeply and for longer than the rest of Europe. While colonialism allowed the Atlantic nations to re-invent themselves, the Holy Roman Empire increasingly became an anachronism and ultimately was served a death-blow by Napoleon's armies in 1806.

CLINGING TO TRADE

Another empire that struggled to adapt following the discovery of the New World was Venice. A merchant society, according to Pope Pius II in the 15th century the Venetians were dedicated to "the sordid occupations of trade." It was this devotion to commerce that kept the empire in good health for many years. Venice put nothing in the way of business. For most of its imperial history the city-state was at war with the Ottoman Empire. Yet it depended on Muslim trade and defended its eastern

colonies as fiercely as if they were home territories. Like the Holy Roman Empire, Venice's *raison d'être* diminished as markets moved elsewhere. Nevertheless, it survived as an independent state well into the 19th century.

Wordsworth wrote a sonnet called "On the Extinction of the Venetian Republic":

Once did She hold the gorgeous East in fee;
And was the safeguard of the West: the worth
Of Venice did not fall below her birth.
Venice, the eldest Child of Liberty.

Yet shall some tribute of regret be paid,
When her long life hath reach'd its final day:
Men are we, and must grieve when even the Shade
Of that which once was great is pass'd away.

Holy Roman Empire, 1400
Venetian commercial empire, c.1430
Major Venetian trading routes
Spanish Empire, 1750

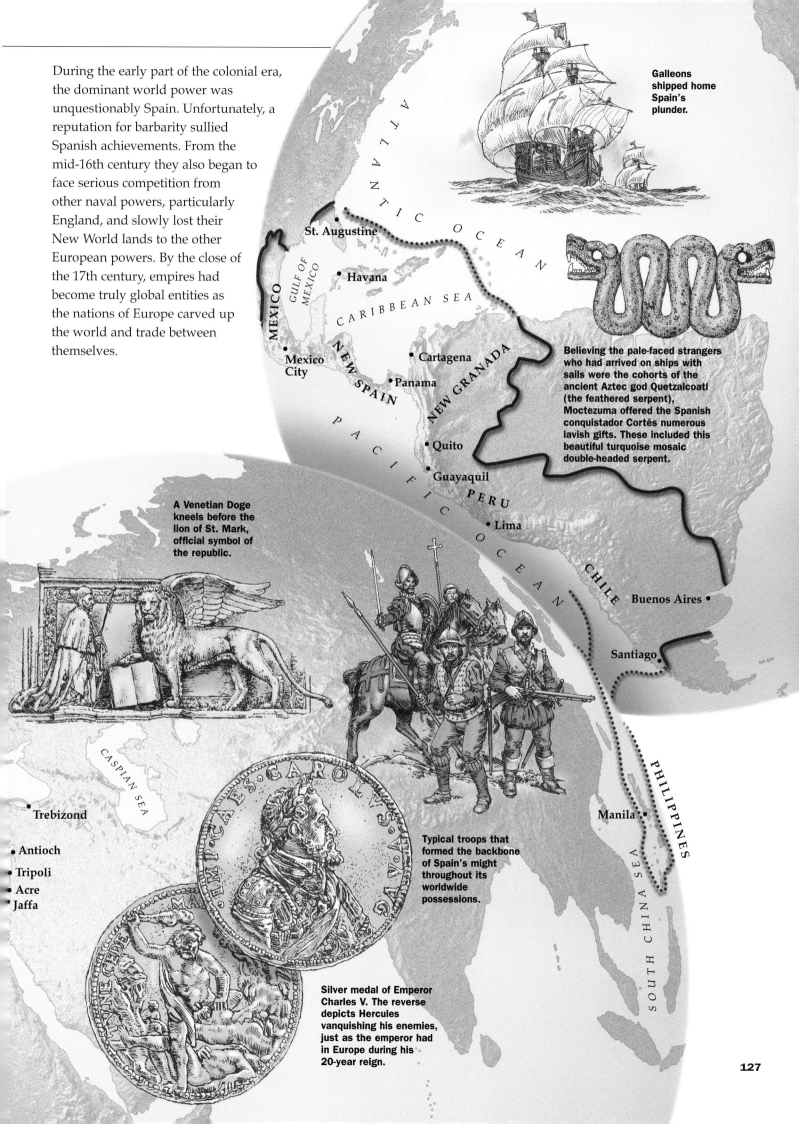

During the early part of the colonial era, the dominant world power was unquestionably Spain. Unfortunately, a reputation for barbarity sullied Spanish achievements. From the mid-16th century they also began to face serious competition from other naval powers, particularly England, and slowly lost their New World lands to the other European powers. By the close of the 17th century, empires had become truly global entities as the nations of Europe carved up the world and trade between themselves.

Galleons shipped home Spain's plunder.

Believing the pale-faced strangers who had arrived on ships with sails were the cohorts of the ancient Aztec god Quetzalcoatl (the feathered serpent), Moctezuma offered the Spanish conquistador Cortés numerous lavish gifts. These included this beautiful turquoise mosaic double-headed serpent.

A Venetian Doge kneels before the lion of St. Mark, official symbol of the republic.

Typical troops that formed the backbone of Spain's might throughout its worldwide possessions.

Silver medal of Emperor Charles V. The reverse depicts Hercules vanquishing his enemies, just as the emperor had in Europe during his 20-year reign.

The Holy Roman Empire

As Europe emerged from the Dark Ages, the expansionist kingdoms of the Franks coalesced into first the Carolingian Empire and then, through political accommodations with the Roman Church, into the most powerful Continental force.

According to Voltaire the Holy Roman Empire was "…neither Holy, nor Roman, nor an Empire." His statement was not without substance, since by Voltaire's time in the 18th century the empire was an anachronism, with no worthwhile religious or political function. Yet this empire lasted a thousand years, from the crowning of Charlemagne in 800 as Roman Emperor until 1806, when Napoleon redrew national boundaries. In between, it survived by adapting to change and evading direct involvement in risky conflicts.

Despite Charlemagne's coronation in AD 800 with the historic title "Roman Emperor," the term "Holy" had not yet been added. The transformation from Carolingian to Holy Roman Empire began

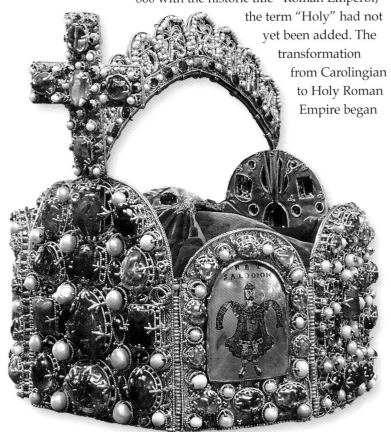

The power and the glory: the imperial crown of the Holy Roman Empire.

when Charlemagne's son, Louis the Pious, died in 840 and his three sons fought over succession. The empire divided into the East and West Frankish kingdoms. For a period, the title of emperor moved between them until West Francia went its own way and became something more recognizably like modern France. The story of the Holy Roman Empire centers on the German East Franks.

As has been shown (*see caption, page 72*), Charlemagne desired that the secular side of the partnership with the Church keep its identity, but the Carolingian dynastic split meant that the monarchs were divided against a single papal authority. Few of Charlemagne's successors possessed sufficient conviction to marginalize the papacy and it became customary for popes to officiate at coronations. In the tenth century a new dynasty seized the East Frankish throne under Otto I (r.936–73). He was crowned emperor in 962, even though the lands he ruled were just a small part of the original, unified Frankish Empire.

CHURCH AND STATE IN CONFLICT

Otto I's son succeeded him, and Otto II (r.973–83) was the first to actually call himself *Holy* Roman Emperor.[†] By this time the empire comprised of German provinces, some of (modern) France and Italy, and all the Netherlands. However, relations between pope and emperor were becoming increasingly antagonistic. When the Hohenstaufen dynasty took control with Henry IV (r.1056–1106), there were long-running disputes between Church and State. Frederick I Barbarossa (red beard), who was emperor for 38 years from 1152, was so frustrated by Pope Alexander III (p.1159–81), whose policies stood in the way of his ambitions, that he established an "antipope" —Victor IV (p.1159–64)—and was duly excommunicated. However, he was

962	c.1000	1190	1228	1247–50	1254–73	1278	1279
Saxon-Salian dynasty takes over Holy Roman Empire from Carolingians with crowning of Otto I	Peak of the Holy Roman Empire	Henry VI becomes Holy Roman emperor after Barbarossa drowns on the journey to Palestine	Frederick II leads Crusaders in the recapture of Jerusalem	Deposed Frederick II is at war with papal allies	The Great Interregnum	Ottakar of Bohemia is killed by Rudolf I at the Battle of Marchfeld	Rudolf surrenders Sicily and the papal states

[†] A disputed matter; some historians suggest that Frederick I Barbarossa was the first to put the word "Holy" before "Roman Emperor."

Division of the Frankish Empire of the Carolingians, 875.

Vikings—or Norsemen—settle, 800–1000, creating the independent state of Normandy.

Hamburg

Utrecht

Magdeburg

EAST FRANCIA (GERMANY)

Rouen

Reims

BRITTANY

Paris

Mainz

Nantes

Orléans

Regensburg

WEST FRANCIA (FRANCE)

Salzburg

CAROLINGIAN EMPIRE

BURGUNDY

St. Gall

Bordeaux

Milan

PROVENCE

Venice

Arles

Toulouse

KINGDOM OF ITALY

Republic of Venice

UMAYYAD EMIRATE

Barcelona

Mediterranean Sea

Rome

Patrimony of St. Peter

The Holy Roman Empire and Habsburg lands, c.1400.

ENGLAND

London

Hamburg

Utrecht

Magdeburg

POLAND

Bruges

HOLY

Rouen

ROMAN

Prague

Reims

Brittany

Paris

Mainz

EMPIRE

FRANCE

Regensburg

Nantes

Orléans

Salzburg

Vienna

St. Gall

HUNGARY

Bordeaux

Lyons

Aquitaine

Milan

NAVARRE

Dauphine

Venice

Toulouse

Arles

Genoa

Republic of Venice

ARAGON

CASTILE

Corsica (Genoa)

PAPAL STATES

BOSNIA

Barcelona

Rome

NAPLES

Mediterranean Sea

Naples

Balearic Islands (Aragon)

Sardinia (Aragon)

▨	Holy Roman Empire
▨	Habsburg lands
▨	Luxembourg lands
▨	Burgundy lands
▨	English territory
—	borders, c.1360

reconciled with Alexander in 1170 and led the Third Crusade against Saladin in 1189. Frederick II (r.1215–50), last emperor of the Hohenstaufen line, competed with Popes Honorious III (p.1216–27) and Gregory IX (p.1227–41) for power in Italy. He was excommunicated no less than three times, but increased the empire's power and prestige by becoming king of Sicily, Germany, and Jerusalem.

The passing of the Hohenstaufens left the empire in a state of flux. Eventually, the Habsburg family stepped into the breach. From Sigismund's death in 1437, with the exception of Charles VII (r.1742–5), the Holy Roman Emperors were all Habsburgs. The title was not hereditary but decided by an imperial Electoral College composed of powerful German princes. For a while the papacy insisted it had the right of veto. However, from 1356 the decree of the Golden Bull established the identity of the electors, including the Archbishop of Mainz, the King of Saxony, and the King of Bohemia. After this time the empire was only a federation of German states with a fragile loyalty to the Habsburg dynasty.

Having taken control of Burgundy through marriage to Beatrice of Burgundy, Frederick I Barbarossa moved on Lombardy in northern Italy. The province, under nominal imperial control, had been left to its own devices for too long. Frederick's ambitions threatened the Papal States, and so began the fight with Popes Adrian IV and Alexandar III. Frederick left behind a strengthened empire after a critical period in German development.

1314	1327	1338	1370	1438	1552	1555	1806
Civil war between new emperor Louis IV and rival Frederick of Austria	Pope John XXII is deposed when Louis IV invades Italy	The Holy Roman Empire votes to become independent of the papacy and forms alliance with England	The Peace of Stralsund gives the Hanseatic League power over Denmark	Albert II is the first of the Habsburg emperors	The French invade Lorraine, causing a war with the Holy Roman Empire	The Peace of Augsburg allows each prince to choose his people's faith	Napoleon abolishes the Holy Roman Empire

Portrait of Martin Luther by Lucas Cranach the Elder. Luther's blast of religious disgust at the excesses of the Roman Church turned into an expression of German nationalism. Luther, who was rude and whose words were often unrepeatable, was shocked when he visited Rome, and after ten years as a Professor of Theology, his protesting developed into a reformation of the faith. The movement affected imperial power as well as the Church, but German nobles quickly began to adapt the reformed faith to their own political ends.

Reformation and Rebellion

When dissent against the Roman Catholic Church spread across Europe in the 15th century, it seemed that the Holy Roman Empire would come to a swift and inevitable end. In 1414 the emperor Sigismund (r.1410–37) summoned Church leaders to a council at Constance in Switzerland with the aim of saving the empire by reinstating strong bonds between the Christian nations of Europe. It was the last time the Roman Church met as a single commonwealth.

The Roman Church, increasingly corrupt and out of touch with commoners, provoked outrage among critics. Condemnation became more vocal. The perceived greed and lascivious behavior of monks and clerics caused friction, but the main reasons for open dissent lay at the very heart of the Catholic faith. John Wycliffe (1320–84) challenged the notion that priests turned bread and wine into the body and blood of Christ. Soon, others also questioned various sacred tenets of the Christian faith.

By the time Martin Luther (1483–1546), a disenchanted German friar, challenged the Catholic faith by nailing his 95 *theses* to the door of a chapel in Wittenberg on October 31, 1517 it was too late to stop the haemorrhage of support. Loyalty to the Holy Roman Empire and the papacy was rapidly diminishing, although devotion to Christian ideals remained strong. When Holy Roman Emperor Charles V (r.1519–56) opened the Diet of Worms in 1521 he said that "the empire from of old had not many masters but one and it is our intention to be that one." He believed that a strong central leadership of Europe was needed and that he could provide it, yet he was fooling himself. The empire was torn with religious strife and internal quarrels and no individual or assembly could halt the slide to open warfare.

WEAKENED BY RELIGIOUS WARS

In 1555 at the Diet of Augsburg Charles V accepted an agreement that permitted each member state to pursue the religion of its choice. He vainly hoped it might reunite Christian nations. Indeed, he continued to foster a dream of one grand union incorporating England, Holland, Spain, and the lands that then comprised the Holy Roman Empire. In fact, the treaty removed papal authority still further from the daily lives of Europeans. Crushed, he abdicated and retired to a monastery. Seventy percent of the empire's population was Protestant by 1570.

Naturally, there was a concerted Roman Catholic attempt to claw back control. Religious diversity, it was believed, could only bring weakness and decline. After 1618 Ferdinand II (r.1612–37), financed by the papacy and by Spanish and German Catholics, made war on the Bohemian Protestants. Success resulted in Catholicism becoming the only faith permitted in Bohemia and Moravia. In 1629 Ferdinand acted against Germany's Protestant princes, reclaiming large tracts of land.

Only aid from Sweden prevented the wholesale abolition of Protestantism in Germany. Now both sides gathered support from elsewhere. France, although largely

Catholic, seized the opportunity to attack its neighbors and sided against the Holy Roman Empire. Europe was in crisis, stricken by acts of terrible barbarity. What came to be known as The Thirty Years War ended with the Peace of Westphalia in 1648, which allowed the survival of both Catholicism and Protestantism. From it emerged more than 300 sovereign German principalities. The Holy Roman Empire was fatally weakened. It kept the title, but from this point on, history more generally refers to it as the Habsburg Empire (*see pages 154–157*).

A further 150 years passed before the death blow came in the form of an expansionist French general. Napoleon Bonaparte cast greedy eyes on the crown of the Holy Roman Emperor (*see pages 160–163*). Believing himself to be a latter-day Charlemagne, he felt the adoption of the title was only fitting. The incumbent, Francis II (r. from 1792), thought differently and promptly resigned from the imperial role on August 6, 1806. The title had been made hereditary just two years previously, so it was impossible for Napoleon to assume it even though he had married Francis's daughter. As Napoleon's armies marched east and the map of Europe was redrawn, the Holy Roman Empire was assigned to history.

In Fortune's Eye—Venice

A geographical advantage gave the Adriatic city of Venice a unique opportunity to forge a long-lasting empire built on maritime commerce, and managed by a practical oligarchy.

A fragment of a carved relief from Aigues-Mortes, France, shows a typical Venetian oared galley of c.1240. It is in this kind of vessel that French crusaders should have crossed the Mediterranean to Egypt in the Fourth Crusade. Instead, the Venetians had made arrangements to ship them to the Bosphorus in an operation that ended with the sack of Constantinople.

By the end of the 12th century the maritime fleet of Venice was master of the Mediterranean and enjoyed a monopoly on east-west trade. Venetians proved themselves smart businessmen and they made full use of their enviable geographical position. In the centuries before the discovery of sea routes to the orient, Venice enjoyed a virtually unchallenged monopoly in the region.

Venice became a republic under an elected doge—or chief magistrate—in 697. In its early years, the Venetian Republic had to cope with attacks from both Saracens and Hungarians. However, the signing of a commercial treaty with the Muslim Saracens in 991 laid the foundations for centuries of prosperity. The town at this time was a center for the increasing trade with Asia, standing as it did at the western end of the

Silk Road (*see map, page 50*). But Venice brokered deals on two religious fronts. In 1082, Venetians were granted the right of unrestricted trade throughout the Christian Byzantine Empire in reward for aiding the Byzantines against Norman invaders. Venetians established a highly successful base in Constantinople.

With the advent of the Crusades in 1095, Venice's fortunes boomed. Almost all the nobles and their assorted armies passed through Venice in order to muster supplies. However relations were soured by the arrogance and aggression of the Venetian traders themselves, who assumed they would always retain their monopoly in Byzantine markets. Soon the Byzantine authorities invited rivals Genoa and Pisa to bid for trade in an effort to drive down prices through competition. Venice was further humiliated in 1171, when the emperor arrested all Venetian residents in his territories and confiscated their goods. When the Fourth Crusade got underway in

1203	1253–99	1310	1354	1380	1405	1427	1440
Venice directs the Fourth Crusade to the sacking of Constantinople	War between Venice and Genoa over trading rights	Council of Ten is established	Venetian fleet defeated by that of rival city-state Genoa	Venetian fleet destroys Genoese fleet; recaptures Chioggia	Venice conquers Padua	Venice conquers Bergamo	Milan defeated by Venice-Florence alliance

1202, Venice saw an opportunity to punish Byzantium by providing galleys for the operation on credit. Crusaders were legally bound to repay their debts with the plunder they gained in Egypt, the target of the expedition. However, unknown to the other countries contributing men and money to the operation, Venice had recently signed a trading treaty with Egypt and had no wish to see it destroyed. Instead, Constantinople was its target.

DUPLICITOUS TACTICS PAY OFF

The aging doge, Enrico Dandolo, suggested a visit to Constantinople and engineered delays to keep the hosts of knights there for months. Men from northern Europe were amazed at the wealth of the city, which had no equal in the west. With every delay the debts owed to Venice mounted. Finally frustrations erupted into a three-day sacking of Constantinople, the center of eastern Christianity and ironically the very city the Crusaders were supposed to protect. Pope Innocent III was outraged:

"It was not against the Infidel but against Christians that you drew your swords. It was not Jerusalem that you captured but Constantinople. It was not heavenly riches upon which your minds were set but earthly ones. Nothing has been sacred to you. You have violated married women, widows, even nuns. You have despoiled the very sanctuaries of God's Church, stolen the sacred objects of altars, pillaged innumerable images and relics of saints."

Despite Innocent's chastisement of the "unholy warriors," Venice rejoiced in its act of revenge.

Most of the loot from Constantinople went back to Venice, much of it to grace the treasury of St. Mark's Cathedral. Venice also emerged with a trading empire in the eastern Mediterranean, including the island of Crete. Venetians carved out for themselves a colony in Constantinople for the purposes of trade and, flushed by their success, the doges adopted the pretentious title of "Lord of One-Quarter and One-Eighth of the Entire Byzantine Empire." Venetians remained the prime traders in Constantinople until 1261 when they were evicted once more by the Byzantines, with the help of the Genoese.

Once the center of Venetian power and government, the Palazzo Ducale (Doge's Palace) stands on St. Mark's Square in Venice. It was built in AD 814, but suffered damage in four fires over the years. Each time, the palace was rebuilt on a larger scale and with greater magnificence. Suited to its position at the crossroads of eastern and western trade, the architecture displays many oriental features alongside European and early Renaissance styles.

1454	1479	1509	1539	1571	1656	1684	1848
Peace agreed between Venice, Milan, and Florence with the Lodi treaty	Venetians cede territory and make peace with the Ottoman Turks	An alliance led by the French takes Venice's territories in northern Italy	Venice cedes territory to make peace with Turkey	Venetians and Spaniards defeat Ottoman Turks in the Mediterranean	Venetians defeat Ottoman Turk fleet at the Dardanelles	The Holy Alliance of Venice, Poland, and Austria unite against the Turks	Venice becomes a republic; Austrians later besiege the city

HOLY
ROMAN
EMPIRE

Mercantile Republics of the Mediterranean, 1430.

- Venetian territory
- Genoese territory
- Ottoman Empire
- Venetian routes
- Genoese routes
- • Venetian trade centers
- • Genoese trade centers

Milan
Venice •
• **Genoa**
• Marseilles

HUNGARY

Corsica

PAPAL
STATES
• Rome

Adriatic Sea
• Split

WALLACHIA

Moncastro

Kiliya

Varna

Tana •

Sea of Azov

Kerch •
Kaffa •   • Canapa

Black Sea

Sinope •
Amastris •   • Amsun

Constantinople •

Sardinia
(Aragon)

NAPLES
• Naples

Thessalonika •

Aegean Sea

• Phocea

Mediterranean Sea

• Palermo

Sicily
(Aragon)

Tunis •

Syracuse •

Preveza
Lepanto ✕
1571
Argos •

Athens •

Modon •
• Monemvasia

Crete Candia •

TURKISH EMIRATES

Adalia •

Antioch •

Famagusta •
Cyprus   Tripoli •

Beirut •

Decline and End

In 1571, the forces of the Holy League, or the League of Cambrai, defeated an Ottoman fleet at the Battle of Lepanto. Having been effectively annexed to the League's cause, many of the ships in the battle were Venetian galleys. It was a rare victory for the Christians against the might of the Muslim Turks.

When Syria fell into Muslim hands at the end of the 13th century, Venice was forced out of its lucrative Middle East holdings and forced to turn to the Black Sea for access to the Far East and new business. This brought the republic into conflict with its arch-rival Genoa, which had received trading privileges in the Black Sea region. The situation sparked a series of minor wars between the two Mediterranean sea powers. After the Peace of Turin, signed in 1381, Venice was finally ceded the trade routes in the Mediterranean and the East. The Venetian Empire, comprising strategic islands and coastline, was now at its zenith.

In 1291 Venetian merchants contemplated the difficulties created by the perpetual hostilities with the Muslims of the eastern Mediterranean. Correctly, they reasoned that there must be a route to by-pass the threat, although they could not even begin to estimate the task of sailing around Africa. It was agreed to dispatch a captain by the name of Vivaldi to find an alternative route to India. He was never heard from again. In 1315 his son embarked on the same ambitious voyage and also disappeared without trace. As the political climate changed in the Mediterranean and trading once again became relatively safe to conduct, Venice abandoned further attempts at exploration. It would be almost two centuries until the sea route to the Indies was finally found and exploited.

At home, Venetian citizens benefited

from a strong system of government. Starting in 1140 there was an overhaul of the political system, which lasted for 20 years. At the end of this period the previously all-powerful doge had his powers curtailed. Governmental responsibility now lay with a body called the Great Council of 45.

The powerful families of Michiel and Falier jostled for supreme power, but the political reforms produced a remarkable system that diminished the possibility of tyranny. Unlike other Italian states, which fell into the pockets of prominent families, Venice introduced laws that separated the government from the judiciary and prevented any individual from assuming total power. However, the oligarchy was run by the wealthy and the conditions endured by the working classes were predictably grim. Like all European cities of the time, Venice was a hazardous and filthy place in which to live. The streets were simply muddy tracks, and to combat the total absence of a sewage system, pigs were placed between the houses to scavenge the waste. Presumably the fragrance of exotic spices imported from the East helped to mask the stench.

CUT OUT OF TRADE

In 1499 Vasco da Gama returned from India to Portugal with his cargo of peppers, cloves, and cinnamon. A new maritime era had dawned and Venice was suddenly no longer the center of cross-continental trade. Ottoman ships triumphed over the Venetian fleet in the same year. The sudden decline in fortune must have been a great shock to Venetian merchants.

Venice's problems were compounded in 1508 when the empire was confronted by the might of the League of Cambrai, comprising the Holy Roman Empire, the Pope, France, and Spain. After defeat at the Battle of Agnadello, Venice was forced to relinquish some of its valuable overseas possessions, which were split among League members. In 1569 Crete was lost to the Ottoman Turks.

Since Italy remained a patchwork of independent political entities, Venice stayed as a city-state long into the era of nation-states. In the War of the Holy League (1683–99) Venice allied itself with Austria,

Poland, and Russia against the Ottomans. In the treaty of Karlowitz Venice gained several eastern Mediterranean lands, including the Peloponnese and the Albanian and Dalmatian coastlines. But Venice found these territories a burden that yielded few financial returns. The Peloponnese was signed back to the Ottomans in 1718.

In 1797 the Venetian Republic was overrun by Napoleon who awarded the territory to Austria. The union with Austria was not a happy one and after several mishaps, Venice became part of the newly established Italian nation in 1866.

This masterpiece of c.1501 by Venetian artist Giovanni Bellini, is a portrait of the Doge Leonardo Loredon. By this period, the doge was more of a figurehead of the republic, the position's powers having been relegated to a council in earlier centuries. Nevertheless, all the wealth and majesty of a king accrued to the role.

THE LION AND THE SAINT

Saint Mark was adopted as the symbol of Venetian spirit. The saint, who is visually linked to the form of a lion, is believed to have died in Alexandria. Venetian merchants are said to have smuggled his bones out of Egypt in a barrel of salt pork in order to avoid scrutiny by Muslim guards.

Spain in the Americas

Santa Fe 1609

San Francisco

Mississippi

St. Augustine 1565

ATLANTIC OCEAN

San Antonio 1716

Rio Grande

Bahamas

Cuba

Puerto Rico

Havana 1515

Gulf of Mexico

Hispaniola

Jamaica

The fleet of Columbus: the Santa Maria, Pinta, and Niña.

YUCATÁN 1524

Caribbean Sea

Cumana 1520

Vera Cruz 1519

Cartagena 1533

Paramaribo

Orinoco

PACIFIC OCEAN

Tenochtitlan 1546 **Mexico City**

Panama 1519

Amazon

Madeira

Line drawn by the Treaty of Tordesillas, 1494

PORTUGUESE TERRITORY SPANISH TERRITORY

Acapulco

When an Italian-born, Spanish-financed explorer landed in the New World on October 12, 1492, he had no conception of either the extent of the lands or the wealth he was claiming for the Spanish crown.

Quito 1534

Guayaquil 1535

Credited with the discovery of America, Columbus only sighted the mainland on his third voyage, never set foot on it, and died convinced he had found the Orient. Painting by Sebastiano del Piombo.

Christopher Columbus believed he had landed on islands off the coast of Asia. Even after four voyages, during which he discovered Puerto Rico, Jamaica, the Virgin Islands, the Windward Islands, the Bahamas, Cuba, and other Caribbean islands, Columbus remained convinced he had found the other route to China and India's riches. In only decades, the true extent of his discovery became apparent.

Columbus missed out on the ultimate accolade of having two entire continents named after him. The new lands were named for Amerigo Vespucci, a fellow Italian who explored the coast of South America for Spain and Portugal in 1501. Vespucci was long branded one of history's villains for eclipsing Columbus. However, Columbus himself said of

Cuzco 1536

La Paz

The expansion of Spanish territory in the Americas to:

▢ 1650
▢ 1750
▢ frontier lands, 1750

Conquest and exploration:

→ Juan Ponce de León, 1513

→ Hernán Cortés, 1519, 1524–26, 1535–36

→ Francisco Pizarro, 1526–36

→ Alvar Núñez Cabeza de Vaca, 1528–36

→ Francisco Vasquez de Coronado, 1540–42

Buenos Aires 1536

Valparaiso 1541

Santiago 1541

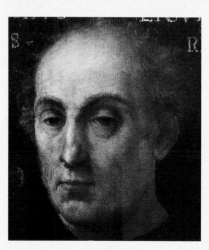

1492	1493	1494	1496	1500	1503	1513
Spanish conquest of Granada, ending Muslim presence in Iberia	Founding of the first Spanish settlement in the Americas, Hispaniola	The Treaty of Tordesillas divides the New World between Spain and Portugal	Santo Domingo, heart of the Spanish Caribbean, is established	Juan de la Cosa publishes the first map of the world	Foundation of Puerto Real, the first permanent Spanish colony in the New World	Vasco Núñez de Balboa is the first European to see the Pacific Ocean

Vespucci: "It has always been his wish to please me; he is a man of good will; fortune has been unkind to him as to others; his labors have not brought him the rewards he in justice should have had."

Within two years of Columbus's discovery, the Treaty of Tordesillas formalized the division of land in the region between Spain and its colonial rival Portugal. The treaty drew an imaginary line down the Atlantic and awarded all lands west of the line to Spain and east of it to Portugal. It was thought at the time that this would leave Portugal with just a few islands, but in fact only a few years later Portuguese explorers discovered that much of the South American continent fell on their side of the line, and the land that is now Brazil was duly claimed by Portugal.

Life for the early colonists was tough, and many succumbed to disease, starvation, or a grisly death at the hands of Indians. Although supplied with agricultural tools brought from Spain, colonists failed to grow enough food in their new environment. They were also stricken with tropical diseases and badly governed by Columbus and those who followed him.

AGE OF THE CONQUISTADORS

Even after the bases of Hispaniola and Panama were firmly established, the Spanish continued to strike out in search of the Orient, certain that it lay nearby. However, dialogue with natives quickly established that there were riches to exploit nearer to hand, particularly gold and silver. Soon, the vast treasures of the Inca and Aztec Empires were seized and hoarded by the Spanish. The most valuable of the silver mines at Zacatecas in Mexico and Potosi in upper Peru (now Bolivia) fell into Spanish hands.

Spain quickly increased its domain and overcame resistance. Although small in numbers, with their cannon and firearms, the invaders speedily brought the native

peoples to their knees. European diseases decimated many more (*see page 108*). During this time the first discussions about the legal and moral implications of conquest took place. A debate was recorded between the Dominican friar Bartolomé de Las Casas, giving the case for

the Indians, and theologian Juan Gines de Sepulveda, supporting the conquistadors. This reveals that intellects of the day were disturbed by questions of religious conversion and the imposition of foreign rule on indigenous people.

In 1542, legislation based on the arguments of Las Casas was passed that was designed to prevent the wholesale enslavement of Indians. While Indians could be forced to work on behalf of the Spanish Empire, the new laws said they had to receive payment and good treatment in return. During the reign of Carlos I (d.1701), all colonization was suspended until it could be decided in law whether the activity was just. Ultimately, of course, it was impractical to police the actions of colonists, and the exploitation and cruelty continued unabated.

1492 was a good year for Spain. Queen Isabella and King Ferdinand of Aragon cleared the last Muslims from Granada and invested in Columbus's exploration for the Orient. The monarchs' investment paid off handsomely, and rapidly as an enormous quantity of Aztec and then Inca gold flooded their treasury. It meant Spain could afford the best quality in newly minted gold coins, like the "4-excelentes" pictured above (and actual size), with Ferdinand and Isabella on the front. Gold and silver transportation from the New to the Old World reached a peak of over 40 tons per annum in the 1550s.

1514	1521	1522	1524	1525	1527	1530	1533
Panama colony is established; Panama City is founded five years later	Conquistadors conquer the Aztec Empire, renaming it New Spain	The Spanish found Mexico City on the ruins of Tenochtitlán	Spanish conquest of the Mayan civilization	Spain captures Francis I and defeats France at Pavia, Italy	King Charles V of the Habsburgs sacks Rome	The annual "treasure fleets" begin taking the riches of the New World to Spain	Francisco Pizarro completes his conquest of the Incas

The Savage Empire

Las Casas was known among the Spanish as the "saintly fanatic." In 1514 he had "a sudden illumination" that left him determined to work for "the justice of these Indian peoples and to condemn the robbery, evil, and injustice committed against them." Although it is widely believed that he was prone to exaggeration regarding Spanish savagery, it is nevertheless true that many of the claims he made about the conquistadors' atrocities were founded on fact.

However, he had taken part in the conquest of Cuba in 1513 and saw at first-hand the atrocities that occurred. It was not only that natives were killed, but the killers' barbarity deeply troubled him despite the fact these Carib Indians were thought to be cannibals. He reported that:

"The Spaniards with their horses, their spears and lances, began to commit murders and strange cruelties. They entered into towns and villages, sparing neither children nor old men, neither women with childe, neither them that lay in, but that they ripped their bellies and cut them in pieces... they laid wages with such as with one thrust of a sword would paunch or bowell a man in the middest or with one blow of a sword would most readily and most deliverly cut off his head or that would best pierce his entrails at one stroke."

Las Casas branded the Spanish soldiers *"men so without all manhood, emptie of all pitie, behaving them as savage beasts, the slaughterers and deadly enemies of mankind."* His journal includes an account of the Spanish training their dogs to attack Indians:

"They taught their hounds—fierce dogs—to tear them in pieces at first view and in the space that one may say a Credo assailed and devoured an Indian as if it had been a swine. These dogs wrought great destructions and slaughters."

That every massacre was justified as the work of God caused particular offense to Las Casas. The religious fanaticism and zeal of the conquistadors, who proceeded in the name of "God and King," was unquestionably intense but their interpretation of the Bible was suspect. Each

Two faces of Spanish conquest: Bartolomé de Las Casas (1474–1566) was the first Roman Catholic cleric to be ordained a priest in the New World. De Las Casas (above) bitterly opposed conquistador brutality and the leadership of men like Hernán Cortés (right).

man also had one eye open for his own fortunes. As one soldier accompanying Hernán Cortés put it: "We want to give light to those in darkness and to get rich." Indeed the plunder was plentiful and matched all expectations.

TWO MIGHTY CULTURES CLASH

Cortés was a man at odds as much with the Spanish authorities as with the Indians. He is remembered for obliterating the Aztec

1538	1545	1565	1568	1569	1571	1581	1591
The Spanish gain control of Colombia	Silver mines in Potosi, Peru, are worked for the Spanish	Spain establishes St. Augustine to stop French Huguenots colonizing Florida	Alvaro de Mendaña de Neyra discovers the Solomon Islands	Former Muslims revolt but are defeated	Spain conquers the Philippines and founds Manila	Philip II of Spain annexes Portugal	Spain integrates the former Inca Empire into the Spanish Empire

conquistadors were driven out. In 1521 the Spanish returned and took Tenochtitlan by force, and the great sack and pillage began.

Religion was central to Aztec existence, and the focus of their worship was the sun god Huitzilopochtli. They made human sacrifices to appease him, the victims usually being defeated enemies. Numbers sacrificed on a single occasion ranged from a few to hundreds. To European eyes, the visceral barbarity of these sacrifices was appalling— many conquistadors would not have encountered the excesses of the Catholic Inquisition's torture chambers back home. It prompted a religious backlash, which well suited the needs of Cortés. As the heathen temples and statues were pulled down, so the gold and silver treasures flowed into bloodied Spanish hands.

The wealth returning to Spain would result in an increased flow of coinage, which in turn would promote massive inflation, religious unrest, and continent-wide political upheaval.

civilization, which was at its greatest when the Spanish arrived. The Aztec capital Tenochtitlan had a population to match that of any major European city, and the surrounding farmland produced sufficient food for surpluses to be stockpiled.

The Aztec emperor Moctezuma II at first believed Cortés to be the returned god Quetzalcóatl (*see pages 94–97*). He welcomed Cortés to Tenochtitlan, but Spanish ambitions were all too clear and the

RIGHT: Illustration of de Las Casas kneeling, from a page of the "Historical Treatise of the Destruction of the Indians," published in Spain in 1522.

1678
Wars between Spain, Germany, France, and the Netherlands ended by the Treaties of Nijmegen

1700
End of the Habsburg dynasty, beginning of the Bourbons

1702
The Grand Alliance— England, Austria, and Holland—declare war on Spain and France; beginning of War of Spanish Succession

1713
War of Spanish Succession ends when Britain and France agree Treaty of Utrecht

1733
Spain enters an alliance with France; War of the Polish Succession against Austria and Russia

1739
Spain and Britain at war over territory in Florida; later part of War of Austrian Succession

1779
Gibraltar under siege. Spain declares war on Britain

1816–21
Argentina, Chile and Mexico become independent of Spain

Wealth and Exploitation

By 1659, Spanish possessions stretched unbroken from San Francisco to the Rio de la Plata in Argentina. In today's terms the empire embraced the western and southern United States, Central America, Venezuela, Peru, and Chile. In the empire's heyday the colonists were pushing back frontiers all the time, staking out new territories, and discovering new tribes. The Spanish Empire remained the largest and most successful until the start of the 17th century. By this time other nations, particularly England, France, and Holland, were rapidly gaining New World territories for themselves.

The lands of New Spain yielded an immense quantity of treasure. In the late

for cruelty in the New World—their European territories were also governed with an iron hand. In Europe the empire extended to the Netherlands, Milan, Naples, Sardinia, and Sicily, and also the Canary Islands in the Atlantic. During the sack of Antwerp in 1576 an estimated 17,000 men, women, and children were killed by a Spanish army that lost just 600 men. English poet George Gascoigne witnessed the carnage:

"They spared neither age nor sex, time nor place, person nor country, profession nor religion, young nor old, strong nor feeble but, without mercy, did tyrannously triumph when there was neither man nor means to resist them." The Spanish wars in the Netherlands were characterized by such brutality.

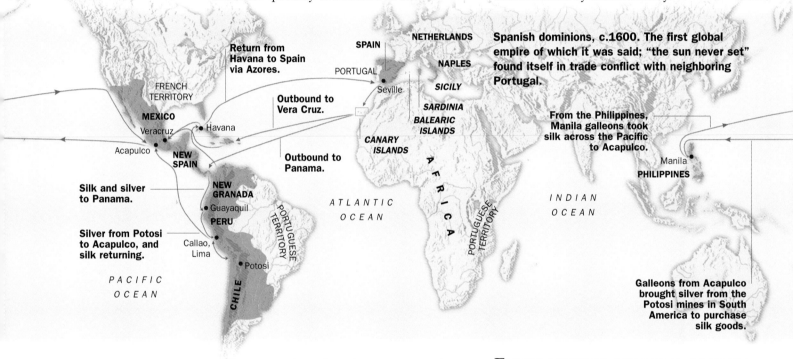

Spanish dominions, c.1600. The first global empire of which it was said; "the sun never set" found itself in trade conflict with neighboring Portugal.

Return from Havana to Spain via Azores.

Outbound to Vera Cruz.

Outbound to Panama.

Silk and silver to Panama.

Silver from Potosi to Acapulco, and silk returning.

From the Philippines, Manila galleons took silk across the Pacific to Acapulco.

Galleons from Acapulco brought silver from the Potosi mines in South America to purchase silk goods.

FACING BELOW: This 16th-century illustration from a copper engraving depicts the mass execution of Dutch freedom fighters by the Spanish at Haarlem. Catholic Spain's militant Counter-Reformation movement hit hardest in its increasingly Protestant Netherlands province. Here, Reformationists were fomenting continual revolt against the invaders. Spanish reprisals were swift and ferocious.

16th century the value of items imported from the Americas was estimated at more than 29 million pesos. Spanish ships were the favorite targets of British buccaneers, the Barbary pirates, and the French. After 1543 Spanish ships traveled in fleets of ten to protect themselves from attack. Despite the obvious wealth, restrictions on trade shackled the Spanish economy. Centuries of sporadic warfare against European rivals also helped to empty Spain's once bulging coffers. The loss of the Armada, comprehensively destroyed by British naval resistance and storms in 1588, cost Spain dearly. As time went on, financing the empire also became increasingly expensive.

The Spanish did not only have a reputation

ELITISM STIFLES COLONIAL SOCIETY

The best jobs in the Americas always went to Spanish immigrants. The Creoles—those born of the colonial Spanish—were restricted to more minor roles. In the long-term, of course, this policy was untenable and ultimately loyalty to Spain in all the colonies waned and independence movements sprang up. Among slaves, the Church encouraged education and marriage, after which the family unit was preserved. The practice of releasing slaves during public celebrations was also encouraged, and slaves were permitted to buy their freedom. Finally, relationships between Europeans and slaves also became accepted. While the opportunities for slaves and working

Flush with the wealth of its New World dominions, Spain was at the peak of European power during the reign of Philip II (r.1556–98). Despite being able to pay for the finest army in Europe, Philip was less lucky in naval matters. His plan to invade and conquer England with the Armada, a massive fleet of ships, fell apart when the outnumbered but unbowed English Royal Navy counter-attacked. Under Philip II's feeble successors, Spain fell into disrepair so rapidly that some imagined the short days of glory had been nothing but an illusion.

Indians were few, the wanton barbarity associated with the treatment of both ethnic groups in North America was largely absent.

When Napoleon swept through Europe the colonies were cut off from Spain, and nationalism openly surfaced throughout the Spanish Empire for the first time. In Brazil the Portuguese permitted and even assisted their colonies' independence. The Spanish, however, resisted and faced violent battles in all the territories. Ultimately, independence for all the Spanish territories came within the space of a decade, with Chile breaking free in 1818, Peru and Mexico in 1821, and Bolivia in 1825.

Jesuits did much to assist Indian tribes by setting up missions in remote areas of the tropical rainforests, but the Jesuits were expelled from Spanish America in 1767 because their true loyalty was deemed to be with Rome rather than Spain. At the time of independence an estimated 7 million people out of a population of 17 million were pure-blooded Indians.

Rivals in the Old World

When the Bolshevik Revolution of 1917 overthrew the Russian Royal family, the event was mourned as the passing of a long-standing European institution. Indeed, the Romanovs had been in power since 1613, but in dynastic terms the Muscovite monarchs were quite recent arrivals. The Habsburgs, a prominent family in Europe since the 11th century, were in power in central Europe from 1452 until 1918, no fewer than 466 years. Habsburgs occupied the thrones of the Holy Roman Empire, Spain, and the Austro-Hungarian Empire during this time.

However, the Osmans were the most enduring of all the dynastic families. They were the hereditary rulers of the Ottoman Empire. From about 1300 until 1923 the family held sway. There can be no doubt that the continuity provided by the long-lasting royal lines helped to keep their empire intact.

WEST VERSUS EAST

Despite the similarities in their structure, there was continual friction and warfare between the empires forged in Europe. The Ottomans were regarded with suspicion and hatred for supporting a different faith, Islam. Although the Habsburgs and the Romanovs were united in Christianity—albeit different branches—they also were rivals, frequently targeting the same regions for expansion.

Europe was traumatized by the Thirty Years War, which began in 1618. The Habsburgs waged war on the Protestants of the Holy Roman Empire. By the time the Peace of Westphalia was agreed in 1648 large areas of central Europe had been laid waste.

In the 19th century nationalism arose in Europe, and this directly affected the old-style empires of Russia, Austria, and the Ottomans. It grew ever more difficult to keep minorities content. The notion of awarding regions their independence was not a popular one. After all, small nations could quickly succumb to other rival empires and as such pose a direct threat. The desire to maintain the existing balance of power in Europe was strong.

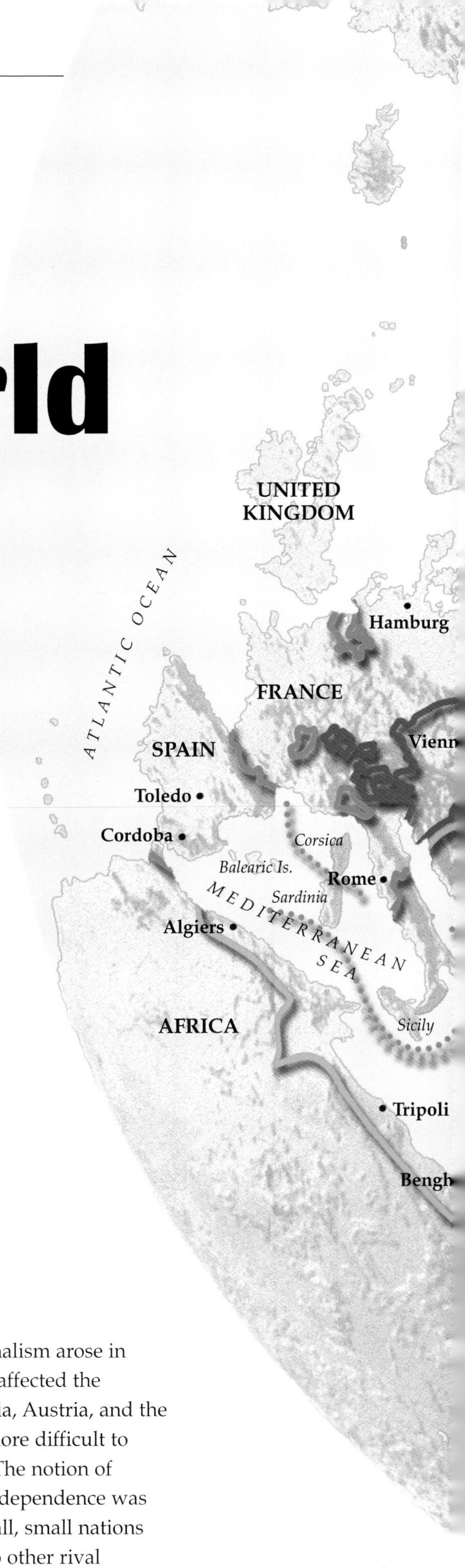

UNITED KINGDOM

Hamburg

ATLANTIC OCEAN

FRANCE

Vienn

SPAIN

Toledo •

Cordoba •

Corsica

Balearic Is.

Rome •

Sardinia

MEDITERRANEAN SEA

Algiers •

AFRICA

Sicily

• Tripoli

Bengh

Vladimir Ilyich Lenin, the founder of Bolshevism, was a major force behind the October Revolution, which in 1917 toppled the last Romanov czar.

NORWAY

SWEDEN

FINLAND

BALTIC SEA

Reval

St. Petersburg

Moscow

Warsaw

Kiev

Buda

Franz Josef, who ruled the Austro-Hungarian Empire from 1848 until his death in 1916, would be its last emperor.

World War I not only brought vast scale and new technology to conflicts, it ended the old order in Europe.

Ottoman Empire, 1520–1720
Habsburg European territories, 1600
   Austrian
   Spanish
Russian Empire, 1815–1917

Varna   Sebastopol

BLACK SEA

CAUCASUS MOUNTAINS

CASPIAN SEA

Constantinople

Anatolia

Rhodes

Crete   Cyprus

Tripoli

Damascus

Jerusalem

Cairo

ARABIA

PERSIA

PERSIAN GULF

RED SEA

This gold *ashrafi* coin struck in the first year of the reign of Suleiman the Magnificent (also spelled Süleyman) reflects the affluence of the period for the Ottoman Empire (1520–66). It was struck at one of more than 20 mints throughout the realm. As with many Turkish coins of the period, it bears no religious inscriptions. The inscription shown reads: "Striker of the glittering money and Lord of might and victory at sea."

The Ottoman Empire

In less than a century, a petty state in northwestern Anatolia amalgamated the Turks, overthrew the Byzantine Empire, and made territorial moves on the Christian countries of Europe.

The Knights of St. John, also known as the Knights Hospitaler, held grimly onto the island of Rhodes. In 1480, Mehmet II dispatched forces to besiege the Hospitalers. The picture depicts Mehmet's grand vizier viewing the Turkish troops. This siege failed, but the Hospitalers were finally evicted in 1522.

Among the eastern European nations, the predominantly Islamic Ottoman Empire's reputation for barbarity was widely believed in—and not without some reason. Selim I, for example, had all his brothers, seven of their sons, and all but one of his own five sons killed to eliminate any rivals. While internal intrigue fueled aggressive expansionism, the growth of the Ottoman Empire also owed much to the weakness of its neighbors. To the east the Mongols were in retreat, to the west, the sacking of Constantinople in 1204 had fatally damaged the Byzantine Empire.

The Ottomans emerged as rulers of a small Turkic Anatolian province, sandwiched between the Seljuk Turks and the Byzantine Empire, under the leadership of Ertoghrul. In 1281, he was succeeded by his son Osman, after whom the dynasty was named. Osman and his successors began the expansion by absorbing immediate neighbors under the banner of a Holy War. Ottoman ideals impressed the *ghazis*, seasoned warriors fighting for Islam, and they swelled the ranks.

After the capture of the Bosphorus town of Bursa in 1326 by Osman's successor Orkhan, the fledgling empire began to modernize its undisciplined and under-equipped army. Through a combination of diplomacy and brute force the Ottomans edged into Europe. Orkhan's son Murad I captured Thrace, Macedonia, central Bulgaria, Serbia, and Adrianople, which was re-named Edirne and made the capital. At first the Ottomans controlled their conquered lands through local rulers. This saved them from having to impose and maintain an unwieldy, costly administration. However, an uprising in the Balkans in 1390 meant that Bayezid I (r.1389–1402) was compelled to institute direct rule.

HOLDING GROUND AGAINST MANY
Expansion attracted attention—Europe in the west and Tatars to the east. Tamerlane (*see page 91*), ruler of the Tatars in Central Asia, sensed a threat and attacked. During the Battle of Ankara (1402) Bayezid was taken and soon died in captivity. Fortunately for the Ottomans, Tamerlane's ambitions in India soon took him away. It gave breathing space to build up the Ottoman army again before European powers counter-attacked.

A seven-year war with Venice began in 1423, then a crusade initiated by the

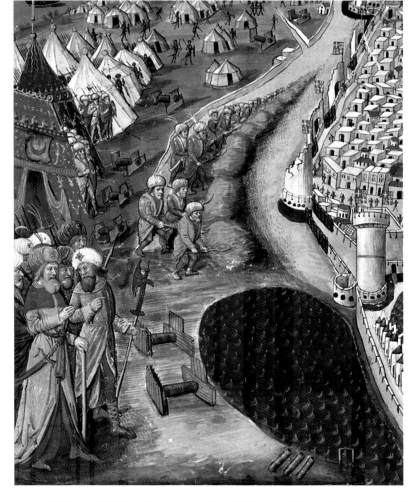

1299	1326	1337	1345	1356	1365	1371	1391–98
Ottoman Empire founded by Osman I	Ottoman Turks, led by Orkhan I, begin to seize Byzantine territory	Byzantine presence in Asia Minor eradicated as Turks take Nicaea	Ottoman Turks enter Europe through the Bosphorus strait	The Ottoman Empire gains control of the Dardanelles	Ottomans make Adrianople, Thrace, their capital	Ottoman Turks conquer Macedonia	Constantinople sieged by Turks, who are paid tribute

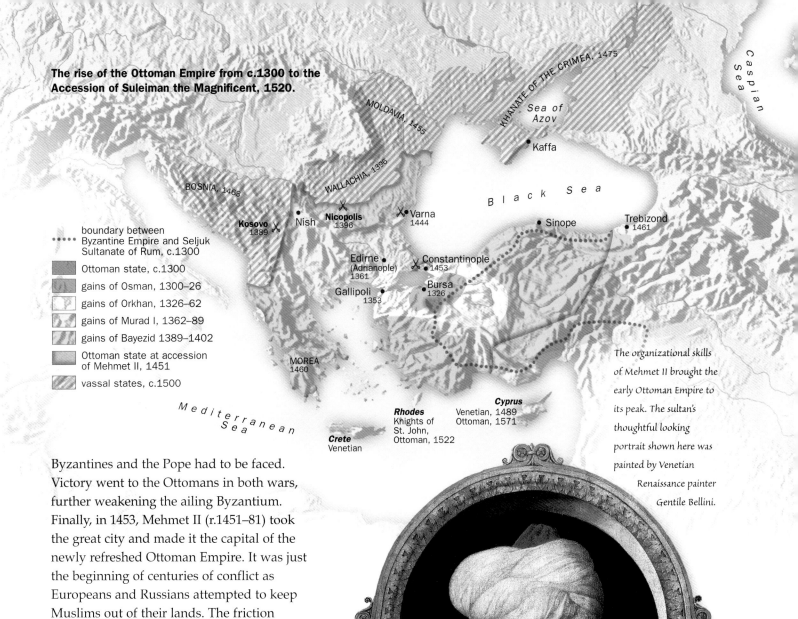

The rise of the Ottoman Empire from c.1300 to the Accession of Suleiman the Magnificent, 1520.

MOLDAVIA, 1455
KHANATE OF THE CRIMEA, 1475
Sea of Azov
Kaffa
BOSNIA, 1468
WALLACHIA, 1396
Black Sea
Kosovo 1389
Nish
Nicopolis 1396
Varna 1444
Sinope
Trebizond 1461

boundary between
Byzantine Empire and Seljuk
Sultanate of Rum, c.1300

Ottoman state, c.1300

gains of Osman, 1300–26

gains of Orkhan, 1326–62

gains of Murad I, 1362–89

gains of Bayezid 1389–1402

Ottoman state at accession
of Mehmet II, 1451

vassal states, c.1500

Edirne (Adrianople) 1361
Constantinople 1453
Gallipoli 1353
Bursa 1326

MOREA 1460

Mediterranean Sea

Rhodes
Knights of St. John,
Ottoman, 1522

Cyprus
Venetian, 1489
Ottoman, 1571

Crete
Venetian

Caspian Sea

The organizational skills of Mehmet II brought the early Ottoman Empire to its peak. The sultan's thoughtful looking portrait shown here was painted by Venetian Renaissance painter Gentile Bellini.

Byzantines and the Pope had to be faced. Victory went to the Ottomans in both wars, further weakening the ailing Byzantium. Finally, in 1453, Mehmet II (r.1451–81) took the great city and made it the capital of the newly refreshed Ottoman Empire. It was just the beginning of centuries of conflict as Europeans and Russians attempted to keep Muslims out of their lands. The friction would last until the demise of the Ottoman Empire after World War I (WWI).

POPULAR CONQUERORS

An advantage the Turks enjoyed in the Balkans, was that their rule was less oppressive than the feudal system they were replacing. Under European feudal government the lower orders were taxed heavily. Therefore, the Ottomans were often seen as liberators, certainly welcome conquerors. Jews also looked toward the Ottomans for protection and, in some measure, they received it. Although the empire—comprised of many different ethnic groups—was predominantly Muslim, other religions were tolerated.

1396	1397	1402	1405–13	1412	1413–21	1430	1453
Ottoman Turks conquer Bulgaria	The Turks invade Greece	Collapse of Ottoman Empire in Asia after Tamerlane defeats them at Ankara	Civil war	Ottomans regain control of Asia Minor under Sultan Mohammed I	Ottoman Empire consolidated under Mehmet I	Ottoman Turks take Thessalonika from Venetians	End of the Byzantine Empire as Constantinople falls to the Turks

Suleiman the Magnificent

When Selim I (r.1512–20), mentioned on the previous page, resorted to infanticide to secure his throne, the sole surviving son was Suleiman. As if marked by destiny, Suleiman (r.1520–66) became the most noted ruler of the empire, receiving the sobriquet of "magnificent"—not from his own people, but rather from his foes in Europe.

At first, it must have been hard to improve on the successful reign of his father. Selim had overwhelmed the Safavids of Persia, who had been blocking eastward expansion. Syria, the Lebanon, and Egypt were also acquired but not colonized, and Medina and Mecca, Islam's holiest cities, were made vassals, although Selim modestly refused to become caliph (religious leader).

Yet with Suleiman at the helm, the Ottoman Empire reached greater heights than before. He more than doubled his territorial inheritance, campaigning successfully in Greece, Hungary, and Transylvania against the Holy Roman Empire. He even put the Austrian capital

*Under Suleiman I, the
Turkish army became the
scourge of Europe—
proudly victorious,
disciplined, and glittering
in battle formation, as this
lively illumination
suggests. The Sultan did
not have everything his
own way, however. While
the janissaries and the
powerful navies reduced
Europe, the religious
differences between Sunni
Turkey and Sh'ia Persia
split the Muslim world.
The Ottomans made allies
of Habsburg-hating
France, but Persia sought
treaties with the Austrian
Habsburgs. The Ottomans
found themselves fighting
a war on two fronts, which
reduced the economy and
power of Suleiman's
successors.*

Vienna under siege in 1529, but the strain on supply lines saved the Habsburgs from humiliation on this occasion.

When action by the Venetian navy prevented Islamic pilgrims from reaching Mecca, Suleiman called on a fearsome piratical Turkish seaman called Khayr ad-Din, who turned the tide of the conflict. It resulted in the Ottomans annexing Algiers in North Africa, further extending the empire's influence. Khayr ad-Din constructed a fleet

for Suleiman that was a match for any in the Mediterranean of the era. Suleiman assisted by building naval bases at Basra to control the Persian Gulf, after taking Iraq, and at Suez on the Mediterranean. The temptation to invade Italy by sea was only postponed when the French reneged on a commitment to aid the Ottomans.

At home Suleiman embarked on a building program that included mosques, schools, baths, and gardens using the astonishing talents of the architect Sinan. Suleiman was renowned for his respect for and protection of civil society and law. He also encouraged the revival of the Muslim tradition for literature and the arts and sciences. In so doing he paid due heed to the cultures of occupied territories, and Ottoman arts were a blend of Persian, Arab, and even Christian influences rather than strictly Turkish.

AN UNCONVENTIONAL ALLIANCE

Suleiman's relations with France were generally good. Ottoman incursions on the eastern borders of Europe kept the Austrians busy, and that kept the French king Francis I (r.1515–47) happy. The Capitulations Treaty (1536) gave French subjects extraordinary freedom of operation within the Ottoman Empire, while other nationals were compelled to seek French protection. At a time when Christians and Muslims were locked in mutual distrust and outright

hatred, this was an extraordinary relationship. Since both powers were in conflict with the Habsburgs and Venetians, the alliance was of mutual benefit.

The Ottoman Empire's strength lay in its army. Among Turkish forces the *devshirme* were prized. These Christian youths drawn from the Balkans were given indoctrination in Islam while being trained as fighters. The influence exerted by the *devshirme* in both the army and domestic politics became legendary after they joined the Sultan's household. The elite infantry known as the Janissaries also enjoyed an awesome reputation.

Suleiman I is remembered as the champion of the Muslim world because he brought the Ottoman Empire to its peak of prestige. The titles lavished on him included Sultan of Sultans in all the lands of Persians and Arabs; The Lawgiver; The Shadow of God over all Nations; Master of the Lands of Caesar and Alexander the Great; even Slave of God, Master of the World.

He was indeed a remarkable man, spiritually rich, culturally gifted, intellectual, innovative, and a strategic genius. His

The Ottoman Empire from Suleiman the Magnificent, 1520, to 1720.

The unsuccessful Turkish siege of Vienna in 1529 marked the end of Ottoman domination of its European territories. The Balkans now became a century-long battlefield between the Habsburgs and Ottomans.

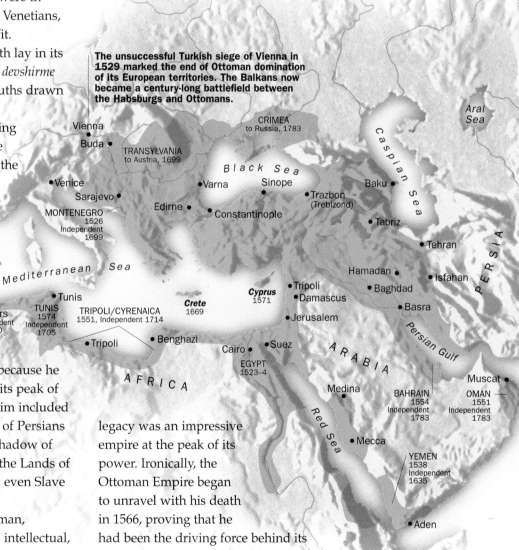

legacy was an impressive empire at the peak of its power. Ironically, the Ottoman Empire began to unravel with his death in 1566, proving that he had been the driving force behind its success.

1479	1509	1533	1538	1571	1593	c.1600	1648
Venetians cede territory and make peace with the Ottomans	A Turkish-Indian fleet at Diu island is defeated by the Portuguese	Ottoman Turks conquer Mesopotamia	Turks conquer the west coast of Arabia	Venetians and Spaniards defeat Turks in the Mediterranean	Ottomans and Austrians are at war in Transylvania	Decline of the Ottoman Empire begins	Sultan Ibrahim I is deposed when slave soldiers revolt in Turkey

Ottoman Decline

The decline of the Ottoman Empire was a long, drawn-out affair. In fact, it could be said to have started immediately after the death of Suleiman the Magnificent. Three hundred years later, Czar Nicholas I of Russia famously said of the Ottoman Empire: "We have on our hands a sick man, a very sick man." Even then, the end did not come until 1922 when the charismatic Kemal Ataturk abolished the sultanate.

Suleiman's descendants failed to match his leadership, and instead of traveling the world, gaining experience and insight, the heirs kept to their palaces. A policy designed to protect them from assassination effectively imprisoned them in their own land and handed the real reins of power to chamberlains. The leadership became insular and so in time did the empire. The Arab empires of earlier had enforced conversion to Islam, which helped cohere their equally far-flung lands, but Ottomans followed the word of Mohammed and showed tolerance to other faiths. The opposite policy would have bound the empire together for longer.

In their position as the middlemen of east-west trade, the Turks benefited financially. When new sea routes opened after the 16th century this role became less lucrative, and Ottoman wealth slumped. At the same time, a brewing conflict with Russia turned into a border war. The Turks flanked the shores of the Black Sea, barring Russian southward expansion and access to the Mediterranean for international maritime trade. Under the leadership of Catherine II the Great (r.1762–96), Russia finally gained the Black Sea and Russian hegemony in the region closed the marketplace. After Peter the Great's reform of the military (*see page 152*) at the end of the 17th century, Russia had become an increasingly organized and effective fighting force. On the other hand, the Ottoman army, even at its zenith under Suleimen, failed to

keep abreast of advances in military technology. In any event, modernization was hindered by the empire's sheer extent. Stretching from Algeria to the Crimea, communications were too extended. Regions furthest from Constantinople were wide open for raids by nearby Christian forces. Uprisings by Christian subjects immediately attracted the support of the European powers, always hungry for territory. Internal divisions, not least the split in the Muslim world between Sunnis and Shi'ites, contributed to the collapse.

A EUROPEAN PAWN

During the first half of the 19th century, the economic crisis deepened until the point that in 1854 the Ottoman Empire borrowed foreign capital. Within 20 years, loan repayments accounted for over half the empire's revenue. The specter of nationalism sprang up in the provinces, and in outlying regions central government control began to crumble. Territories started slipping away, particularly in the Balkans and North Africa.

Not all European powers wished the empire's demise. Since the Ottomans were a

1656	1669	1683	1684	1768–74	1799	1866–87	1923
Venetians defeat the Ottoman fleet at the Dardanelles	Ottomans take Crete from the Venetians	Germany and Poland stop the Turks' attempt to take Vienna	The Holy Alliance of Venice, Poland, and Austria unite against the Turks	Turkey at war with Russia	Napoleon thwarts the Turks' attempts to take Egypt	Cretans revolt against the Turks but are defeated	Ottoman Empire dissolved under the Treaty of Lausanne

strategic counter-weight to expansionist Russia, Britain and France went to their aid during the Crimean War (1854–56). A once-proud empire was now dependent on the patronage of former enemies for its very survival. Within 60 years, the empire found itself in opposition to French and British interests during WWI. The Allies supported rebel Arab interests against The Ottomans, and eventually they were defeated along with the central European powers. The empire was now carved up by the victors. Turkish nationalism accounted for its final death throes. The dynamic Kemal Atatürk declared Turkey a Republic in 1923.

Many traditional foes had reason to celebrate its passing. The Balkan states had been repressed, Christians were ideologically opposed to it, Arab national aspirations had been thwarted by it, and later Turkish nationalists viewed it as an anachronism. All empires have limited lifespans, and the Ottoman time had come to an end. In 1930 Constantinople was renamed Istanbul, the capital of the new nation of Turkey.

CONSTANTINOPLE—WHAT'S IN A NAME?

Although Constantinople became Istanbul in 1930, there is evidence that the modern name had already existed for centuries. To Byzantines, a trip to the sprawling metropolis was simply referred to as going "to the city," or in ancient Greek *eist enpolin* (is-tin-polin). By the mid-15th century, this had become simply "Istanbul," and is the name by which the Turks knew Constantinople.

ROMANIA
RUSSIAN EMPIRE
BULGARIA
Black Sea
Istanbul
Sinope
Ankara
Caspian Sea
RUSSIAN EMPIRE
Mediterranean Sea
Baghdad
Damascus
PERSIA
Cairo
EGYPT
Al'Aqabah
Medina
Red Sea
Mecca
BRITISH TERRITORY 1914
Aden

Ottoman Empire, 1914
Arab influence, 1914
Turkey, 1923

From Muscovy to Behemoth

By the end of the 13th century the Mongols held sway across most of Russia. Muscovy was only a petty state within the Grand Principality of Suzdal-Vladimir. Here, isolated from the outside world, Moscow steadily increased its own power.

A cavalry skirmish as Russians chase Bulgars, from a Slavonian manuscript. These early wars and conquests were fought with armies and a state apparatus that had little in common with those of western Europe. They were not medieval but owed more to Mongol and subsequently to Ottoman Turkish inspiration.

Muscovy absorbed neighboring Russian principalities and by 1478 had taken over the vast Republic of Novgorod. This brought it to the Arctic Ocean and the frontiers of a similarly expanding Swedish empire in the Baltic. Far greater growth was still to come, but before that could happen, Moscovy had to throw off the relics of Mongol-Tatar overlordship, which it did in 1480. Now the tables were turned and it was the Russians who started to seize the weakened remains of what, centuries earlier, had been Genghis Khan's world empire.

The conquest of the Khanate of Kazan in 1552 opened the way to the Ural Mountains and beyond them to the vast expanses of Siberia. Russia's destiny seemed to pull it inevitably eastward, yet its bitterest wars were fought in Europe against Sweden in the northwest, Poland in the west, and the mighty Ottoman Turkish Empire in the southwest. Nor were the Mongol Tatars a spent force. Their days of world conquest were over, but as an ally of the Ottomans, the Khanate of the Crimea, Tatars repeatedly struck back at Muscovy. Crimean Tatars even sacked Moscow itself in 1571.

Periodic chaos within Muscovy also slowed Russian expansion. Nevertheless, Russian merchants still ventured further in search of valuable furs while Cossack adventurers pressed deeper into Siberia. One of the most astonishing of these men was Yermak Timofeyevich, an almost mythical Cossack chief who led his men into western Siberia during the blood-stained reign of Ivan IV the Terrible (r.1533–84). In the process he himself became a hero of folk-song and legend.

DYNASTY DESTINED TO RULE

The chaos that followed the death of Ivan the Terrible put the new empire in jeopardy. Having killed one of his sons in a fit of rage, Ivan left his sickly son Fyodor I to take the reins. During a 14-year tenure, his brother-in-law Boris Godunov acted as the power behind the throne. In the opening years of the 17th century there were a series of assassinations, uprisings, and invasions which endangered the Muscovite throne. However, in 1613 some measure of stability returned with the crowning of Michael Fedorovich Romanov—great nephew by marriage to Ivan the Terrible and founder of the Romanov dynasty, which would last until the Bolshevik revolution of 1917.

The growth of Russia continued apace. Crucially Muscovy added Smolensk and the eastern Ukraine to the empire in 1667, following a war with Poland. The strategic significance of this region was that it

1471–78	1485	1501–7	1534–6	1557–71	1572	1580s	1590–93
Ivan III (the Great) of Moscow conquers Novgorod	Ivan the Great takes Tver; he assumes the title "Czar of all the Russians"	Massive Russian imperial expansion into east and south Asia	Poland at war with Russia.	Prolonged hostilities break out between Russia, Poland, Sweden, and Denmark	Moscow sacked by invading Tatar forces	Russian imperial expansion eastward	Russia wins war with Sweden over access routes to the Baltic Sea and also occupies parts of Finland

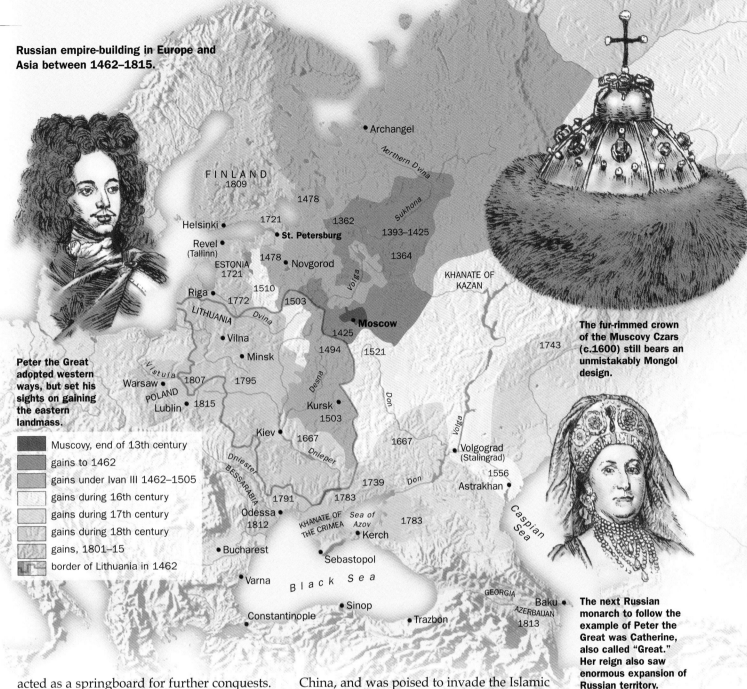

Russian empire-building in Europe and
Asia between 1462–1815.

Peter the Great
adopted western
ways, but set his
sights on gaining
the eastern
landmass.

Muscovy, end of 13th century
gains to 1462
gains under Ivan III 1462–1505
gains during 16th century
gains during 17th century
gains during 18th century
gains, 1801–15
border of Lithuania in 1462

• Archangel

FINLAND
1809
Helsinki •
Revel •
(Tallinn)
ESTONIA
1721
Riga •
LITHUANIA
• Vilna
• Minsk
Warsaw •
POLAND
Lublin •

1721
1478
• St. Petersburg
1478 • Novgorod
1510
1503
Dvina
1807 1795
1815

1362
1393–1425
1364
KHANATE OF
KAZAN
•Moscow
1425
1494 1521
Kursk •
1503
Kiev •
1667
Dnieper
Odessa •
1812
KHANATE OF Sea of
THE CRIMEA Azov
• Kerch
• Bucharest
Sebastopol
• Varna
Black Sea
Constantinople •
• Sinop
Northern Dvina
Sukhona
Volga
Desna
Don
Vistula
Dniester
BESSARABIA
1791 1783
1739 Don
1667
Volga
• Volgograd
(Stalingrad)
1556
Astrakhan •
1783
• Trazbon
1743
GEORGIA Baku •
AZERBAIJAN
1813
Caspian Sea

The fur-rimmed crown
of the Muscovy Czars
(c.1600) still bears an
unmistakably Mongol
design.

The next Russian
monarch to follow the
example of Peter the
Great was Catherine,
also called "Great."
Her reign also saw
enormous expansion of
Russian territory.

acted as a springboard for further conquests.

Then in 1682 a new Czar came to the
throne and almost immediately started what
can only be called a Russian revolution. He
was Peter I, one day to be called Peter the
Great. Not only did his armies break
through to the Baltic Sea in the west and the
Sea of Azov in the south but, more
importantly, his own travels in Western
Europe had convinced Peter that the whole
fabric of Russian government had to be
"westernized."

By the time he died in 1725, Russia had
reached the Pacific Ocean, the frontiers of
China, and was poised to invade the Islamic
heartlands of Central Asia. It was also fast
becoming a unique state in which a
superficially westernized ruling elite could
make use of European technology while
remaining almost Mongol in their reliance on
absolute autocratic power. For over a century
they could also expect the total obedience of
increasingly oppressed serfs and an Orthodox
Church committed to the glory of Mother
Russia. By the mid-18th century Russia was,
in fact, already the vast half-European,
half-Asiatic empire it remains today.

1609–18	1613	1618–48	1632–34	1648–54	1672	1695	1698
Russo-Polish War sees Moscow briefly occupied by the Poles	Poles driven out of Moscow, Romanov dynasty begins	Thirty Years War begins in western Europe	Russo-Polish War; with surrender of 40,000 Russian troops at Smolensk	Cossack-Polish War; uprising of Cossacks in Polish-held Ukraine, over 150,000 Jews lose lives in reprisals.	Czar Peter I (the Great) is born.	Russo-Turkish War launched by Peter the Great.	Peter the Great suppresses rebellion by the ultra-conservative Strelsy

This lampoon pokes fun at the progressive Czar Peter and the traditional Russian Boyar, whose beard is being scissored by the monarch. Peter's need to raise money for expensive projects like building a new capital city, or sponsoring mammoth expeditions to uncover the secrets of Siberia (see box on the facing page), resulted in excessive taxation. His famous "beard tax" was a two-edged shearing—the westernized, cultured Peter wanted nobles at court who looked fashionable, not long-bearded Boyars. Either they filled his coffers, or smartened up the court, either way, Peter won.

Headlong to Disaster

In pursuit of French culture, and English and Dutch trade, Czar Peter moved his capital from Moscow to a new city built with access to the Baltic Sea, St Petersburg. New industry brought state-run metalworks to the Urals, armories, shipyards and a navy— an innovation for a previously landlocked nation. The re-armed military achieved swift victory against the Ottomans in the Crimea. This opened up the Black Sea and so the Mediterranean to Russian trade. The tax burden, however, was great. Peter even levied a tax on beards.

After Peter's death, a series of five short-term rulers were eclipsed by Catherine II the Great (r.1762–96), who shared a similar global vision to Peter. She was an admirer of French culture and welcomed artists and musicians to her court, which quickly became the envy of all European monarchs. The empire expanded into the Caucasus, the Aleutian Islands, into Alaska, and made further inroads in Poland and the Crimea. Catherine also turned on the Ottoman Empire to win Black Sea ports in support of

Russia's growing maritime trade.

Her grandson, Alexander I (r.1801–25), attempted domestic reforms but became wholly taken up with foreign wars. In 1809, he captured Finland from Sweden. The Finns were not displeased, since Alexander allowed them more autonomy than had the Swedes. Much later, when urged to curtail Finnish freedom, Czar Nicholas I said: "Leave the Finns in peace. Theirs is the only province in my great realm that during my whole reign has not caused me even a minute of concern or dissatisfaction."

In 1812, Russia suffered Napoleon's ruinous invasion, although Alexander shared in the spoils of war on the French emperor's defeat: the remainder of Poland was awarded to Russia to add to the gains of Georgia, Bessarabia, and Baku on the Caspian Sea.

END OF THE CZARS

Despite its size Russia had a small population. When Catherine came to the throne she had fewer than 20 million subjects in her realm. With each territorial acquisition, the strain of garrisoning increased. When Russian expansion brought it into conflict with the Western powers supporting Ottoman claims on the Black Sea, Czar Nicholas I (r.1825–55) was unable to muster sufficient forces to resist French and British power. Russia was forced to concede, withdraw from seized Ottoman territory, and accept that the Black Sea would remain a neutral trade zone.

Nicholas's successor, Alexander II (r.1855–81), revised the army, providing manpower through emancipation of the serfs (an act also intended to curb popular unrest). His life was claimed by a bomb thrown by a Polish anarchist in protest at Russian rule. Expansion across the steppes continued throughout the reign of Alexander III (r.1881–94). The khanates lying between the Aral Sea and Lake Balkhash were subdued, which opened better access to east Asian trade. The Trans-Siberian Railway was built to be the main artery.

Back in the west, discontent grew among the oppressed masses suffering under a system where a tiny percentage owned all the wealth. It was fueled among the educated classes by the new doctrine of communism. In the face of radicalism, Nicholas II (r.1894–1917) inevitably clamped down on political freedoms. The increasing repression merely ushered in an age of secret societies, underground revolutionaries, and anarchists. Acquisition and empire did nothing to appease those committed to communist government. In 1904–05, Russia's eastward ambitions met bitter humiliation at the hands of the Japanese, infuriated at Russia getting Port Arthur from them (*see page 180*). Nicholas was forced to give up the port and south Manchuria, news that increased the unrest in European Russia.

The Romanov dynasty rushed toward its own end, when Nicholas disastrously meddled in Balkan affairs, supporting Serbian factions opposed to Austrian imperialism in the region. It sparked the crisis that in 1914 turned into World War I. Unable to counter the forces of Austria and Germany with an army seething with anti-Czarist feeling and fueled by communist sympathies, the empire of the Russian Czars collapsed. Russia withdrew from the war and Nicholas II, his wife and children notoriously met their end at the hands of Bolshevik revolutionaries in 1918.

The Russian Empire was a volcano waiting to erupt. In 1917, Czar Nicholas II and Czarina Alexandra were deposed by the very Bolsheviks they had imprisoned in Siberia, and executed a year later, bringing the largest single-landmass empire in history to its end.

BELOW: The beginning of the end—warships of the Russian fleet sunk at Port Arthur by the Japanese. The humiliation would wait 40 years for revenge.

The empire outlived the Romanovs. Despite their rigid political doctrine, the communists saw the economic advantages of retaining lands already conquered, and a secret service to maintain security in them. Russia in the form of the Union of Socialist Soviet Republics would continue to expand through most of the 20th century.

THE ALASKA LAND SALE

In the late 18th century, Russia crossed the Bering Strait and colonized Alaska. By 1812, forts had been built as far south as Fort Ross in California. When Alexander II needed to raise money in 1867 for the development of Siberia, he sold Alaska to the United States of America for US$7.2 million. It made sense at the time, but doubtless his communist successors during the Cold War period regretted the loss.

Alaska was discovered by Vitus Bering, a Danish mariner in the service of Peter the Great, in 1741. Bering's second Siberian expedition cost him his life.

The Russian Empire, 1815–1917

Bolshevik dissident Stalin imprisoned in labor camp.

Bolshevik dissident Trotsky imprisoned in labor camp.

Bolshevik dissident Lenin imprisoned in labor camp.

Mongolia, under Russian influence 1900–14.

Manchuria, occupied by Russia, 1900–05, then under Japanese authority.

RUSSIAN AMERICA sold to United States, 1867

The Habsburg Empire

In a time-span of over 400 years, Habsburg borders were thrust forward and withdrawn, wars won and lost, there was revolution and retrenchment. Yet few families wielded such authority during the centuries that shaped modern Europe.

The "Habsburg Empire" is a complex affair, more of a family business than an empire in the sense that most others described in this book were empires. In medieval times, the Habsburgs ruled

The Battle of Kahlenberg at the Second Siege of Vienna, detail of a painting by Franz Geffels. In 1619 and again in 1645, Vienna was besieged by forces of the Ottoman Empire, but succeeded in keeping the Turks at bay.

disconnected estates, semi-autonomous within the Carolingian Empire. Later, leading lights of the dynasty had themselves crowned Holy Roman Emperors, though not always contiguously. At one point, Habsburgs also owned everything that comprised the Spanish Empire. Eventually, Habsburg holdings were reduced to what became known as the Austro-Hungarian Empire.

Their name appears to derive from Habsburg castle, which was built by Bishop Werner of Strasbourg on the River Aar in

what is today Switzerland. Literally translated, the name means Hawk's Castle. The Bishop's nephew, also called Werner (d.1096), became the first count of Habsburg. A subsequent Habsburg, Count Rudolf (r.1273–91), became Holy Roman Emperor and acquired additional lands, including Austria, Styria, and Carinthia. Thereafter, Habsburgs consistently provided candidates for the throne of the Holy Roman Empire.

Through various means, including intimidation, diplomacy, and tactical marriages, Habsburg lands swelled until, by the 16th century, it was a fully-fledged empire embracing, among other lands, Bohemia, Hungary, and Croatia. Many different ethnic groups fell within the empire's borders including Magyars, Germans, Czechs, Slovaks, Poles, Romanians, Serbs, and Italians. Their religions were likewise numerous—Greek Orthodox, Protestant, and Muslim—although the Habsburgs themselves remained staunchly Roman Catholic. Present-day Austria was only one small constituent of the empire.

ENEMIES ALL AROUND

As with all dynasties, the Habsburgs faced continual aggression from rival neighbors. To the north, Muscovy's expansionist policies made the Russians sometime-allies, more-frequently bitter foes. To the west, French Bourbon ambitions were in direct conflict. During the 19th century there were problems provoked by Prussia. But the most feared enemy lay to the south—the Ottoman Empire. In a long history, the Muslim Ottomans forged treaties with other European powers, but the Habsburgs never entertained an accord with a people they regarded as infidels.

The architect of the empire is often said to be Holy Roman Emperor Maximilian I (r.1493–1519) whose marriage brought the

10th century	1400s	1452	1477	1516	1519	1526	1576
First records of Habsburg family.	Habsburg territories expand and are united politically by Frederick V (renamed Frederick III).	Frederick III is crowned Holy Roman Emperor.	Maximilian marries Mary of Burgundy, incorporating Burgundy into the Habsburg Empire.	Charles becomes King of Spain.	Charles takes title of Holy Roman Emperor and becomes Charles V.	Austria, Hungary, and Bohemia are united under the Habsburgs.	A rebellion in the Netherlands is put down with great cruelty by Habsburg Spanish soldiers.

Low Countries under his control while the wedding of his son, Philip, drew Spain into the Empire. Thereafter Habsburgs enjoyed dual power, with one line ruling in Spain and the other in Vienna. The Spanish Habsburgs lost Spain (and its huge empire) in 1701, when the death of Charles II sparked the War of Spanish Succession (1701–13), after which the throne went to a member of the French Bourbon family.

The Austrian and Spanish Habsburgs, 1600–48.

See map on page 129 for Habsburg territories, c.1400.

Austrian Habsburg territory, 1620	
Spanish Habsburg territory, 1620	
France, 1620	

The same fate could have befallen the Austrian Habsburgs without the foresight of Charles VI (r.1711–40). He had a daughter but no sons to inherit the crown. In 1713 he decreed that his daughter, Maria Theresa, would succeed him. Her accession was opposed by Frederick I of Prussia (r.1713–40) and he gathered together an impressive coalition to fight Austria. Defeat would have meant the end of the empire.

Maria Theresa consulted all her late father's senior advisors. Blighted by a lack of funds, the advisors—and even her husband—felt it was wisest to seek peace with her enemies. She was, she said later, "without money, without credit, without an army, without experience, and finally without advice." However, she refused to surrender and somehow her resolve paid off. There were a series of diplomatic compromises so that the army could be focussed on Bohemia, which was occupied by French and Bavarian troops. In 1745 she won a defensive victory that proved the worth of the empire and banished its feeble image.

ONE THAT GOT AWAY

Irritatingly for Habsburg self-esteem, one nation retained independence, even at the realm's center. In 1291, the Treaty of Rütli united three tiny Swiss cantons against Habsburg oppression. After the Swiss defeated the Habsburg army at Morgarten (1315), five other Swiss cantons joined the Confederation. By the mid-14th century, the Habsburgs had renounced any claims over the fiercely independent Alpine nation.

1579	1606	1635	1664	1687	1740–92	1806	1918
The Habsburg Netherlands are divided by the Treaty of Utrecht.	The Ottoman and Habsburg Empires conclude a peace treaty.	The armies of the German states of Saxony and Brandenburg under Habsburg control.	The Ottoman advance into Austria is halted.	The Austro-Hungarian Empire begins under Leopold I's Habsburg army.	High point of Habsburg culture under Maria Theresa, Joseph II, and Leopold II.	Francis II abdicates and Holy Roman Empire is dissolved by Napoleon.	After WWI Habsburg empire splits into Austria, Hungary, Czechoslovakia, and Yugoslavia.

María Theresa (1717–80) proved to be the most capable of the Habsburg rulers. She overshadowed her husband Francis I (r.1745–65), who was the elected Emperor, and held the titles of Archduchess of Austria and Queen of Hungary in her own right.

Compromise and Catastrophe

After the war with Prussia, Maria Theresa devoted her energies to pressing domestic matters. She brought in a new, more centralized system of government in a bid to create some cohesion among the scattered peoples she ruled. Her reign was also notable for its contribution to national education, which had previously been in the hands of the Catholic Church. By her death more than 6,000 state schools catering for 200,000 students had been established. She also made the first tentative steps toward dismantling the repressive feudal system that persisted in many regions.

However, she is perhaps best remembered for the cultural richness that accompanied her reign. Noble families attracted by life at the Habsburg court built new palaces in Vienna. It attracted artists aplenty and the capital emerged as an exciting cosmopolitan city. By the second half of the 18th century Vienna had become the center of European music, favored by luminaries like Joseph Haydn and Wolfgang Amadeus Mozart in what many scholars regard as the high point in the history of Western music. The

atmosphere of creativity led to emperors Ferdinand III, Leopold I, and Joseph I becoming composers themselves. Drama too was enjoying a renaissance. Typically, the Baroque theater of the era (which still remain dotted around Vienna, Salzburg, and other Austrian cities) was lavishly decorated and boasted advanced stage machinery.

A mother to 16 children, Maria Theresa died in 1780, enabling her eldest son—who had been co-ruler for 15 years—to take sole authority. Joseph I made his mark with the Edict of Toleration in 1781 which offered Lutherans, Calvinists, Orthodox Christians, and Jews a far greater level of equality. He also attempted to abolish serfdom. However, he was not wholly popular due to somewhat tactless handling of some of the empire's minorities.

The first half of the 19th century was characterized by numerous wars— frequently led by inept commanders—which drained the coffers. It culminated in the revolutions of 1848. Inspired by the actions of the French who had risen against their government, the fervor for revolution spread across the empire, with the most serious incidents occurring in Hungary and Italy.

WEAKENED BY NATIONALISM

Ultimately the Italian provinces were lost and Italy was unified into a nation-state. The Hungarians were finally appeased by the *Ausgleich* (compromise) of 1867 in which the Magyars were given control of Hungary, although they still had to recognize Francis Joseph as king. However, the emperor was

European alliances on the eve of war, 1914.

North Sea

UNITED KINGDOM

Amsterdam

Antwerp •
Brussels •

• Hamburg   • Stettin

            • Berlin

GERMAN EMPIRE

RUSSIAN
EMPIRE

• Cologne

• Frankfurt

• Prague

AUSTRO-HUNGARIAN
EMPIRE

FRANCE

Strasbourg
        Munich •   • Salzberg

SWITZERLAND

Geneva •

• Vienna

• Budapest

annexed
1908

ROMANIA
• Bucharest

independent
1878

• Milan   Venice •

• Genoa

Bosnia
Herzegovina

Sarajevo •

independent
1878

SERBIA

independent
1878

BULGARIA

independent
1908

SPAIN

Adriatic Sea

ITALY

GREECE

Corsica
(French)

• Rome

Sardinia

Sicily

Mediterranean
Sea

FRENCH
ALGERIA

Central powers, 1914

Allied powers, 1914

borders

under no illusions. He knew the deal was merely for political expediency to shore up the Habsburg Empire, at least in the short term. By this time he ruled more than 34 million subjects. He wrote to his daughter: *"I do not conceal from myself that the Slav peoples of the monarchy may look on the new policies with distrust but the government will never be able to satisfy every national group. This is why we must rely on those who are the strongest... that is, the Germans and the Hungarians."*

The compromise was a symptom of the empire's decline. Unlike its major rivals, it did not acquire colonies in the 19th century. So while others were basking in newly exploited wealth and had a population united in pride, the Habsburg Austro-Hungarian Empire lagged behind.

More than one quarter of the population was ethnically German. When Bismarck's neighboring Prussia distinguished itself as the premier German state in Europe, many of those in the Austro-Hungarian Empire cast envious glances north and instinctively veered toward it. It was to be an alliance of vested interests that would prove disastrous for Europe, as a threatened Russia—aware of German desires for Russian territory—and an allied France and Britain began arming for war.

Divisions between ethnic groups in Austria-Hungary became increasingly apparent. When Serbs in occupied Bosnia began agitating for independence, the old enemy Russia supported the Serbs, which in turn inflamed Germany. Archduke Francis Ferdinand, heir to Emperor Francis Joseph, was assassinated in Sarajevo, Bosnia in June 1914. To satisfy honor, the Habsburgs pressed for war. The final outcome of WWI was catastrophic internationally, but the losers were also made to suffer. After the armistice of 1918, the Austro-Hungarian Empire was dismembered and the Habsburg monarchy dissolved.

Sometimes, currency can outlive the dynasty that minted it. Among the most durable of currencies, Maria Theresa thalers have remained in production and circulation ever since her death. Thalers have been struck since the 16th century from Austria's rich silver deposits, but the position of the Habsburgs by the mid-18th century provided so much confidence in the coins, that they were in widespread use outside the empire as well. The dies of the 1780 coin, struck in the year of Maria Theresa's death, were even used in India by the British during WWII. The obverse face shows the double-headed imperial eagle of the Habsburgs.

CHAPTER TEN

Rivals in a New World

The urge for empire became a driving force among the European nations at the end of the 19th century. It was an era when much of the world was still shrouded in mystery. David Livingstone was still charting central Africa when he died in 1873. Equally ill-fated, Percy Harrison Fawcett and his entire party vanished in 1925 while forging a path through the hostile Mato Grosso in South America. The last uncharted regions of the world were finally opening up to intrepid explorers.

The lure of new lands and seemingly unlimited wealth proved irresistible, despite the dangers. The maintenance and extension of empires became a matter of national prestige. Africa was largely virgin territory and its land became prized among Europeans. Even small countries like Belgium made their presence felt in Africa, and it was here that Germany gained its late entry to the colonial era. Europe also looked greedily at Asia, where local imperial power was waning. Britain had long since colonized Australia, opening up the world's most southerly inhabitable continent.

STAMP OF POWER

With the colonists came soldiers, administrators, merchants, and missionaries. There was no part of life left unaffected by colonization. Colonists generally paid scant regard to the consequences of their inevitably high-handed actions. Boundaries were declared with a cursory line on a map. It meant families were split between dominions, or a village belonged to one nation while its water supply was the property of the next. Borders drawn during colonial times are still the source of friction today in many parts of the world.

Grenadier of Napoleon's army.

While the king or queen was the figurehead of the British Empire, business barons were the people who built and managed it. Men like Cecil John Rhodes (1853–1944), who made a fortune in South Africa's Kimberley gold mines and then went on to carve out an almost personal empire, named Rhodesia after him, to the north of the Union of South Africa. God-fearing, upright, fiercely pragmatic, these were the conquering warriors of the new age.

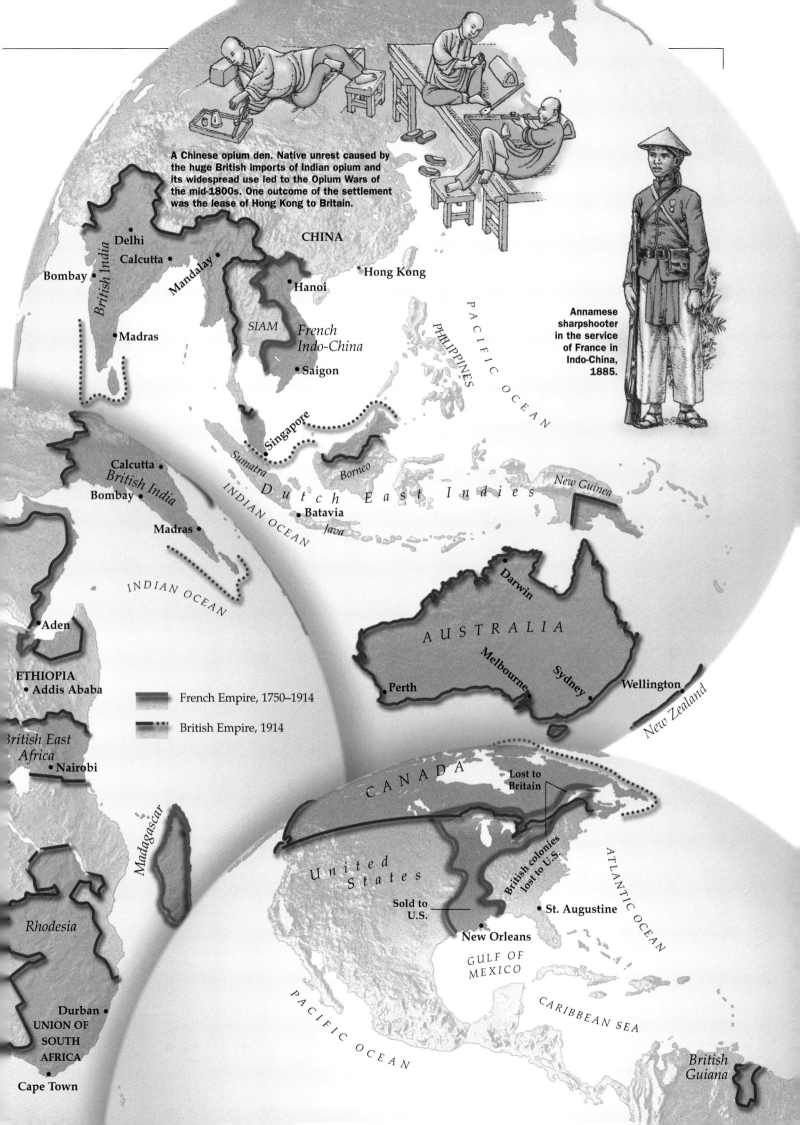

A Chinese opium den. Native unrest caused by the huge British imports of Indian opium and its widespread use led to the Opium Wars of the mid-1800s. One outcome of the settlement was the lease of Hong Kong to Britain.

CHINA

Delhi

Calcutta

Bombay

British India

Mandalay

Hong Kong

Hanoi

SIAM

French Indo-China

Madras

Saigon

PHILIPPINES

PACIFIC OCEAN

Annamese sharpshooter in the service of France in Indo-China, 1885.

Singapore

Sumatra

Borneo

New Guinea

D u t c h   E a s t   I n d i e s

INDIAN OCEAN

Calcutta

British India

Bombay

Madras

Batavia

Java

INDIAN OCEAN

Darwin

Aden

A U S T R A L I A

Melbourne

Sydney

ETHIOPIA

Addis Ababa

Perth

Wellington

French Empire, 1750–1914

British Empire, 1914

New Zealand

British East Africa

Nairobi

Madagascar

C A N A D A

Lost to Britain

Rhodesia

United States

British colonies lost to U.S.

ATLANTIC OCEAN

Sold to U.S.

St. Augustine

New Orleans

GULF OF MEXICO

Durban

UNION OF SOUTH AFRICA

PACIFIC OCEAN

CARIBBEAN SEA

British Guiana

Cape Town

Napoleon—General of Genius

In 18th-century Europe, a popular demand for representative government clashed with reactionary *ancien régime* thinking. The French Revolution of 1789 swept away all vestiges of monarchy and order. In this vacuum, a young, gifted soldier rose to prominence to lead the nation—toward conquest.

Napoleon I, Emperor of the French; detail from the sculpture by Antoine Denis Chaudet, c.1798. The young Bonaparte was not an emperor at the date of this work, but his political ambitions were riding hard on the successes of his Italian and Austrian campaigns.

Napoleon was born to the Bonaparte family in Corsica in 1769, French-speaking but with Italian heritage. At 16, he joined the army as a second lieutenant, and by 1797 had emerged with a reputation built on a series of successful campaigns in Italy and Austria. Rising through the ranks, he became First Consul in a regime that bore all the hallmarks of a new dictatorship.

Deeply nationalistic, he was an imperialist at heart. Yet although conservative and militaristic, he preferred meritocracy to aristocracy, which made him popular. He once declared with typical confidence: "I found the crown of France on the ground and I picked it up with my sword."

By Napoleon's time France already had a mighty overseas empire, with colonies in the Americas and Middle East. Soon Napoleon also commanded the European coastline from Genoa to Antwerp, and rather than strengthen his colonies in the New World he concentrated instead on gaining new territories in Europe and the Middle East. This policy was furthered by his 1803 sale of France's vast North American territories to the United States in what is known by Americans as the Louisiana Purchase.

1798	1799	1800	1801	1802	1803	1804	1805
Napoleon loses the Battle of Aboukir Bay to Nelson	Napoleon seizes power in France and prevents the Turks taking Egypt	He wins the Battle of Marengo; France invades Austria	France is defeated by Britain at Alexandria	Napoleon makes peace with Britain through the Amiens treaty	Napoleon sells Louisiana and New Orleans to the USA to finance his war efforts	Napoleon becomes emperor of France	Battle of Trafalgar

ANGLO-FRENCH RIVALRY

Napoleon posed a serious threat to Britain, his main colonizing and naval rival. He aided the Irish in their struggle against British rule and, in 1798 attacked Britain's India trade route by invading Ottoman Egypt. In turn, Britain worked hard to muster coalitions against Napoleon. Napoleon even plotted the invasion of Britain across the Channel in 1804, but his lack of understanding of, and impatience with naval strategy led to delays and the abandonment of this daring plan. However, Napoleon's poor record at sea was countered by his genius in land battles. Typically, while he lost at sea in 1798 at Aboukir Bay (Battle of the Nile), he was victorious in the Battle of the Pyramids and Mount Tabor in the same year.

In 1802 the Treaty of Amiens brought peace to the delight of the war-weary French. Both sides agreed to return to the other any conquests made since 1793 and there was also trading of African colonies. The peace held for barely a year, during which time Napoleon organized a referendum with the question: "Shall Napoleon Bonaparte be consul for life?" The answer was an overwhelming "yes."

The French Empire came into being on May 28, 1804, and Napoleon crowned himself emperor at Nôtre Dame cathedral, Paris on December 2, 1804, in the presence of Pope Pius VII. The lavish ceremony outraged both the remaining revolutionaries and the ousted aristocracy. Yet Napoleon did not see himself as a career dictator: *"When I put myself at the head of power... all the most powerful peoples of Europe were united against [France]. To resist... the head of state had to have at his disposal all the strength and all the resources of the nation,"*

Soon France was at war again, but the French navy was now in a poor state after its severe buffeting by the British in the last years of the 18th century. Poor morale affected officers and men. The "gang of brothers" that Britain's Horatio Nelson fondly referred to under his command could not be matched on French ships. The French fleet was soundly defeated by Nelson at the Battle of Trafalgar in 1805, scuppering all hope for an invasion of Britain. On land, again it was a different story. Napoleon's army defeated the combined might of Austria and Russia in the Battle of Austerlitz just a few months later.

The Napoleonic Wars
- French victory
- French defeat

Central Europe, 1805–9
- 1 Austerlitz, 1805
- 2 Ulm, 1805
- 3 Jena-Auerstadt, 1806
- 4 Königsberg, 1807
- 5 Friedland, 1807
- 6 Ratisbon, 1809
- 7 Ebersburg, 1809
- 8 Wagram, 1809
- 9 Aspern (Vienna), 1809

Peninsula War, 1808–12
- 10 Torres Vedras 1808
- 11 Vitoria #1, 1808
- 12 Madrid, 1808
- 12 Valencia, 1808
- 14 Bailen, 1808
- 15 Ocana, 1809
- 16 Talavera, 1809
- 17 Lisbon, 1809
- 18 La Coruña, 1809
- 19 La Albuera, 1811
- 20 Badajoz, 1812
- 21 Salamanca, 1812
- 22 Vitoria #2, 1812
- 23 Toulouse, 1812

Russian campaign, 1812–13
- 24 Smolensk, 1812
- 25 Borodino, 1812
- 26 Moscow, 1812
- 27 Maloyaroslavets, 1812
- 28 Krasnoi, 1812
- 29 Berezina, 1813
- 30 Bauzern, 1813
- 31 Dresden, 1813
- 32 Leipzig, 1813
- 33 Hanau (Frankfurt), 1813

Final campaign, 1814–15
- 34 Montereau, 1814
- 35 Montmirail, 1814
- 36 Champaubert, 1814
- 37 La Frère Champenoise, 1814
- 38 Paris, 1814
- 39 Thierry, 1814
- 40 Reims, 1814
- 41 Laon, 1814
- 42 Ligny, 1815
- 43 Waterloo, 1815

Europe, 1801–15
- French Empire
- French ally
- dependent state
- → French campaign
- → British campaign

Napoleon's army lived off the land, which created problems in the Peninsula War, where the British were plentifully supplied by sea from home. In the bitterly cold Russian campaign, this same tactic proved fatal for the French.

Mount Tabor 1798
Aboukir Bay (Battle of the Nile) 1798
Alexandria
Battle of the Pyramids 1798

1806	1807	1808	1809	1810	1812	1813	1815
Under Napoleon the Holy Roman Empire becomes the Confederation of the Rhine	Following defeat at Friedland, Russia and Prussia make peace with France	Charles IV abdicates after the French invade Spain; Napoleon's brother, Joseph, is made king	France defeats Britain in Spain and invades Portugal	Napoleon marries Marie Louise, daughter of the Austrian emperor	Invasion of Russia fails due to severe winter	Napoleon is defeated at Leipzig by a coalition	He escapes from exile and overthrows Louis XVIII but is defeated at Waterloo

The Russian Folly

In 1811 Napoleon was riding high. His empire included the Illyrian Provinces, Tuscany, some of the Papal States, Holland, and the German states bordering the North Sea. In addition there were vassal states in the hands of his close relatives, and dependencies including Spain, the Swiss Confederation, the Confederation of the Rhine, and the Grand Duchy of Warsaw.

His buoyancy was not to last. On June 24, 1812, Napoleon marched into Russian territory with an army of over 400,000, and made rapid progress. After triumph in the blood-soaked Battle of Borodino in September, Napoleon headed toward Moscow. On this occasion he was shrewdly outmaneuvered by Russian forces led by Mikhail I Kutuzov, who melted away before him, luring him onward to Moscow. Encouraged by this apparent success, Napoleon was unaware until he walked into the city that the occupants had been evacuated. Czar Alexander I refused to negotiate and the victory suddenly rang hollow. Baron Claude Francois de Menval, who was with Napoleon's forces described what happened next:

"Hardly had the Emperor entered the Kremlin than fire broke out in the Kitaigorod [Chinese suburb], an immense bazaar surrounded by porticoes in which were heaped up, in large shops or in cellars… goods of every kind, such as shawls, furs, Indians, and Chinese tissues. Fruitless efforts were made to extinguish the flames and the burning of the bazaar became the signal for a general conflagration in the city. This conflagration, spreading rapidly, devoured three-quarters of Moscow in three days."

By now Napoleon realized he had been cheated. Worse, the bitter Russian winter was setting in, permitting him little time to withdraw. The retreat is a sorry tale of woeful hardship. With supply lines broken, in the fierce cold the weary French troops were subjected to continuous guerilla-style attacks. Only 25,000 French troops returned; the vast majority died from the cold.

BEGINNING OF THE END

The Russian escapade sent shock waves around the empire. The Peninsula War, waged to support an invasion of Iberia, was so unpopular it was known as "the Spanish ulcer." Anti-Napoleon sentiments soon spread and became manifest as unrest in France and its territories. A united front among France's enemies forced a capitulation and Louis XVIII, brother of the executed Louis XVI, was awarded the French throne.

The Treaty of Fountainebleau drawn up in April 1814 permitted Napoleon possession of the island of Elba and the Duchies of Parma, Placentia, and Guastalla as well as a pension and the right to retain his rank. He became something of a draw for English tourists on the Grand Tour of Europe. One of them, Member of Parliament Hugh Fortescue, recorded:

"His manner put me quite at my ease almost from the first and seemed to invite my questions, which he answered upon all subjects without the slightest hesitation and with a quickness of comprehension and clearness of expression beyond what I ever saw in any other man."

Napoleon's charm offensive lulled the British into a false sense of security. On February 26, 1815, Napoleon escaped from Elba and returned to France to wreak havoc for 100 days until his defeat by Wellington at Waterloo. This time the British took no chances. Napoleon was dispatched to the distant island of St. Helena in the South Atlantic where he lived the life of a recluse.

He died in 1821, apparently of cancer, leaving these last instructions:

"I wish my ashes to rest on the banks of the Seine in the midst of that French people I have loved so much… I die before my time, killed by the English oligarchy and its hired assassins."

Napoleon was dead but a legend was born. His body was returned to Paris for a state funeral in 1840.

The retreat from Russia: few pictures have captured the sense of grim reality of Napoleon's 1814 debacle at the hands of the winter weather as well as Ernest Meissonier's famous painting of 1864. The French Emperor leads his officers along the churned up tracks away from Moscow and toward a bleak destiny.

NAPOLEON'S LEGACY

One of the greatest legal documents in history, the *Code Napoleon*, was produced under Napoleon's auspices. Flawed by today's standards, it was striking for its time. It ensured equality for all, freedom, tolerance, and trial by jury. He also established military academies, a national bank, universities, and an administrative system that endured. While thousands of soldiers died in his name in some misconceived campaigns, Napoleon is also remembered for his foresight and vision. A rift with Rome was healed with the Concordat of 1801. Despite his ultimate military failure, Napoleon's legacy to French culture and society was immense.

The British Empire

Despite initiating its colonial efforts a century after Spain had begun empire-building, over the next 300 years Britain's empire equaled and then surpassed those of the other European powers.

In the decades leading up to World War I the British Empire was unparalleled in extent. At its height it comprised almost a quarter of the globe's territory and exercised control over the lives of no fewer than 400 million people. By this time Britain held influence, to varying degrees, on every continent in the world.

The key to British success in acquiring and maintaining land overseas lay in its strong maritime tradition coupled with relatively efficient organization. Britain's huge navy resulted from centuries of competition with other European powers; chiefly Spain, France, and the Netherlands. By the late 19th century no other nation could match Britain's global influence.

The driving force was trade. As Napoleon had observed, Britain was a nation of shopkeepers and fiercely protected the routes it saw as essential for conducting business. As Halford MacKinder (1861–1947) observed at the turn of the 20th century: "Free trade is the policy of the strong." It was only sense for the British to establish strategic strongholds around the world to safeguard shipping lanes and trading ports. Often, these ports served as stepping stones

When Victoria mounted the British throne in 1837, she was taking command of a powerful empire. It was about to get bigger: not only was she Queen of Britain but in 1876 she was crowned Empress of India as well. Her Diamond Jubilee in 1897 was a moment for her people to celebrate the apogee of British imperial power.

to inland colonization. The foundations of the United States, Canada, Australia, New Zealand, Singapore, and many other nations were laid in this way.

The figurehead of the realm was the British monarch and during the empire's peak days Queen Victoria (r.1837–1901) held the throne. Victoria was crowned at 18 and ruled for more than 60 years. A staunch imperialist, her much-vaunted affection for those overseas under British rule was tempered with pragmatism: "If we are to retain our position as a first rate power we must, with our Indian Empire and large colonies, be prepared for attacks and wars, somewhere or other, continually," she wrote to one of her prime ministers.

A DISPARATE REALM

Attacks and wars were indeed a constant problem. In 1776 Britain had its first taste of a major colonial uprising when its 13 American colonies united, and after a bloody seven-year war, won full independence. This shocked many in the British government, since it had not been thought possible that a guerilla campaign fought by an upstart colonial army could threaten highly-trained and well-equipped

ALASKA to United States 1867

DOMINION OF CANADA from 1867

UNITED STATES

BRITISH HONDURAS 1859

Bahamas

1607	1620	1656	1661	1664	1707	1713	1756–63
Jamestown is established, England's first permanent American settlement	Protestants from England establish a colony in Massachusetts	War begins when England takes Jamaica from Spain	The English East India Company establishes a base in Bombay	The Dutch lose New Amsterdam to the English, who rename it New York	The Act of Union combines England, Wales, and Scotland into the United Kingdom of Great Britain	The Treaty of Utrecht gives Nova Scotia and Newfoundland to Britain	Seven Years' War: England and Prussia defeat France, Russia, Austria, and Sweden

British forces. Strengthened by military help from France, the American revolutionary forces had shown that a determined and well-organized colonial army could ultimately win a long war of attrition against even the strongest imperial power in the world. For the first time, the British were forced to recognize the fragility of their hegemony.

Nevertheless, the American Revolution did not mark the beginning of the decline of the British Empire. Indeed, the empire was destined to expand and become even more successful over the following century. While the fledgling United States pushed westward, the British Empire continued to gain new colonies around the world and expanded its presence in established colonies. Lessons were learned from the American wars and the British kept a tighter grip on their most troublesome colonies, such as India. Not all colonies were kept in check by military power alone, however. Power was devolved to the larger colonies, such as Australia and Canada, and these new and large nations drew up their own constitutions, with most decisions taken in their own legislatures.

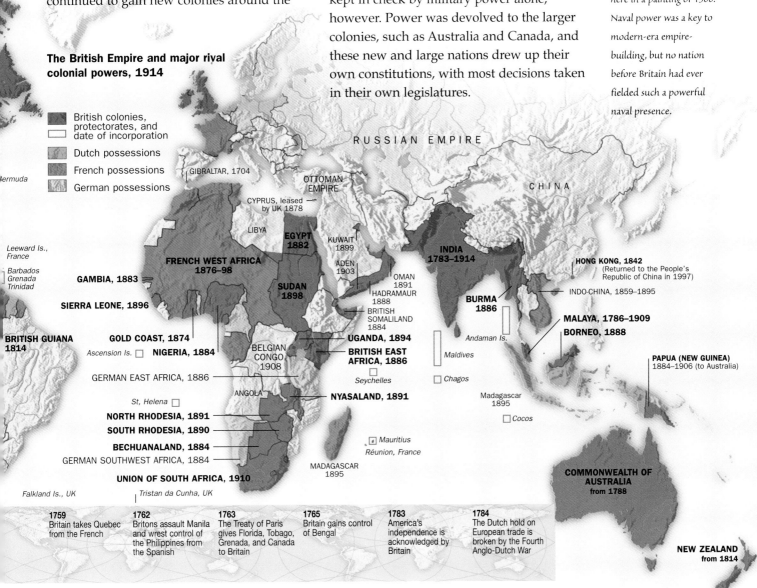

Launched in 1892, the 10,500-ton battleship HMS Centurion *became the British flagship in the Far East Fleet, pictured here in a painting of 1900. Naval power was a key to modern-era empire-building, but no nation before Britain had ever fielded such a powerful naval presence.*

The British Empire and major rival colonial powers, 1914

- British colonies, protectorates, and date of incorporation
- Dutch possessions
- French possessions
- German possessions

RUSSIAN EMPIRE

CHINA

OTTOMAN EMPIRE

GIBRALTAR, 1704

CYPRUS, leased by UK 1878

LIBYA

EGYPT 1882

KUWAIT 1899

ADEN 1903

INDIA 1783–1914

HONG KONG, 1842 (Returned to the People's Republic of China in 1997)

Leeward Is., France

Bermuda

Barbados Grenada Trinidad

GAMBIA, 1883

FRENCH WEST AFRICA 1876–98

SUDAN 1898

OMAN 1891

HADRAMAUR 1888

BRITISH SOMALILAND 1884

BURMA 1886

INDO-CHINA, 1859–1895

SIERRA LEONE, 1896

MALAYA, 1786–1909

BRITISH GUIANA 1814

GOLD COAST, 1874

Ascension Is. ☐ NIGERIA, 1884

BELGIAN CONGO 1908

UGANDA, 1894

BRITISH EAST AFRICA, 1886

Andaman Is.

BORNEO, 1888

Maldives

GERMAN EAST AFRICA, 1886

ANGOLA

St. Helena ☐

NYASALAND, 1891

Seychelles

☐ Chagos

Madagascar 1895

PAPUA (NEW GUINEA) 1884–1906 (to Australia)

NORTH RHODESIA, 1891

SOUTH RHODESIA, 1890

BECHUANALAND, 1884

GERMAN SOUTHWEST AFRICA, 1884

MADAGASCAR 1895

☐ Cocos

Mauritius

Réunion, France

UNION OF SOUTH AFRICA, 1910

Falkland Is., UK

Tristan da Cunha, UK

COMMONWEALTH OF AUSTRALIA from 1788

1759	1762	1763	1765	1783	1784
Britain takes Quebec from the French	Britons assault Manila and wrest control of the Philippines from the Spanish	The Treaty of Paris gives Florida, Tobago, Grenada, and Canada to Britain	Britain gains control of Bengal	America's independence is acknowledged by Britain	The Dutch hold on European trade is broken by the Fourth Anglo-Dutch War

NEW ZEALAND from 1814

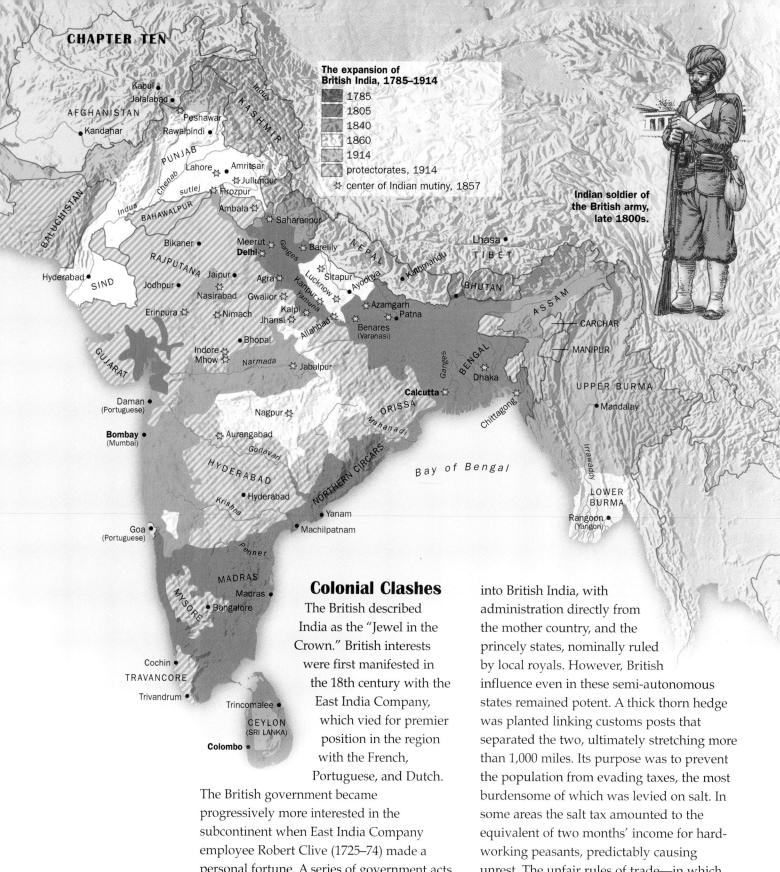

Colonial Clashes

The British described India as the "Jewel in the Crown." British interests were first manifested in the 18th century with the East India Company, which vied for premier position in the region with the French, Portuguese, and Dutch.

The British government became progressively more interested in the subcontinent when East India Company employee Robert Clive (1725–74) made a personal fortune. A series of government acts brought in after 1784 levered power away from the Company until control of India was wrested entirely by the state in 1858.

This vast subcontinent was then divided into British India, with administration directly from the mother country, and the princely states, nominally ruled by local royals. However, British influence even in these semi-autonomous states remained potent. A thick thorn hedge was planted linking customs posts that separated the two, ultimately stretching more than 1,000 miles. Its purpose was to prevent the population from evading taxes, the most burdensome of which was levied on salt. In some areas the salt tax amounted to the equivalent of two months' income for hard-working peasants, predictably causing unrest. The unfair rules of trade—in which British goods were allowed into India duty-free but Indian goods exported to Britain bore a substantial tariff—caused further dissent.

CHAPTER TEN

The expansion of British India, 1785–1914
- 1785
- 1805
- 1840
- 1860
- 1914
- protectorates, 1914
- ☆ center of Indian mutiny, 1857

Indian soldier of the British army, late 1800s.

1788	1796	1802	1806	1808	1812–15	1815	1818
Britain founds Sydney to hold convicts in Australia	Ceylon (Sri Lanka), India, is conquered by the British	The Treaty of Bassein gives Britain control of central India	A British colony is established at the Cape of Good Hope	France fights Britain, Spain, and Portugal in the Peninsula War	War of 1812 between the US and Britain	Napoleon is defeated by Britain and Prussia at Waterloo	The Maratha Hindu warriors finally succumb to English rule in India

No serious attempt was made by the British to bring equality to India. The British themselves filled all the key jobs in their unwieldy bureaucracy. Nevertheless, Britain did leave the legacy of its legal system and institutions in India. Reflecting the attitudes of the time, one observer said: "trained by us to happiness and independence and endowed with our learning and political institutions, India will remain the proudest monument of British benevolence." Indians, however, felt differently. The colonists and Indians stayed in their own communities and integration was not tolerated. English was introduced as the country's official language.

MUTINY AND OPEN REBELLION

During the 19th century rifles were greased using beef or pork fat, and Hindu and Muslim soldiers serving under the British were understandably offended by this. Ultimately it proved to be the final straw in a catalog of discontent. So began the Indian Mutiny of 1857, the most damaging challenge to British rule in India up to that time. Nevertheless, despite winning popular support in some key areas the mutiny failed, partly because of the political and religious rifts between Indians, who it must be remembered had never been united as a single nation before—politically, India was a

British invention.

British interest had also grown in East and West Africa (*see map on page 173*), but it was in the more agreeable climate of South Africa that trouble first brewed. The Boers, Dutch colonists whose ancestors had arrived in the region long before the British, rejected British rule. They rebelled in 1880 and again in 1899. Early attempts to contain the Boers failed. However, after reinforcements arrived, the Boers were finally defeated despite the resourceful and devastating use of guerilla tactics. Novelist HG Wells noted: "Our empire was nearly beaten by a handful of farmers amidst the jeering contempt of the whole world." It was a sign that the empire was beginning to fray at the edges, although few at the time could have recognized this.

Britain's international reputation was sullied by its use of concentration camps that claimed the lives of some 20,000 Boer women and children. Many more black Africans were killed, though their numbers were never recorded. India and South Africa were not the only colonies to rise up against British rule. The quest for independence in Ireland was also a bitter one and attracted the most brutal responses from Britain.

LEFT: The military skill of First Lord Robert Clive (1725–74), or "Clive of India," led to Britain's first acquisition of Indian territory. A local ruler had captured the East India Company's Calcutta base in 1756, imprisoning 145 Englishmen in the so-called "Black Hole." All but 23 died. Clive attacked and defeated the prince at Plassey (1757), and established British control over Bengal.

The British invented the concentration camp in South Africa to house captured and interned Boers. Thousands died.

COLONIAL CARE

While some European colonial powers, such as Portugal, left virtually no legal framework in their colonies, Britain established comprehensive systems of law in all its colonies. Lord Kitchener (1850–1916) wrote a constitution for the Sudan after he took control there in 1899 that endured until Sudan's departure from the empire in 1956. Many former colonies around the world have chosen to retain systems based on British law to the present day.

1825	1839–42	1840	1842	1854–56	1876	1902	1901
England has the world's first passenger railway	In the First Afghan War Britain prevents Russia spreading south	Britain gains sovereignty over New Zealand	At the end of the first Anglo-Chinese War Britain gains Hong Kong and trading rights on a lease	In the Crimean War Britain and France fight Russian expansion	Queen Victoria becomes Empress of India	The British and Afrikaners end the Boer War with the Peace of Vereeniging	Australia becomes a commonwealth; New Zealand later becomes a dominion (1907)

A statue of Thomas Stamford Raffles in heroic pose stands near the Empress Landing, where he arrived in Singapore, having acquired the strategic island for the East India Company in 1819. The memory of Raffles is strong in the thriving modern Singapore, especially at the famous hotel that bears his name, and where visitors to the Long Bar can celebrate old imperialist attitudes by blithely discarding peanut shells on the floor for the local staff to clear away.

Sunset of the Empire

Paternalism and the prestige of holding an empire had largely replaced the profit motive in Britain by the dawn of the 20th century. Indeed, Britain's net profit out of India—which was costly to administrate— was negligible. All the while the expenses of empire continued to mount. As early as 1852 a British politician voiced the feelings of a growing number when he commented: "These colonies are millstones around our neck." The British Empire had been the most successful in recent history, but its day was drawing to a close. World War I would weaken it; World War II would deliver the death blow.

In Victorian times the British population was remarkably loyal to monarch and empire. However, unconditional faith in royalty diminished after Victoria's death in 1901. Correspondingly the population's interest in imperial matters waned. By this time Britain enjoyed prosperous trade links with North America and had facilitated the development of self-government for many of its major colonies, including Australia and Canada, which became dominions of the empire rather than being governed directly from Britain.

At the turn of the 20th century, society remained painfully unequal in Britain, and despite many well-intentioned reforms at home, emigration to the colonies was often literally a passage to a better life for British citizens. Some half a million men and women in Britain were employed in

The British and Dutch East Indies (Netherlands India), 1800–1914. During the Napoleonic wars, with the Netherlands under French control, Britain felt justified in attacking Dutch interests.

Tenasserim

Andaman Sea

Kutaraja

Strait of Malacca

Simeulue

Nias

Padang

Siberut

Sipura

Benkulen

Enggano

INDIAN OCEAN

Sumatra

Malaya

Tembilahan (Indragiri)

Jambi

Bintan

Lingga

Singkep

Bangka

Belitung

Palembang (Srivijaya)

SOUTH CHINA SEA

Sarawak

SARAWAK, 1888

BRUNEI, 1888

BRITISH NORTH BORNEO, 1888

Jesselton (Kota)

Sandakan

Sukadana

Banjarmasin

Borneo

Makassar Strait

Philippines (United States)

Kepulauan Talaud

Celebes Sea

Morotai

Manado

Ternate

Celebes

Kasiruta

Obi

Kepulauan Banggal

Kepulauan Sula

Ceram

Buru

Makassar

Band

1811, British attacked Batavia and took Java from the Dutch. The Dutch regained Java 1814–16.

Bantam

Batavia (Jakarta)

Java Sea

1824, British ceded Benkulen and Sumatra in return for Dutch recognition of British sovereignty over Malacca, Penang, Port Wellesley, and Singapore.

Yogyakarta

1825–30

Java

Surabaya

Denpassar

Bali Sea

Bali

Lombok

Sumbawa

1881–94

Flores Sea

Flores

Sumba

Alore

Timor

Wetar

Dili (Portuguese)

In 1824, Britain received from the Dutch recognition of its control of the Straits Settlements (underlined). In 1896, the Federated Malay States were set up under British governorship. The Unfederated States were acquired from Siam (Thailand) in 1909.

Gulf of Thailand

Andaman Sea

Kedah 1909
Port Wellesley 1800
South China Sea
Perlis 1909
Kota Baharu
Kelantan 1909
Penang 1786
Kuala Terengganu
Ipoh
Perak
Kelantan
Terengganu 1909
Perak 1874
Pahang
Kuantan
Selangor 1874
FEDERATED MALAY STATES
Kuala Lumpur
Pahang 1887
Negri Sembilan 1874
Malacca
Johore 1885
Johor Baharu
Malacca 1795
Singapore (Singapura) 1819
Singapore Strait
Bintan
S U M A T R A

domestic service, earning pitiful wages for hard labor but probably better off than those in the workhouse, the accepted method of poverty relief until the 1920s. The British government paid citizens with skills needed in the colonies—carpenters, teachers, nurses, and many other vocations—to emigrate, especially to Canada and Australia.

The British Empire could well have survived longer, but the two world wars drained its resources—killing many of its most skilled citizens—and gave independence movements the chance they needed to assert themselves. The Atlantic Charter of 1941 signed by President Roosevelt of the United States and Prime Minister Winston Churchill endorsed, among other things, the freedom for people to choose their own government. It was the beginning of a recognition in Britain that the age of empire was over.

A WIND OF CHANGE

Indians inspired by Mahatma Gandhi embarked on a campaign of civil disobedience that piled pressure on for independence in that country. The end of the British Raj finally came on August 15, 1947, just under 200 years after it had begun.

The separation of Ireland from Britain was achieved in 1922, except for six counties who found the formula for the Irish Free State unacceptable and chose to remain under the British umbrella—creating a political conflict in Northern Ireland that continues to this day. South Africa became an independent state in 1961, notoriously choosing to develop a system of apartheid. In 1960 the British Prime Minister Harold Macmillan called the massive movement toward decolonization "the wind of change."

By the 1970s most British colonies had achieved independence. The British Commonwealth, created in 1931, is a loose group of some 50 former-empire nations who have signed up to common principles and policies. This organization—comprising over a quarter of the world's population—continues to carry some political weight and remains on the world stage as the last significant vestige of the British Empire.

Mahatma Gandhi—small of stature, but able to bring the British to heel.

The East India Company had been minting silver rupees since the 1640s. This coin came from the first year of the Calcutta New Mint (1835). The British monarch's head remained on Indian rupee coins until independence in 1947. The word rupee is the English version of the Hindi word "rupya," meaning "silver coin."

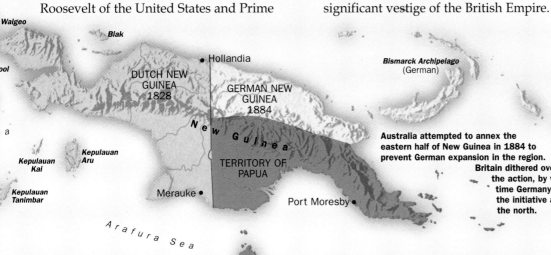

Waigeo
Biak
Hollandia
DUTCH NEW GUINEA 1828
GERMAN NEW GUINEA 1884
Bismarck Archipelago (German)
sool
New Guinea
Kepulauan Aru
Kepulauan Kai
TERRITORY OF PAPUA
Kepulauan Tanimbar
Merauke
Port Moresby

Australia attempted to annex the eastern half of New Guinea in 1884 to prevent German expansion in the region. Britain dithered over the action, by which time Germany had seized the initiative and claimed the north.

Solomon Islands

Arafura Sea

AUSTRALIA

French Colonialism

Compared to the Spanish and Portuguese, France was a slow starter on the colonial land grab. However, imperial aspirations soon led to the acquisition of a powerful empire.

Ho Chi Minh (1890–1969) was President of the Republic of Vietnam (North Vietnam) from 1945 until his death. A founding member of the French Communist Party in 1930 (at the time of this picture), he visited Moscow, was imprisoned in China, and led his people to victory over the Japanese at the end of WWII. After throwing out the French, he became a thorn in the side of U.S. Asian policy in the Vietnam War.

From the 16th to the 18th centuries France was one of the main players of the European colonial age. French explorers made major discoveries in the New World and gave France a huge empire. However, by the end of this period, most gains had been lost or sold off. Eastern Canada, probed by French explorers in the 16th century, had been settled but following the French and Indian War with Britain and the subsequent Treaty of Paris in 1763, Canada became a British dominion.

On the Mexican Gulf, France laid claim in 1682 to Louisiana, named after Louis XIV. In 1803 Napoleon sold the territory to the United States to concentrate on his European ambitions. By the end of Napoleon's rule the ruined French Empire amounted to the Caribbean islands of Martinique and Guadeloupe, two islands off Newfoundland, and trading posts in Senegal, India, and the island of Réunion. French Guiana was later added, and became one of the most dreaded penal colonies in the world.

A decade after the trauma of Napoleon's defeat confidence returned, and in 1830 the French established themselves in North Africa. Dominated by desert and the Atlas Mountains, and once part of the Ottoman Empire, Algeria had become a pirate state. From 1881, the French moved in thoroughly: not only was the north of the country colonized, but it was also incorporated with France under French law.

Defeat in the Franco-Prussian War of 1870–1 further spurred the desire to enhance national pride. Given growing Prussian strength, there was little France could do in Europe, so the acquisition of overseas territories became a priority—colonies would increased the nation's prestige *and* wealth.

INVADING SOUTHEAST ASIA

French missionaries and traders had been involved with Vietnam since the 17th century, but the first imperial expansion began in 1858. Napoleon III used the persecution by native rulers of Catholic missionaries as an excuse for invasion. By 1862, France had overrun the south of Vietnam. The country's population was sparse but the region clearly had potential for plantations. Encouraged by these commercial possibilities France went on to subdue the rest of Vietnam, finally taking Hanoi in 1883. Cambodia had been a protectorate since 1863 and Laos was absorbed by 1893. Local monarchs remained in place in most areas but they were merely political puppets, with French officials installed in administrative strongholds to take the key decisions. The region was christened the Indochinese Union.

1615	1681	1682	1699	1721	1758–83	1809	1830
The Portuguese prevent the French establishing a colony in Maranhao, Brazil	Strasbourg is annexed by the French	Robert La Salle claims the Mississippi region for France	The French establish the Louisiana colony	The French gain Mauritius from the Dutch	France and Britain fight over Senegal	France defeats Britain in Spain and invades Portugal	France begins its conquest of Algeria

Until now settlers had tended to be single men ready to brave the hardships of an unpredictable life. Now entire French families were shipped out and with them came European technology, French culture, education, and Catholic Christianity. These were imposed wholesale on the indigenous communities. The French-built colonial quarter of Hanoi became famous for its gardens, broad boulevards, and luxury living quarters. However, the same considerations were not extended to the native sector of the city where dwellings were rundown, jobs were menial, and wages low.

THE LOST TERRITORY

Not everyone in France was enamored with the idea of colonies. France lost Alsace-Lorraine—a valuable border area—to the Prussians in 1871. The loss was lamented in France and appeared to many to be a greater priority than gaining land overseas. "I have lost two children and you offer me 20 servants," exclaimed the poet Paul Deroulede. Ironically, refugees from Alsace-Lorraine boosted the French population of Algeria. By 1871 there were some 300,000 colonists in the North African country.

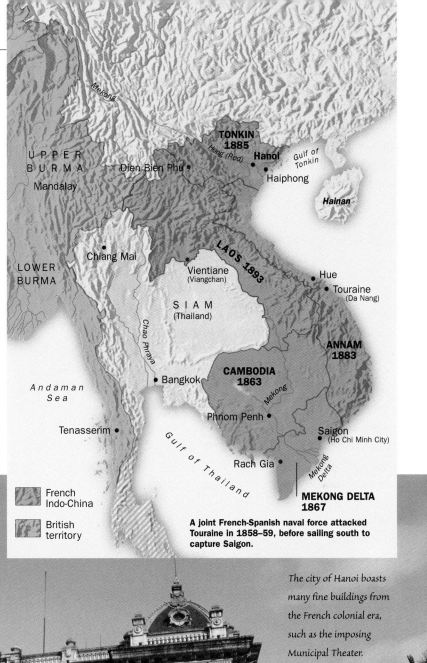

A joint French-Spanish naval force attacked Touraine in 1858–59, before sailing south to capture Saigon.

French Indo-China

British territory

The city of Hanoi boasts many fine buildings from the French colonial era, such as the imposing Municipal Theater.

1862	1870	1883	1887	1893	1894	1904
Southeast Vietnam is annexed by the French	Second French empire ends when Napoleon II surrenders at Sedan	France begins its conquest of Madagascar	Foundation of the French Indo-Chinese Union	France establishes Guinea colony, Africa	The Triple Alliance of Germany, Austria-Hungary, and Italy leads to a counter-alliance between France and Russia	France's African empire is controlled from Dakar

The Struggle for Freedom

In the late 19th century the major European powers rapidly and ruthlessly divided the continent of Africa among themselves in a huge colonial land-grab. France was well-placed to participate in this action. It was the beginning of a golden era of colonialism for France, but it would only last a few decades before independence movements sprang up around the world and put an end to the colonial era for France and the other European powers.

Three areas of Africa—Gabon, French Congo, and Ubangi-shari—became collectively known as French Equatorial Africa. On the western seaboard the Ivory Coast, Dahomey, and Guinea came under French dominion, as did Senegal, Djibouti, and Chad. After a bitter dispute with the inhabitants of Madagascar this island also fell under French control in 1896. In an effort to expand its Algerian territories France took over Tunisia on Algeria's eastern border and Morocco on its west.

Below: The most famous manifestation of French colonial rule is probably the *Légion Étrangère*, or French Foreign Legion, portrayed here in a print of 1906 at Sidi-Bel Abbès, south of Oran.

At the outbreak of World War I, the French Empire boasted some 50 million people living in four million square miles of territories. However, it was plagued by some of the most vicious and protracted struggles for self-determination. Among the first to try for independence were the countries of Indo-China. In World War II, Vietnam was occupied by the Japanese. After their defeat France attempted to return the region to its pre-war colonial status. The French government, however, underestimated the power and determination of English- and French-educated Vietnamese revolutionary Ho Chi Minh. Having led the fight for freedom against the Japanese, he had little intention of swapping oriental colonialism for older French masters.

Full-scale war broke out in 1946 and lasted until 1954, when the Geneva Convention settled the dispute and ended French influence in the region. This agreement split Vietnam along the 17th parallel, creating communist North Vietnam and capitalist South Vietnam. In doing so, the seeds of another long-running conflict were sown, which erupted that same year and lasted until 1976, famously drawing in American firepower and troops.

TO THE BRINK OF CIVIL WAR

Just as the Indo-China war finished, an equally fierce and costly conflict erupted in North Africa, in Algeria, Tunis and Morocco.

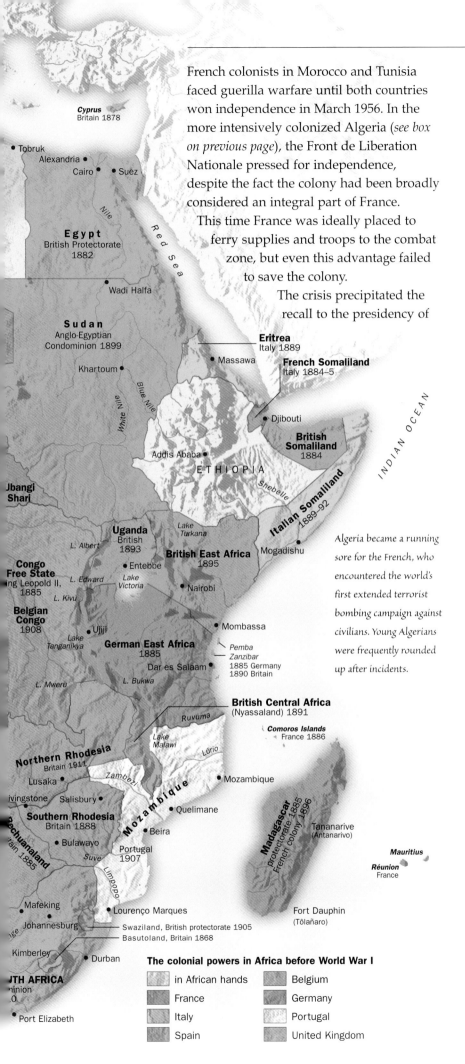

French colonists in Morocco and Tunisia faced guerilla warfare until both countries won independence in March 1956. In the more intensively colonized Algeria (*see box on previous page*), the Front de Liberation Nationale pressed for independence, despite the fact the colony had been broadly considered an integral part of France.

This time France was ideally placed to ferry supplies and troops to the combat zone, but even this advantage failed to save the colony.

The crisis precipitated the recall to the presidency of

Algeria became a running sore for the French, who encountered the world's first extended terrorist bombing campaign against civilians. Young Algerians were frequently rounded up after incidents.

The colonial powers in Africa before World War I

in African hands	Belgium
France	Germany
Italy	Portugal
Spain	United Kingdom

war hero and right-wing politician Charles de Gaulle. In the war years de Gaulle had insisted that colonies might be self-governing but would always remain the property of France. Now the reality of sustaining a long-term dispute in Algeria hit home. He insisted that Algerians had the same rights as the French and was open to ideas on self-determination. The situation was now aggravated by French settlers. Fearing the unhappy outcome of negotiations between the government and Algerian dissidents, they staged a revolt that also included the armed forces stationed there. The mutiny by army leaders—branded "prejudiced, ambitious, and

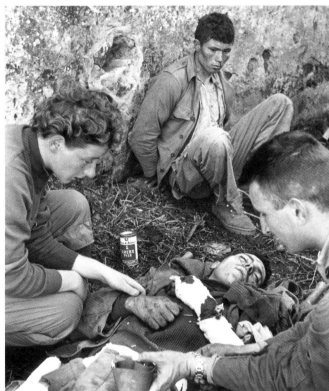

fanatical" by de Gaulle—collapsed, but its long running campaign brought France to the brink of civil war. A referendum held in both Algeria and France established that the overwhelming will of both peoples was for independence, which was finally declared in the summer of 1962.

Other African countries in the empire were content to be self-governing within the French community before achieving overall independence by peaceful means. The last African colonial territory to be granted independence from a European country was Djibouti, previously known as French Somaliland, in 1977.

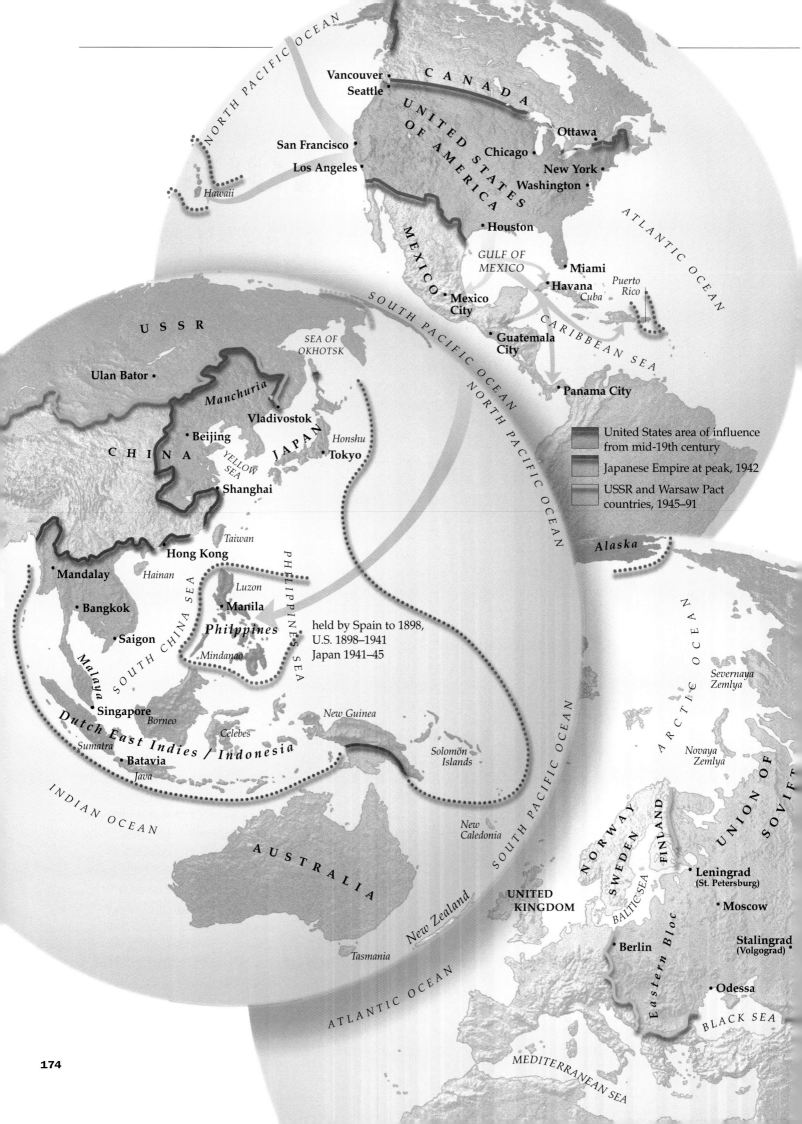

NORTH PACIFIC OCEAN

Hawaii

C A N A D A

Vancouver
Seattle

UNITED STATES OF AMERICA

San Francisco

Los Angeles

Chicago

Ottawa

New York

Washington

M E X I C O

Houston

GULF OF MEXICO

Mexico City

Miami

Havana
Cuba

Puerto Rico

ATLANTIC OCEAN

CARIBBEAN SEA

Guatemala City

SOUTH PACIFIC OCEAN

NORTH PACIFIC OCEAN

Panama City

U S S R

SEA OF OKHOTSK

Ulan Bator

Manchuria

Vladivostok

Beijing

Honshu

C H I N A

YELLOW SEA

J A P A N

Tokyo

Shanghai

Taiwan

Hong Kong

Hainan

PHILIPPINES SEA

Mandalay

Luzon

Manila

Bangkok

Philippines

Saigon

SOUTH CHINA SEA

Mindanao

held by Spain to 1898,
U.S. 1898–1941
Japan 1941–45

Malaya

Singapore

Borneo

Dutch East Indies / Indonesia

Celebes

New Guinea

Sumatra

Batavia

Java

Solomon Islands

INDIAN OCEAN

A U S T R A L I A

New Caledonia

SOUTH PACIFIC OCEAN

New Zealand

UNITED KINGDOM

Tasmania

ATLANTIC OCEAN

Alaska

ARCTIC OCEAN

Severnaya Zemlya

Novaya Zemlya

N O R W A Y

S W E D E N

F I N L A N D

UNION OF SOVIET

BALTIC SEA

Leningrad
(St. Petersburg)

Moscow

Eastern Bloc

Berlin

Stalingrad
(Volgograd)

Odessa

BLACK SEA

MEDITERRANEAN SEA

United States area of influence from mid-19th century

Japanese Empire at peak, 1942

USSR and Warsaw Pact countries, 1945–91

174

The Modern Empires

At the dawn of the 20th century it seemed that the empires Britain, France, and other European nations had built would last for centuries. No one could have foreseen that over the next 50 years two world wars and a host of independence movements around the globe would put an end to the European colonial era. The world was entering a new, dynamic, and dangerous phase, characterized by rapid technological development in sea and land transport, communications, and aviation that would alter the balance of power and create enormous global instability. As traditional imperialism reached its zenith, empires rose and fell—not over centuries or millennia as before, but in a matter of decades.

The experience of the United States with colonialism was unique. From the original 13 states that had declared independence from Britain in 1776, the nation grew rapidly, reaching the west coast of North America by the mid-19th century and going on to colonize Hawaii, Alaska, and the Philippines. By the 1850s, American warships had forced Japan to open its markets to the U.S., and Americans were vying with British and French for access to Asian trade. The country that had founded itself on principles of independence and self-determination had ironically founded an empire of its own.

The opening of Japan soon had profound effects on the global status quo. Within decades Japan transformed itself from a feudal agricultural state into an industrialized nation, becoming the first Asian country to compete directly with Europe and America. In the 1930s, Japan's new-found power threatened world peace. It invaded China and later made a dramatic entry into World War II with its attack on Pearl Harbor. In the Pacific war, the old empires of Britain and France were eclipsed by the new might of Japan. In attacking the U.S., however, Japan sealed its fate. In the wake of Pearl Harbor Japanese Admiral Yamamoto recognized the huge gamble his nation had taken: "I fear we have only awakened a sleeping giant and his reaction will be terrible," he correctly prophesized. The U.S. was the only participant to gain from the Pacific war in that it established the nation as the leading global power; a status it enjoys to this day.

THE SUPERPOWERS

The conclusion of WWII also brought another nation to global prominence, the reborn Russia, the USSR. As eastern Europe fell under Soviet domination, so began the Cold War, and now there were only two major players. The U.S. and the Soviet Union faced each other as "superpowers," dividing the world into antagonistic blocs held together by the threat of the atomic bomb. For decades the world held its breath as the very real threat of nuclear holocaust loomed. The fate of humanity lay in the hands of a small number of individuals in two hostile camps. The age of empire had reached a dramatic conclusion.

Siberia

Manchuria

Ulan Bator •

Mongolia

SOCIALIST

REPUBLICS

Kazakhstan

ARAL
SEA

CASPIAN
SEA

The United States of America

Although the U.S. had fought the British to free the nation from the colonial yoke, and despite the Founding Fathers' guarantees of equality and human rights for all citizens under the American Constitution, for a period, the U.S. itself set about becoming a colonial power.

In 1867 the United States seemed an unlikely candidate for colonial expansion. The bitter civil war, over only two years previously, loomed large and the matter of healing internal divisions appeared far more pressing than acquiring new dominions. Yet the U.S. was a changed nation, with renewed self-confidence and a new doctrine called *Manifest Destiny*—the belief that expansion throughout the North American continent and into the Pacific was both desirable and necessary.

Americans expected to expand to the western seaboard, but Secretary of State Seward's 1867 purchase of Alaska from Russia took many by surprise. Formerly known as Russian America (*see also page 153*), the price was reasonable—$7.2 million in gold. Yet many Americans were scornful about the purchase. Alaska was dubbed "Seward's Icebox." Gold finds in the Yukon region soon appeased critics.

Any hopes that the new territory was a stepping stone toward the ownership of all of North America were in vain. Canada had no intention of being integrated into the U.S. The Dominion was expanding in the same direction, acquiring Manitoba and British Columbia, effectively keeping Alaska as a severed state. However, American imperialists were satisfied that they had "a

Theodore "Teddy" Roosevelt, 26th president of the United States, embodied U.S. imperialism with his motto: "Speak softly and carry a big stick." Roosevelt, who was responsible for building the Panama Canal, came to prominence as a leader of the volunteer Rough Riders in the Philippines during America's "splendid little war" against Spain, which began when the U.S. battleship Maine sank in Havana Harbor (FAR RIGHT) in 1898.

finger pointed at Asia."

At the time of the Alaska purchase, most of the continent was a wilderness. Railroads did not yet connect the east and west coasts—there remained much to be done at home. But to restless minds in government the acquisition of overseas territory was a logical step in protecting American interests. A finger pointing at Asia was not enough.

As stepping stones in the vast Pacific, the strategic significance of the various island groups was not missed by acquisitive French and British eyes. The U.S. lost little time, seizing Midway in 1867, and the Hawaiian Islands in 1895. There had been an American presence in Hawaii since the 1820s, fostering trade and Christianity. When Queen Lilio 'ukalani veered from outright support for the U.S. in 1893, American sugar planter Sanford B. Dole established a government of his own. In January 1895, the queen was imprisoned, and Hawaii effectively became a territory of the U.S., even though President Cleveland disassociated the nation from the warlike actions of a few colonialists. Men similar to Dole also saw the strategic value of small bases like Wake Island and Tutuila (American Samoa), and these were also annexed. But America's most daring colonial adventure was yet to come.

THE SPANISH-AMERICAN WAR

Since its discovery by Columbus in 1492, Cuba had been a Spanish colony. Hostilities between the Cubans and Spanish erupted into the Ten Year's War, during which time the Spanish captured the *U.S. Virginius*, which was bringing aid to the rebels. When eight U.S. citizens were executed in reprisal, Americans were outraged.

When the U.S. battleship *Maine* exploded in Havana Harbor on February 15, 1898, with the loss of 260 lives, furious Americans put the blame squarely on Spain[†]. Spain was anxious

1776	**1777**	**1781**	**1803**	**1818**	**1819**	**1830**	**1846–48**
The Declaration of Independence from Britain is proclaimed	Congress establishes the United States of America	Britain loses its claim to American colonies on surrender at Yorktown	Napoleon sells Louisiana and New Orleans to the U.S. to finance his war efforts	The 49th Parallel marks the border of the U.S. and Canada	Spain cedes Florida to the U.S.A	The Indian Removal Act forces native Americans into the center of the U.S.	Mexico loses territory in a war triggered by U.S.A annexing Texas

† In 1969, U.S. Navy divers confirmed that a defective boiler on the *Maine* exploded and caused the tragedy.

to avoid war but refused to comply with demands to withdraw from Cuba. War was completely avoidable, and politicians on both sides worked hard to prevent hostilities, but a fervent jingoistic newspaper campaign in the U.S. made the outcome inevitable. In April 1898 the U.S. declared war. America,

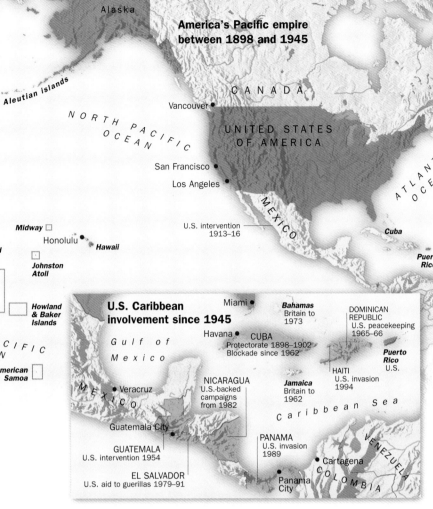

America's Pacific empire between 1898 and 1945

Alaska

CANADA

NORTH PACIFIC OCEAN

UNITED STATES OF AMERICA

Vancouver

San Francisco

Los Angeles

ATLANTIC OCEAN

MEXICO

Aleutian islands

U.S. intervention 1913–16

Cuba

Puerto Rico

Midway

Honolulu • Hawaii

PHILIPPINES to U.S. 1898

Manila

Northern Mariana Islands

Guam

Wake Island

Johnston Atoll

Marshall Islands

Pacific U.S. Islands

SOUTH PACIFIC OCEAN

Howland & Baker Islands

American Samoa

buoyed up by colonial gains since the end of the Civil War, was keen to assert authority over the Old World power of Spain.

The conflict was quickly over. A victory by the small but effective U.S. Navy in the Battle of Manila Bay, Philippines, was both a physical and a psychological blow to the Spanish who were unable to supply reinforcements. Army troops, including Theodore Roosevelt's Rough Riders enjoyed an equal measure of success on land. It was the end of global Spanish power, and as soon as August 1898 America emerged triumphant with remarkably few casualties.

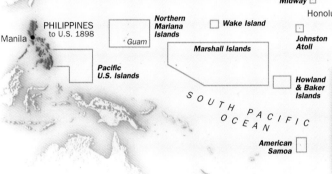

U.S. Caribbean involvement since 1945

Miami

Bahamas Britain to 1973

DOMINICAN REPUBLIC U.S. peacekeeping 1965–66

Gulf of Mexico

Havana • CUBA Protectorate 1898–1902 Blockade since 1962

Puerto Rico U.S.

HAITI U.S. invasion 1994

MEXICO

Veracruz

NICARAGUA U.S.-backed campaigns from 1982

Jamaica Britain to 1962

Caribbean Sea

Guatemala City

PANAMA U.S. invasion 1989

GUATEMALA U.S. intervention 1954

Cartagena

VENEZUELA

EL SALVADOR U.S. aid to guerillas 1979–91

Panama City

COLOMBIA

EMPIRES WITHIN AN EMPIRE—NEWS BARONS

Entrepreneurs like William Randolph Hearst (1863–1951) turned the world of newspapers into financial empires of unprecedented success at the end of the 19th century. The newspaper had long been a powerful political medium in Europe, but in America, Hearst capitalized on the interests of the burgeoning population, rather than the intellects of power brokers as in Europe. Instead of long-winded sentences, Hearst encouraged short, sharp pieces in simple language. Hearst was often accused of cheap sensationalism, or "yellow journalism" (named after the trick of printing huge headlines in bright yellow ink to attract attention), but was not the worst offender in this respect. Yellow journalism is epitomized in the hulabaloo raised over the sinking of the *Maine* in Havana and the subsequent warmongering campaign in many American newspapers.

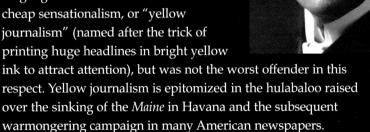

1861–65	1867	1886	1929	1947	1949	1962	1989
American Civil War	The U.S. buys Alaska from Russia for $7.2 million, a fraction of what the Yukon gold mines would soon yield	Native resistance to U.S. government fades after Geronimo surrenders	U.S. and world economic depression is triggered by Wall Street crash	The Truman Doctrine gives U.S. support to free nations threatened by communism	NATO forms after the USSR becomes a nuclear power	Following Cuban Missile Crisis, Cuba is expelled from the pro-peace Organization of American States	The Cold War ends when Mikhail Gorbachev and Ronald Reagan set a nuclear disarmament program

The power of America's role on the world stage was in no doubt after construction began on the Panama Canal in 1904. This picture taken two years before the canal opened in 1914 shows workers digging by hand through the Cucaracha Slide of the Gaillard Cut, now a series of massive locks.

America's 25th president, William McKinley, furthered the colonization process by taking the Philippines from Spain after the successful conclusion of the Spanish-American War in 1898. In this, he paved the way for his successor, Teddy Roosevelt, to increase American influence and begin a series of interventions that would last until today.

Giant Among Nations

"A splendid little war!" exclaimed delighted newspaper magnates and politicians alike at the satisfactory outcome of the Spanish-American War. Cuba was at first made a protectorate but then given its independence in 1902, although American influence remained invasive. At the Treaty of Pars, made in December 1898, Spain ceded Puerto Rico, Guam, and the Philippines, receiving $20m compensation in return. Not all Americans were overjoyed at joining the ranks of the colonial overlords, however. Matters worsened when it became clear that Filipino freedom fighters, who had been waging a war for years against their Spanish oppressors, made no distinction between Spanish and American aims.

Critics pointed out that the very action of occupation of the Philippines contradicted the valued American principle of self-determination, and was contrary to the spirit of the Constitution. President William McKinley had no such misgivings. He reflected on the religious divide in the dispute when he spoke to the Senate on the subject of the Philippines becoming an American colony:

"I am not ashamed to tell you, gentlemen, that I went down on my knees and prayed to Almighty God for light and guidance that one night. And one night later it came to me this way... there was nothing left for us to do but to take them all and to educate [the Filipinos] and uplift and civilize and Christianize them, and by God's grace, do the very best we could by them, as our fellow men for whom Christ also died."

Any further attempt to "uplift and civilize" in other conquered regions was ended in 1901 when an anarchist shot McKinley dead, but he represented a majority view that U.S.-style Protestantism coupled with capitalism was the way ahead. Territories under U.S. control were quickly given the right of self-government but America still dominated policy. The aim was, as ever, to ease the path for American commercial interests.

In America's "backyard"

With this in mind, the U.S. government was convinced of the need to build a canal across the narrow Isthmus of Panama to connect government became increasingly concerned about the territorial violation. Outright war was only avoided when Wilson finally withdrew the U.S. troops.

the Atlantic and Pacific Oceans. Alas, however, at the time Panama belonged to Colombia, whose government was keen to keep America at bay. In 1903 Panamanian rebels, covertly supported by the American government, ousted the Colombians. The agreement the U.S. had been hoping for was swiftly forthcoming and the U.S. Corps of Engineers started to build the 51-mile long canal. When it opened in 1914, America kept control of the land flanking the waterway. The territory was only handed back to Panama in 1979, while the canal itself remained in American hands until 2000.

When some 40,000 American residents of Mexico became at risk from a revolution in 1913, it was only a matter of time before the U.S. became involved. President Woodrow Wilson seized the port of Veracruz the following year, effectively suffocating the rebel Mexican government. The Mexican army—with American support—then occupied Mexico City. Another foreign adventure would have been concluded had it not been for the activities of one Pancho Villa, a renegade who carried out a decisive raid on American territory in 1916, killing 19 U.S. citizens. Wilson sent a column of troops into Mexico to root out Villa but they failed in their mission. Meanwhile, the Mexican

Isolationism ends in WWI

America had every intention of remaining neutral when war broke out in 1914. Natural sympathies with Britain were tempered by fierce isolationism, but American patience was tried when German submarines sank the British liner *Lusitania* in May 1915, with heavy loss of life, including many Americans. The British government put heavy pressure on the U.S., which paid off in 1917. The U.S. joined the now global World War I, suffering some 115,000 fatalities but playing a decisive role in the conflict's outcome.

BRITANNIA TO AMERICA

ON THE SINKING OF THE *LUSITANIA*
In silence you have looked on felon blows,
On butcher's work of which the waste lands reek;
Now, in God's name, from Whom your greatness flows,
Sister, will you not speak?
Punch, London, May 12, 1915

Hero or villain? "General" Pancho Villa leads Mexican rebels on horseback. Villa saw the U.S. as a greedy conqueror of his land. His raids on the U.S. almost led to war with Mexico in 1916.

Rising Sun—Japan

Since 1544, Japan had dealt gingerly with European sailors and missionaries. In 1637, all foreigners were expelled and so began two centuries of isolation, during which time the feudal system was undermined by a growing money economy.

RIGHT: Japanese troops of the 4th Division, 9th Regiment await orders to advance on Port Arthur during the siege of the city in the Russo-Japanese War. Japanese naval and land power took the Russians by surprise. Soldiers (BELOW) load a 500-lb shell into an 11-inch "Osaka Baby" gun. In one day, nearly 2,000 of these shells devastated the Russians' arsenal and many ships in the harbor. Japan had given notice...

In 1854, American gunboat diplomacy opened up Japan to foreigners for the first time since the 17th century. While the new Japanese middle classes relished this intervention, those entrenched in the feudal system did not. In the civil war of 1867–8, the conservatives lost to a new movement that swept away the reactionary *bakufu* (military bureaucracy) and the *shogun* (governor), a system that had prevailed since 1192. The *Meiji* (enlightened rule) movement restored the emperor and, under divine imperial guidance, ministers resolved that Japan should become the pre-eminent nation of East Asia.

This was to be achieved through a wholesale program of modernization:

increased industrialization, international trade, and the creation of a thoroughly modern army. At first the West, assessing the future commercial potential, was eager to help. Almost overnight, Japan created a new socio-economic society, largely based on European judicial laws, with new schools and universities teaching European science and technology.

Japan began to have imperialist ambitions to match those of the West. In 1872—to Chinese alarm—Japan laid claim to the Ryukyu island chain. In 1873, the Bonin Islands were colonized by agreement with Britain and the U.S. In 1875, Japan relinquished the southern half of Sakhalin to Russia in exchange for full ownership of the defensive Kuril Islands. Friction with China increased in 1879, when the strategic Ryukyu Islands were made a full territory. Finally, in 1894 an uprising in Korea sparked intervention by both Japan and China. The Japanese Navy destroyed China's fleet in the Yellow Sea, while the army crushed the Chinese in Manchuria. Japan won for itself Formosa (Taiwan) and the Liaotung peninsula on the mainland, with its ice-free harbor, Port Arthur. Unfortunately, the Russians also coveted Port Arthur.

Now the West also became concerned at Japan's gains. In support of Russia, France

1854	1863	1867	1875	1895	1904	1905	1910
The U.S. Navy forces Japan to trade with other countries	Japanese forts open fire on Western merchant ships; U.S./European retaliatory fleets arrive the next year	Emperor Mutsuhito gains full leadership when the shogun rulership ends	Japan gains Kurile Islands from Russia but cedes Sakhalin	Japan gains Formosa (Taiwan) from China in the Sino-Japanese War	The Japanese start the Russo-Japanese War by attacking Port Arthur	Treaty of Portsmouth ends the war after Russia is defeated at Port Arthur, Mukden, and the Tsushima straits	Korea is annexed by Japan

and Germany pressured Japan to present Port Arthur to the Czar (*see page 153*). As yet incapable of facing down Russia and its allies militarily, Japan unwillingly ceded the port and the Chinese government leased Liaotung to Russia. Russian expansionism soon began interfering with a briefly independent Korea. This was too near to home. Japan began preparations to take on the Russian Bear.

SWEET REVENGE

Weakened at home by the defeat, China found itself beset by the conniving of Western powers. In 1899, the fury of Chinese conservatives was vented against foreigners in the bloody Boxer Rebellion. Western diplomats cowered in the legation quarter and appealed for help. European and American forces finally defeated the Boxers and Beijing was occupied. A humiliating peace treaty was imposed on China, but the incident illustrated the folly of trying to carve up the vast country into dominions. The Russians were noticeably tardy in withdrawing troops from Manchuria. Japan watched uneasily as military activity in the area intensified.

After signing an Anglo-Japanese accord in 1902, which effectively neutralized Russia's ally France, Tokyo put pressure on Russia to quit Chinese territory. In the mistaken belief that the Japanese were merely blustering, Russia indulged in prolonged talks without removing a single soldier from the area. In February 1904 the Russian Navy was woefully unprepared when Japan unleashed a blistering attack on the fleet in Port Arthur. On the same day Japanese troops overran Korea. The subsequent peace deal brokered by America gave Liaotang back to Japan, along with

the southern part of Sakhalin. Crucially Japan was denied the opportunity to take over Manchuria. By 1910, however, it had annexed the whole of Korea.

Map labels

Ryukyu Islands

Sakhalin
Russia 1875
Southern half to
Japan 1905

Trans-Siberian railroad

Kabarovsk

Hokkaido

Otaru

Hakodate

Aomori

Hailar

Chinese eastern railroad under Russian control

Manchuria

Amur

Harbin

Lake Khanka

Akita

Yamagata

Vladivostock

Sea of Japan

Changchun

Manchurian railroad under Japanese control

Mukden

Honshu

Kwangtung Territory
Russia, 1895–1905

Russian surrender, May 26, 1905

Kyoto

Tottori

Osaka

Pyongyang

Matsue

Liaotang peninsula

Seoul

Beijing

Bo Hai

Lüshun (Port Arthur)

KOREA

Hiroshima

Shikoku

Tianjin

Weihaiwei
Leased to Britain, 1898

Battle of the Yellow Sea, 1894

Pusan

Kyushu

Jinan

Quingdao

Mokpo

Nagasaki

Yellow

Yellow Sea

Quingdao
Leased to Germany, 1898

Quelpart Is.

Tanega Shima

Yaka Shima

Lake Hongze

MANCHU EMPIRE

Nanjing

Lake Hu

Shanghai

Hangzhou

Ningbo

Yangtze

Wuhan

Lake Pengli

Nanchang

Lake Dongting

East China Sea

Ryukyu Islands Japan 1879

PACIFIC OCEAN

Fuzhou

Formosa (Taiwan)
Japan 1895

Xiamen (Amoy)

Pescadores Japan 1895

Guangzhou (Canton)

Macao Portugal

Hong Kong Leased to Britain

Edo (Tokyo)

Legend

	Japanese territory, 1850

Situation by 1914

	Japanese gains
	Japanese influence
	Russian Empire
	Russian influence
——	railroads

Timeline

1914
Japan declares war on Germany

1919
Japan adds the Caroline, Mariana, and Marshall Islands to its territory

1933
Japan leaves the League of Nations

1937
The Japanese invade China and take Beijing, Nanjing, and Shanghai

1940
Japan takes Saigon and invades French Indo-China

1942
Japan invades Java but is forced back from Burma

1943
The U.S. expels Japanese invaders from Guam and the Philippines

1945
Japan surrenders after the U.S. drops atomic bombs on Hiroshima and Nagasaki

Architect of war, or pawn in a warmongers' game? Emperor Hirohito of Japan proceeds to the "Mimic War Maneuvers" that took place for several days at the end of November 1931 at Okayama. Japan's preparations for all-out war on China were almost complete.

RIGHT: In mid-1937, Japanese forces attacked Shanghai, swiftly overwhelming Chinese nationalist troops, already wearied of the two-front aggression of Japan and Chinese communists. This picture shows Japanese soldiers clambering up the ramparts along the Soochow Creek on arriving in the Hongkew district of Shanghai.

Road to Disaster

Within decades Japan had developed from an anachronistic feudal state into one of the world's mightiest nations, economically and militarily. When World War I began, Japan focussed again on China, now a republic after the overthrow of the Manchu dynasty. With British consent, Japanese forces took the German settlement in Quingdao. Afterward the Japanese presented the Chinese with 21 demands that effectively reduced whole regions of China to vassals. Despite stout resistance, most of Japan's demands were met, backed by the European powers and confirmed by the Treaty of Versailles in 1919.

In 1921 a tripartite agreement limited the strength of Japanese, British, and U.S. navies. It also barred the Western powers from building major naval bases in Hong Kong or the Philippines. To Japan this felt like power among equals, but it was not. America was at the same time debating laws to limit Japanese immigration to the U.S. Similar laws were passed in Australia and New Zealand. In Japan there was brooding bitterness. A terrible truth was dawning—

that Asians could not expect equality with Westerners in a world dominated by the Anglo-Saxon powers. Such was the political reality during the 1930s.

CHINA MERCILESSLY SUBJUGATED

Rising nationalism and militarism went hand in hand. In 1931 Manchuria was invaded and became a Japanese puppet state under its former emperor. China retaliated with a boycott of Japanese goods. Japan responded with a swift strike against Shanghai that forced China to agree terms favorable to the Japanese—but it was only a respite. In 1937, the full-scale invasion of China began. Any voice of reason went unheard in jubilant Japan, where liberalism had all but disappeared in the wake of an assassination campaign carried out by fringe interest groups.

The League of Nations, at which Japan had a seat until 1933, was powerless to prevent atrocities in China, among the most infamous being the orgy of rape, pillage, and summary execution of thousands in Nanjing after the city fell in December, 1937. Acts of unprovoked aggression left Italy and Germany likewise isolated. The three countries signed the Anti-Comintern Pact in December 1936 to bolster a hard line against communism. Japanese leaders watched and waited following the outbreak of World War II in Europe. The glittering prizes now in their grasp were the British and French colonies of Asia—as long as Soviet Russia and America did not act against them.

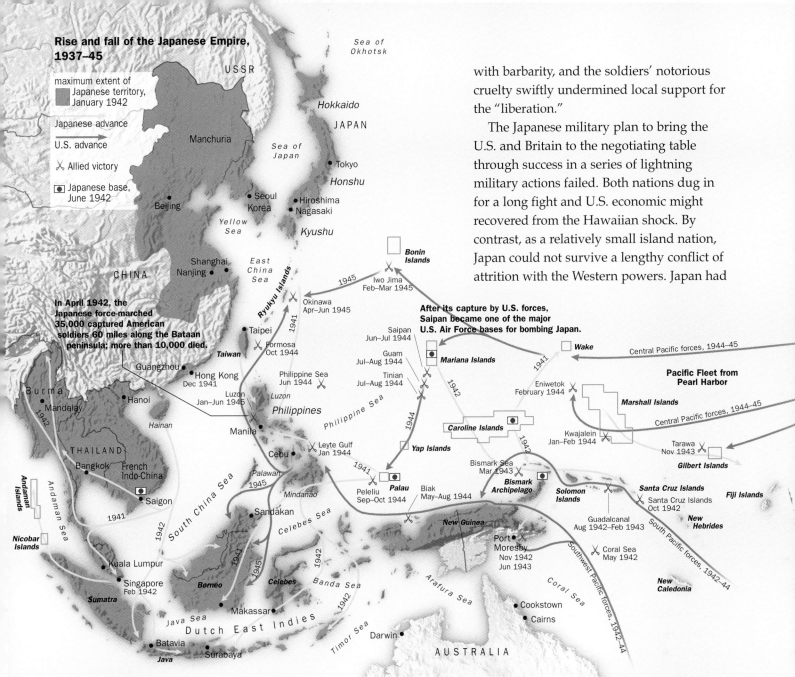

maximum extent of Japanese territory, January 1942

→ Japanese advance

→ U.S. advance

✕ Allied victory

◉ Japanese base, June 1942

USSR

Sea of Okhotsk

Hokkaido

JAPAN

Manchuria

Sea of Japan

• Tokyo

Honshu

• Beijing

• Seoul
Korea

• Hiroshima
• Nagasaki

Yellow Sea

Kyushu

• Shanghai
CHINA
Nanjing •

East China Sea

Ryukyu Islands

In April 1942, the Japanese force-marched 35,000 captured American soldiers 60 miles along the Bataan peninsula; more than 10,000 died.

✕ Iwo Jima Feb–Mar 1945

☐ **Bonin Islands**

1945

• Okinawa Apr–Jun 1945

After its capture by U.S. forces, Saipan became one of the major U.S. Air Force bases for bombing Japan.

• Taipei

✕ Formosa Oct 1944

Taiwan

Saipan Jun–Jul 1944

☐ Wake

Central Pacific forces, 1944–45

• Guangzhou

• Hong Kong Dec 1941

Philippine Sea Jun 1944

✕ Guam Jul–Aug 1944

◉ **Mariana Islands**

1941

Burma

• Mandalay

• Hanoi

Hainan

Luzon Jan–Jun 1945

Luzon

Philippines

✕ Tinian Jul–Aug 1944

✕ Eniwetok February 1944

Pacific Fleet from Pearl Harbor

• Manila

Philippine Sea

Caroline Islands ◉

Kwajalein Jan–Feb 1944 ✕

Marshall Islands

Central Pacific forces, 1944–45

THAILAND

• Bangkok

French Indo-China

◉ Saigon

✕ Leyte Gulf Jan 1944

• Cebu

1941

☐ Yap Islands

Tarawa Nov 1943 ✕

☐

Andaman Islands

Andaman Sea

South China Sea

Palawan 1945

Mindanao

Peleliu Sep–Oct 1944

☐ ◉ **Palau**

Biak May–Aug 1944

Bismark Sea Mar 1943

✕ **Bismark Archipelago** ◉

Solomon Islands

Santa Cruz Islands

Gilbert Islands

Fiji Islands

Nicobar Islands

• Sandakan

Celebes Sea

New Guinea

✕ Santa Cruz Islands Oct 1942

New Hebrides

• Kuala Lumpur

1941

1942

• Makassar

Banda Sea

Guadalcanal Aug 1942–Feb 1943

South Pacific forces, 1942–44

• Singapore Feb 1942

Borneo

Celebes

Port Moresby Nov 1942 Jun 1943

✕ Coral Sea May 1942

Sumatra

Java Sea

Dutch East Indies

Arafura Sea

Coral Sea

New Caledonia

• Batavia

Java • Surabaya

Timor Sea

• Darwin

Southwest Pacific forces, 1942–44

• Cookstown

• Cairns

AUSTRALIA

The Tripartite Axis Pact of 1940, signed with Germany and Italy, was a defense against the U.S., while the 1941 neutrality treaty with Russia defused their ancient enemy. Japan was ready. On December 7, 1941 Japanese fighters struck the American fleet at Pearl Harbor without warning. On the same day the islands of Guam, Singapore, and the Philippines were bombarded. With astonishing ease the Japanese roared through southeast Asia, winning control of Hong Kong, Wake Island, Malaya, Sumatra, Bali, Java, and many small Pacific islands.

To some they seemed like liberators. Japan had long supported the notion of "Asia for Asiatics" and delivered a huge blow to Western colonialism. However, Japanese officers and troops were not fraternal toward any ethnic group. Soon, Japanese occupation became synonymous

The U.S. exploded two atomic bombs over Nagasaki and, BELOW, Hiroshima. In split seconds, two of Japan's largest cities simply vanished. The Allied rationale was that the devastation saved more lives than if the war had continued any longer.

with barbarity, and the soldiers' notorious cruelty swiftly undermined local support for the "liberation."

The Japanese military plan to bring the U.S. and Britain to the negotiating table through success in a series of lightning military actions failed. Both nations dug in for a long fight and U.S. economic might recovered from the Hawaiian shock. By contrast, as a relatively small island nation, Japan could not survive a lengthy conflict of attrition with the Western powers. Japan had also underestimated how enemy submarines could cripple the import of vital supplies. As American troops neared the Japanese home islands, two factions argued over whether to suffer the humiliation of defeat or continue fighting to preserve national honor. This question was resolved when the atomic bombs were dropped on Hiroshima and Nagasaki in August 1945, proving beyond doubt that continued resistance would bring total annihilation.

The Soviet Bloc

"From Stettin in the Baltic to Trieste in the Adriatic an Iron Curtain has descended across the continent. Behind that line lie all the capitals of the ancient states of central and Eastern Europe."
Winston Churchill, WWII British prime minister, 1946

Churchill's words perfectly convey the political post-war reality that confronted battle-weary Europeans. The communist empire built up by the Soviet Union under the premiership of Josef Stalin (1879–1953) seemed poised for further expansion, with western Europe and even

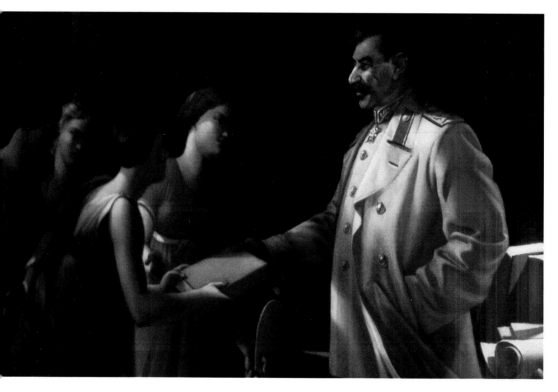

Joseph Stalin created an empire ruled largely through state-sponsored terror, enforced by the vast Red Army and a ubiquitous security apparatus, but propagandists frequently portrayed him as the "Father of the Nation."

North America under threat of attack.

Communism had long been a potent force in Europe, and one of the planks of Hitler's success was the fostering of anti-communist feeling. Indeed, the German army delayed its surrender in 1945 in order that greater numbers of refugees and soldiers could give themselves up to the Americans and British rather than to the advancing Russians, such was the fear of the Soviets. The potent

feelings of dread and paranoia engendered by relentless propaganda were almost universally held.

In six years WWII had claimed the lives of 55 million service personnel and civilians worldwide. An estimated 21 million of the fatalities were Soviet citizens and the western side of their country was laid to waste. But as the war came to an end it became clear that the Soviet Union sought to dominate the countries of eastern Europe it had overrun, and that there was nothing the West could do to stop this from happening.

Wartime relations had been cordial between Churchill, Roosevelt, and Stalin. However, Churchill swiftly returned to his pre-war anti-communist stance, so much so that he was denounced in the Russian state newspaper *Pravda* as an anti-Soviet warmonger. In fact, Churchill played no part in the peace deals agreed after the war, having lost his job as prime minister in the 1945 general election. Roosevelt died just before the war ended and was replaced at the negotiating table by Harry S. Truman (p.1945–53). Stalin's suspicions of the new president were well founded: it was Truman who had ordered the atomic bombing of Hiroshima and Nagasaki.

The wrangling went on for years and the split between the Soviets and the West became increasingly marked. While many countries willingly acepted post-war American aid under the Marshall Plan to help rebuild, Stalin stoutly rejected any U.S. help offers. Others of the so-called Eastern Bloc, such as Poland, Czechoslovakia, and Finland, also refused to accept U.S. funds.

1875	1878	1894	1905	1914	1917–21	1918	1922
Russia gains Sakhalin from Japan but cedes Kurile Islands	The Congress of Berlin gives Russia control of Bulgaria	The Triple Alliance of Germany, Austria-Hungary, and Italy leads to a counter-alliance between France and Russia	Treaty of Portsmouth ends the Russo-Japanese War after Russia is defeated at Port Arthur	Russia, Britain, and France declare war on the Ottoman Empire after they attack Crimean ports	Bolshevik revolution and civil war	The last Czar, Nicholas II, abdicates and is executed by Bolsheviks	Russian Empire becomes the Union of Soviet Socialist Republics

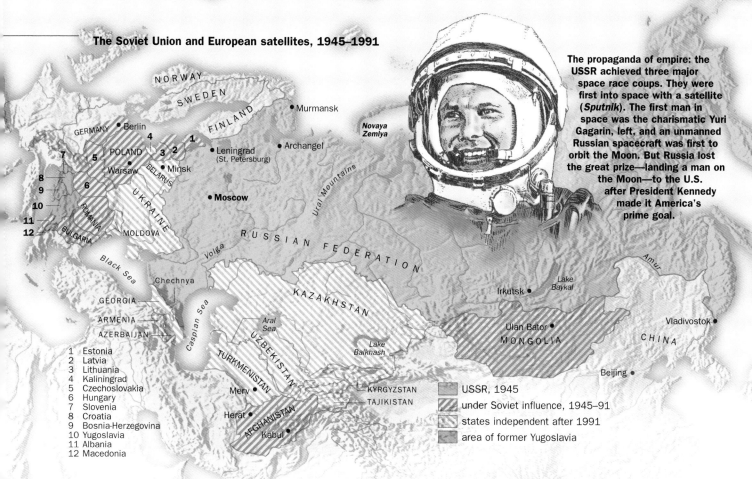

The Soviet Union and European satellites, 1945–1991

The propaganda of empire: the USSR achieved three major space race coups. They were first into space with a satellite (*Sputnik*). The first man in space was the charismatic Yuri Gagarin, left, and an unmanned Russian spacecraft was first to orbit the Moon. But Russia lost the great prize—landing a man on the Moon—to the U.S. after President Kennedy made it America's prime goal.

1 Estonia
2 Latvia
3 Lithuania
4 Kaliningrad
5 Czechoslovakia
6 Hungary
7 Slovenia
8 Croatia
9 Bosnia-Herzegovina
10 Yugoslavia
11 Albania
12 Macedonia

USSR, 1945
under Soviet influence, 1945–91
states independent after 1991
area of former Yugoslavia

RUSSIA BECOMES A SUPERPOWER

Relations deteriorated further when Russia tested its first atomic bomb in 1949, after which followed the onset of ill-concealed hostility between the Eastern Bloc and the "capitalist West." Although there were many minor conflicts (and even major ones in the Korean and Vietnam Wars), because the main protagonists avoided direct hot confrontation on the battlefield, it was aptly named the Cold War, and lasted almost half a century.

Thronged with refugees, displaced persons, freed prisoners-of-war, German fugitives, and Allied troops, it was almost impossible to impose immediate order on the chaos that was Europe in 1945. In this situation, Stalin's strong leadership won the hearts and minds of many people, especially ex-resistance fighters and partisans who were anyway inclined to communist sympathies after fighting Nazi repression. Stalin had hosted the Yalta Conference in 1945 that had agreed "free and unfettered" elections. Although each of the countries in the Eastern Bloc made the journey to communism through the ballot box, these elections were little more than token events designed to rubber-stamp the installation of communists in government and Soviet Russian hegemony over all.

Czechoslovakia had been a democracy before being overrun by Germany in 1938. All reasonable hopes that it might return to this status were dashed when communists won 39% of the vote in 1946. A coalition formed to rebuild the country, but rifts over policy— specifically policing— developed. When non-aligned ministers resigned in protest at the organization of the police in 1948, communists seized their jobs. Many fled, leaving the ranks of the opposition virtually empty. Stalin's shadow loomed. He insisted Czechoslovakia should be governed along Soviet lines, and instigated a purge, subsequent show trials, and a campaign against the Church.

The Soviet regime did not have everything its own way. When in 1968, Russia invaded Czechoslovakia, which was threatening to break away, students demonstrated daily in Prague. Communism prevailed—for a while.

1924–53	1939	1941	1949	1955	1962	1989	1991
Joseph Stalin rules the Soviet Union	The Soviet Union and Germany agree a non-aggression pact	Germany invades the Soviet Union	NATO forms after the USSR becomes a nuclear power	The Warsaw Pact is formed to oppose NATO	The U.S. Navy stops the USSR setting up a missile base on Cuba	The Cold War ends when Mikhail Gorbachev and Ronald Reagan set a nuclear disarmament program	Following an attempted coup, the USSR is dissolved

Lenin's image looks down on the annual Red Army parade of military might in Red Square, Moscow. By 1987, this propaganda display was beginning to look hollow.

Forging a Communist Empire

Given Poland's suffering during WWII at the hands of the Nazis, it was no surprise that post-war Polish politics were by inclination left-wing. Because similar sentiments existed throughout eastern Europe, the Soviet Union easily consolidated its powerbase in the region. And where support was less intensive, Stalin resorted to lies. Russian agents falsified the results of a Polish national referendum that came out in favor of a moderate candidate and also used scare tactics in the 1947 elections. Ultimately the communists absorbed all the other national parties.

Communists were in the minority in Hungary's first post-war government of 1944. However, Soviet agents utilized tactics that had served them well in Russia, and systematically eliminated any opposition. Typically, those who failed to co-operate were branded "fascists." They were shamed and ousted. By August 1949, a Russian-style constitution was introduced and Hungary became a "people's republic."

The communists of Bulgaria helped to

IT NEARLY HAPPENED

The bleakest years of the Cold War were the late 1950s and early 1960s, when the threat of nuclear war dominated. The world came closest to nuclear holocaust in 1962 when the Soviet Union stationed missiles in Cuba and the U.S. reacted by blocking further Russian shipments to the Caribbean island. The whole world waited for WWIII as President John F. Kennedy and Soviet premier Nikita Kruschev played brinkmanship as Russia insisted on sending a blockade-breaking convoy of missile-carrying ships to Cuba, escorted by Soviet attack submarines (like the one below, photographed by a U.S. Navy aircraft at the edge of the exclusion zone). To everyone's relief, Kruschev eventually backed down and agreed to remove all nuclear weapons from Cuba.

consolidate their position by pressing for a series of trials of so-called war criminals. Before they were finished, Bulgarian courts had tried an estimated 11,122 people of whom 2,730 were sentenced to death—an extreme response compared to that of the British and Americans in Europe. Yet Bulgarian democrats won little practical help from the West. An election held in 1946 produced a large communist majority. Prominent opponents of the new regime were expelled or executed.

East Germany, Romania, and the Baltic States were also dominated by Russia. Although communist, Yugoslavia retained a large degree of autonomy, as did neighboring Albania.

WARSAW PACT

The 1955 Warsaw Pact linked the military policies of all the eastern European countries to the USSR's. Protests against Soviet influence and interference did occur and were invariably ruthlessly crushed. The small hopes of freedom from the communist yoke that arose on the death of Stalin in 1953 and his subsequent denunciation in Russia were swiftly shattered. A strike in Poznan, Poland, in June 1956 was quickly suppressed. The new Polish premier, Wladyslaw Gomulka, sought to reform communist rule with Soviet approval. Advances were slow, and finally ground to a halt.

In 1956 Budapest was brought to a standstill by a massive march of Hungary's discontented students reinforced by residents of the capital city. With no experience of facing public protest, the police responded by firing into the crowd. Reformer Imre Nagy swept into power. However, when he attempted to pull Hungary out of the Warsaw Pact, Russia intervened. Soviet tanks rolled into Hungarian streets, causing turmoil. Resistance against Soviet Russia was futile, although the workers satisfied their honor by staging a general strike that took months to settle. Nagy and his cohorts were executed after a secret trial. Hundreds fled to the West while they had the opportunity.

Despite holding this vast empire, Soviet Russia remained poor. It was weighted down by a self-seeking bureaucracy, industrial and agricultural inefficiency, and the huge cost of the space race with America. The launching of the world's first artificial satellite in 1957, ahead of the Americans, was a source of great national pride, but the project drained resources that could have been better used elsewhere.

Held together only by force, the Soviet Union began to unravel as its communist system collapsed. The last attempt to forcibly extend the empire—into Afghanistan in 1979—encountered fierce resistance and the army withdrew ignominiously a decade later. Famously, leader Mikhail Gorbachev's introduction of *glasnost* (openness) and *perestroika* (restructuring) from 1985, caused economic disorder in the decaying USSR. It signaled a new era in which greater freedom could be enjoyed. The Berlin Wall, which had been the most potent symbol of Russian might in the Cold War, was torn down. The USSR itself was then swiftly replaced by a Commonwealth of Independent States.

Churchill's metaphor, the Iron Curtain, was made concrete across Germany. A barbed-wire barricade divided the communist East from the West. Berlin, which sat within East Germany, was divided between the Soviets and the western powers. As the Cold War darkened, East Germany constructed what became infamously known as the Berlin Wall, to cut the city in two. Many East Germans died, shot trying to cross the Wall to the West. And then in November 1989, with Soviet power waning, the Wall was brought down, to universal jubilation.

The State of Empire Today

Empires grew to become costly, unfashionable, politically unacceptable, and anachronistic. What is to become of them?

The United Nations and its symbol (below) are universally recognized. The UN is the antithesis of "empire." It stands for harmony among all peoples and between all nations. The first experiment in global peace-keeping—The League of Nations—was formed after WWI, but came to grief through its inability to deal with empire-building by the Japanese, Nazi Germany, and Fascist Spain and Italy. After WWII, the will of the world proved stronger, and the UN has become a symbol of the time we live in, a time when empires— as they have been detailed in this book—are considered a danger to all. But it is only as long as the will of most people for peace—or if not, at least dialog and concensus— remains focussed that the future of the UN will be assured.

Looking back through the millennia of civilization from our vantage point in the 21st century, it is clear that the longevity of empires slowly diminished over vast tracts of time, as technological advances and competition from other empires created instability and attrition. Ancient Egypt survived more or less intact for 3,000 years. China also survived in splendid isolation for over 2,000 years. By the time the Byzantine empire was brought down in 1453 it had lasted over a millennium. The Ottomans held sway for six centuries in southeastern Europe, between AD 1300 and 1922.

In comparison to these examples, the great European conquering powers of the second millennium AD look positively feeble. The Holy Roman Empire was famously debunked by Voltaire as "…neither holy, nor Roman, nor an empire." The Portuguese theoretically controlled 3.3 million square miles of Brazil (although, of course, saw very little of it), and left in the 1820s after three centuries. Spain's American, Caribbean, and Pacific colonies were equally short-lived; the Dutch managed 250 years in Indonesia; the Italians a half-century in Africa; and the Germans (latecomers to overseas empire-building) merely a few

decades in the Dark Continent.

The French maintained colonies for 229 years in Canada, but lasted less than a century in Africa and Indo-China. The British Empire may have been both immense (13 million square miles) and populous, but it was hardly a long-term structure. Interests on the American seaboard spanned barely 170 years, in India 200 years, and in most of Africa 80. Canada, Australia, and New Zealand all made the transition to autonomy after 100 years or so, and although Afrikaners lost the Boer War in 1902 they won independence eight years later.

So what were the motivations and rewards behind the quest for empire?

Throughout history, the quest for wealth and status have been the driving forces. In ancient times rulers sought new lands from which to extract commodities, and new citizens whom they could tax. The same was true even by the 19th century AD, when European countries needed raw materials, new markets, and more people to power their economies. As the age of empire waned after the world wars of the 20th century, direct rule was replaced by political influence and the growth of the now ubiquitous multi-national company— empires of their own.

National rivalry and religious zealotry are other driving forces in empire-building— although these were often just masks for greed. In the post-Cold War world the ideal that humankind would live in a "global village," devoid of nationalism, has already fallen into disrepute (given the rise of nationalism and ethnic unrest in the former Soviet Union and the Balkans). Even as European Union enthusiasts talk of closer integration, many EU member countries face calls for devolved government within their own borders.

What of the Internet, that unstoppable piece of technology that knows no government or national boundaries—how does this change the concept of empire? As

the Internet grows, so will its capacity to re-invent itself—spreading and blending cultures, ideas, and national identities. Governments will be powerless to resist this (though many will try), but ultimately where we live will become secondary to who we are.

The Internet is merely one factor among many new challenges. In the future, famine and disease may cause huge population shifts and rising sea levels caused by climate warming could re-draw the world's political map. It is on this point that history and geography have much to offer. A study published in January 2001 by Yale University and the University of Massachusetts, Amherst, used ice cores, corals, and sediments to show that the rise and fall of ancient civilizations is closely linked to abrupt climatic changes. The Classic Maya society ended in the ninth century AD during the longest drought of the millennium. Egypt's Old Kingdom, the Akkadian Empire, and the early Bronze Age peoples of Greece,

Crete, and Palestine all peaked around 2300 BC before declining in the drought and climate-cooling that followed. The Late Uruk society of southern Mesopotamia flourished in 3500 BC but collapsed some 350 years later—again due to drought. Do we imagine that we are immune to such cataclysmic events? If so, we are wrong.

As the events of September 11, 2001 have shown, the world is still a volatile and unpredictable place, perhaps more so than at any time since WWII. Following the attacks in the U.S. and the revelation that weapons of mass destruction may now be in the hands of small but fanatical terrorist organizations, it has become apparent to all that the security of even the most powerful nations is no longer guaranteed. Despite the assertion by some historians that with the end of the Cold War came the end of history, more than a decade on we can plainly see that this is not the case. Perhaps, from this realization, a more secure world will eventually develop.

Members of the United Nations Assembly listen to President Jimmy Carter in October 1977. At the time, the U.S. was seeking concensus for various actions in the Middle East. Carter's historical forebears —rulers of their own empires—would never have considered discussing such matters in the open.

Index

A

Abbasid Empire 60, 68–71
Abu Bakr 102, 104
Achaemenid Empire 21, 27, 28–31
ad-Din, Khayr 146
Admonitions of Ipuwer, The 20
Akkadian Empire 10, 11, 12–15, 22
Aghlabids 104
agriculture 10, 107
Ahmose I, Pharaoh 20
Akhenaten, Pharaoh 20, 21
Aksum *see* Axum
al-Mumin, Abd 105
al-Rahman, Abd 68
al-Rashid, Harun 69, 74
al-Rashid, Mamoun 69, 70, 71
Alaska purchase 153, 176
Alexander I, Czar 152, 162
Alexander II, Czar 152
Alexander III, Czar 152
Alexander III, Pope 128
Alexander the Great 20, 21, 27, 30, 32–35, 42
Alfonso VI, King 105
Algeria 173
Almagro, Diego de 108–109
Almohad dynasty 102–105
Almoravid Empire 92, 102–105
Amenemhet I, Pharaoh 20
American Revolution 164–165
Amorites 15, 22, 23
Anabasis 31
Angevin dynasty 111, 118–121
Anglo-Japanese Accord 181
Anglo-Saxons 102
Antefoker 21
Anti-Comintern Pact 182
Ardashir I, King 42
Aristotle 32
Ark of the Covenant 62
Artaxerxes I, King 31
Artaxerxes II, King 31
Artaxerxes III, King 31
Ashurbanipal, King 24
Ashurnasirpal II 11, 23–25
Assyrian Empire 11, 22–25
Atahualpa 107–109
Atatürk, Mustafa Kemal 148, 149
Atlantic Charter of 1941 169
atomic bomb (*see also* Hiroshima) 184–185
Attila the Hun 76, 78–79
Augustulus, Emperor 41
Augustus, Emperor 21, 39, 40
Austro-Hungarian Empire (*see also* Habsburg Empire) 154
Avars 79, 114
Axum, Empire of 60, 62–65, 114
Aztec Empire 94, 95, 97, 127, 137, 138–139

B

Babylonian Empire 22, 63
bakufu 180
ball game 92, 96
Bang, Liu, Emperor 48
Barbarossa, Frederick 128, 129
Basil II, Emperor 116
Batak houses 98
Battle of Austerlitz 161
Battle of Borodino 162
Battle of Manila Bay 177
Battle of Trafalgar 161, 162
Bayezid I 144
"Beard tax" 152
Becket, Archbishop Thomas à 118
Beg, Toghril 76
Belisarius 113
Berbers 68, 92, 102–105
Berlin Wall 187
Bingham, Hiram 106
Bismarck 157
Black Death 110, 111, 122
Black Hole of Calcutta 167
Boer War 167
Bokassa, "Emperor" Jean Bédel 6
Bolshevik Revolution 142, 150, 153
Bonaparte, Napoleon 126, 128, 131, 160–163, 135, 141, 152, 160–163, 164, 170
Boxer Rebellion 181
British Commonwealth 169
British Empire 127, 161, 164–169
Buddhism 43, 51, 54, 56, 58, 59, 91, 99, 101
Bulan, Emperor 82, 83
Byzantine Empire 65, 67, 69, 70, 84, 110, 111, 112-117, 132, 144, 149

C

Caesar, Julius 38
Capac, Huayna 106, 108
Caracalla, Emperor 41
Carlos I 137
Carolingian Empire 60, 72–75, 154
Carthage 37
Catherine II, the Great 148, 151, 152
Celts 36
Chac Mool figures 97
Chagatai Khan 89
Chandragupta I, King 52
Chandragupta II, King 47, 52, 53
Charlemagne 60, 72, 128, 131
Charles V 130
Chepren, Pharaoh *see* Khaefre
Cheops, Pharaoh *see* Khufu
Christianity (*see also* Orthodox Church, Protestant Reformation and Roman Catholicism) 41, 44, 60, 61–65, 66, 73, 83, 105, 111, 112–117, 122
Christopher of Bavaria 125
Churchill, Winston 169, 184
Cicero 38–39
Claudius, Emperor 40
Cleopatra 33, 39
Clive, Robert 166–167
Code Napoleon 163
Code of Hammurabi 23
Cold War 184–187
Columbus, Christopher 136
communism, spread of 182–189
Comnenus, Alexius I, Emperor 116
concentration camps 167
Concordat of 1801 163
Confucianism 48, 51, 56, 58, 59
conquistadors 95, 106–109, 127, 137–139
Constans II, Emperor 115
Constantine I, Emperor 38, 41, 44, 112
Constantine III, Emperor 115
Constantine XI, Emperor 117
Cortés, Hernán 138
Council of Chalcedon 65
Council of Constance 130
Crassus, Marcus 38
Creoles 140
Crimean War 149
Crusades 67, 111, 116–117, 119, 129, 132
Cuban missile crisis 186
Cyrillic alphabet 117
Cyrus the Great 28, 42

D

Daoism 51
Dandolo, Enrico 133
Darius I 27, 28, 29, 30, 42, 43
Darius II 31
Darius III 33
de Gaulle, Charles 173
Devshirme fighters 147
Diet of Augsburg 130
Diet of Worms 130
Diocletian, Aurelius Valerius 112
Dole, Sanford B. 176
Dutch East Indies 168

E

East India Company 166, 168
Eastern Bloc 184–185
Edward I 120, 121
Edward II 121
Edward III, Black Prince 121
Egypt 11, 16–21
    Old Kingdom 16-19; Middle Kingdom 11; New Kingdom 20-21
Einhard 74
Elamites 13
Eleanor of Aquitaine 118
Eric I 124–125
Erik I "Bloodax" 122
Ethiopia *see* Axum
Ezana, Prince 64

F

Fatimid Empire 102
Fawcett, Percy Harrison 158
Ferdinand, Archduke Franz 157
Ferdinand and Isabella 137
Ferdinand II 130
Fertile Crescent *see* Mesopotamia
Five Dynasties period 59
Five Pecks of Rice sect 51
Fortescue, Hugh 162
Francis I 146
Francis II 131
Franco-Prussian War 170

Frederick II 129
French and Indian War 170
French Revolution 160
Front de Liberation Nationale 173
Frumentius, Bishop 64, 65

G
Gagarin, Yuri 185
Gallic Wars 38
Gama, Vasco da 135
Gandhi, Mahatma 169
Gaozong, Emperor 56
Gaozu, Emperor 56
Genghis Khan 76, 86–91, 150
Ghana 102, 104
Gök Empire 80–81, 82
Gomulka, Wladyslaw 187
Gorbachev, Mikhail 187
Gordian Knot 32
Great Cloud Sutra 57
Greek Empire 20, 21, 27, 31
Guifei, Yang 59
Gupta Empire 47, 52–55
Gutians 15

H
Habsburg Empire 75, 129–131, 142, 146, 154–157
Habsburg, Maria Theresa 155–156
Hagia Sophia 113, 116, 117, 147
Hammurabi, King 23
Han Empire 47, 48–51, 78
Hannibal 37
Hanseatic League 111, 124–125
Hatshepsut, Queen 18
Hawaii 176
Haydn, Joseph 156
Hearst, William Randolph 177
Heaven's Mandate, doctrine 8
Henry II 111, 118, 121
Henry III 121
Henry IV 121, 125
Heraclius, Governor 114–115
Hinduism 52, 54, 101
Hiroshima 183, 184
Hittite Empire 21, 23
Hohenstaufen dynasty 128
Holy Roman Empire 75, 124, 126, 128–131, 135, 142, 146
Hormizd III 44
Hou, Lu 48
Hsiung-nu 78
Huangdi, Shi, Emperor 48
Huascar 108
Hunas 55
Huns 76, 78
Hyams, Edward 92
Hyksos 20

I
Ibn Tashfin 102, 104
Ibn Tumart 105
Ibn Yasin 102, 104
Iconoclasm 117
Inca Empire 92, 106–109, 137
Indian Mutiny of 1857 167
Innocent III, Pope 133
Irish Free State 169
Islam 27, 65, 66–71, 82, 85, 102–105, 111, 115, 126, 142, 146

Ivan IV, the Terrible 150

J
Janissaries 147
Japanese Empire 153, 172, 180–184
Java, Kingdom of 101
Jesuits 141
John I 111, 119–121
Judaism 82–85
Julian calendar 39
Justinian I 112–113
Justinian II 84

K
Kama Sutra 55
Kennedy, President John F. 186
Khaefre, Pharaoh 18
Khazaria 82–85, 114
Khosru I 45
Khosru II 45
Khufu, Pharaoh 16
Khwarezm-Shah Empire 88
Kish, Kingdom of 12, 13, 14
Knights Hospitaller 144
Kruschev, Premier Nikita 186
Kublai Khan 87, 89–91
Kumaragupta I, King 52
Kush, Kingdom of 20, 21, 62, 63
Kushans 52, 78
Kutuzov, General Mikhail 162
Kyrgyz Empire 81

L
Las Casas, Bartolomé de 137, 138, 139
Last of the Incas, The 92
League of Cambrai 134, 135
League of Nations 182, 188
Leo I 79
Leo III, Pope 72
Lilio'ukalani, Queen of Hawaii 176
Lingdi, Emperor 51
Livingstone, David 158
Louis XIV 170
Louis XVI 162
Louis XVIII 162
Louisiana Purchase 160
Luque, Hernando de 108
Lushan, An 59
Lusitania, sinking of 179
Luther, Martin 130

M
Machu Picchu 106
MacKinder, Halford 164
Macmillan, Harold 169
Magna Carta 111, 121
Maine, U.S. battleship 176
Mamluks 71
Mang, Wang, Emperor 48, 49
Manichaeanism 43
Manifest Destiny, U.S. doctrine 176
Margaret I, 122-125
Marshall Plan 184
Martel, Charles 66, 73
Marx, Karl 8
Maurice, Emperor 114
Mauryans 52
Maximiam, Emperor 112
Maximilian I, Emperor 154
Mayan Empire 94, 95, 96, 97

McKinley, President William 178
Mecklenburg, Albert of 123
Mehmet II 144, 145
Meiji 180
Menelik, King 62
Menes, Pharaoh *see* Narmer
Menkaure, Pharaoh 18
Mentuhotep II, 19
Menval, Baron Claude Francois de 162
Mesopotamia 10–11, 12–15, 22–25, 41, 43, 68
Midway Island 176
Minh, Ho Chi 170, 171
Mixcóatl 94
Moctezuma II 95, 127, 139
Mohammed 60, 65, 66, 67, 148
Mongol Empire 70, 71, 81, 86–91, 144, 150, 151
Monophysites 65
Montfort, Simon de 121
Moors *see* Berbers
Moses 13, 62-3, 66
Mozart, Wolfgang Amadeus 156
Muscovy 150
Muslims *see* Islam
Mycerinus, Pharaoh *see* Menkaure

N
Nagasaki 183, 184
Naram Sin, King 13, 15
Narmer, Pharaoh 16, 17
Narses, King 44
Nebuchadnezzar, King 25
Nefertiti, Queen 21
Nelson, Admiral Horatio 161, 162
Nero, Emperor 40
Nicholas I, Czar 148, 152
Nicholas II, Czar 153
Nubia 20, 21, 65

O
Octavian, Emperor *see* Augustus
Ogotai Khan 89
Olaf I 123
Olympic Games 112
Ondegardo, Pedro de 106
Orang Laut people 99
Orthodox Church 111
Osman 144
Otto I 128
Otto II 128
Ottoman Empire 111, 117, 126, 134, 135, 142, 143, 144–149, 152, 154

P
Panama Canal 176, 178–179
Parthians 42
Peace of Turin 134
Peace of Westphalia 131, 142
Pearl Harbor, 175
Peninsula War 162
Pepin III 72, 73
Persia (*see also* Achaemenid, Safavid and Sassanid empires) 32–35, 42–45, 68, 84, 146
Peter the Great 148, 151–152
Pheidippides 29
Philip II 32
Philippines 178–179
Phocas, Emperor 114

Phoenicians 102
Pius II, Pope 126
Pius VII, Pope 161
Pizarro, Francisco 107–109
Plantagenets *see* Angevin dynasty
Polo, Marco 90, 91
Pompeius, Gnaeus "Pompey" 38
Port Arthur 153, 180
Portuguese Empire 126–127, 141
Priscus of Panium 79
Procopius 112
Protestant Reformation 126, 130–131, 140
Prussia 157
Punic Wars 37
pyramids (Egyptian) 17–19

Q
Queen of Sheba 62
Quetzalcóatl 94–95, 127, 139

R
Raffles, Thomas Stamford 168
Ramesses II, Pharaoh 20, 21
Rawlinson, Henry 27
Renaissance 117
Richard II 121
Richard the Lionheart 110, 111, 118–121
Robin Hood 120
Roman Catholicism 115, 116, 128,
    130–131
Roman Empire (*see also* Byzantine
    Empire and Western Roman Empire)
    16, 21, 27, 36–41, 42, 44, 48, 78, 102, 112
Romanov dynasty 142, 150–153
Roosevelt, President Franklin D. 169
Roosevelt, President Theodore 176–177,
    184
Rosetta Stone 20, 21
Rough Riders 176–177
Russian Empire 89, 150–153, 162

S
sacrifice 107, 109, 139
Safavids 146
St. Cyril 83
Saladin 111, 129
Samudragupta, King 52
Sargon I, King 10, 12–13
Sargon II, King 25
Sassanian Empire 27, 42–45, 65, 80, 114,
    115
Saxons 72
Scipio, Publius Cornelius 37
Scythians 80
Sea People 21
Secret History of the Mongols 86
Selassie, Emperor Haile 62
Selim I 144, 146
Seljuks 76, 116, 144
Senwosret III, Pharaoh 20
Sepulveda, Juan Gines de 137
Seqenenre II, Pharaoh 20
Severus, Emperor Septimus 41
Seward, Secretary of State 176
Shamshi-Adad I, King 23
Shapur I 27, 43, 44
Shapur II 44
Shar-kali-sharri, King 13
Sheng, Prince Liu 51
Shi'ite Islam 66–71, 148

Shoshenq I, Pharaoh 21
Sigismund, Emperor 130, 131
Silk Road 51, 76, 122, 132
slavery 140–141
Snefru, Pharaoh 18
Solomon 62
Spanish-American War 176–177
Spanish Armada 140
Spanish Empire 95, 126–127, 136–141, 154
Spanish Inquisition 139
Spartacus 38
Sputnik 185
Srivijaya 92, 98–101
Stalin, Josef 7, 184–185
Suleiman I, the Magnificent 143, 146–147,
    148
Sulla, Cornelius 38
Sumerians 12, 22
Sunni Islam 66–71, 148
Switzerland 155

T
Taizong, Emperor 56
Tamerlane 91, 144
T'ang Empire 47, 56–59, 98
Telaga Batu stone 101
Teotihuacán 94
Teutonic Knights 125
Thirty Years War 131, 142
Tiberius, Emperor 40
Tiglath-pileser III 25
Timofeyevich, Yermak 150
Toltec Empire 92, 94–97
Topiltzin, Ce Acatl *see* Quetzalcóatl
Trajan, Emperor 41
Trans-Siberian Railway 152
Treaty of Amiens 161
Treaty of Fontainebleau 162
Treaty of Pars 178
Treaty of Tordesillas 137
Treaty of Versailles 182
Tripartite Axis Pact 183
Truman, President Harry S. 184
Tryggvason, Olav I 122
Tsang, Hsuan 54
Tuareg nomads 103, 104
T'u-chueh 79–81
Tutankhamen, Pharaoh 21
Tuthmosis I, Pharaoh 20
Tuthmosis III, Pharaoh 18

U
Uighurs 81
Umayyad Empire 60, 67, 68
Union of Kalmar 122–125
Ur 12, 14, 22
Uruk 14
Ur-Nammu 22
Ur-Zababa 12

V
Valens, Emperor 112
Valentinian, Emperor 112
Valerian, Emperor 27, 43
Valley of the Kings 18
Varus, General 39
Venice, Republic of 126, 132–135, 146, 147
Vercingetorix 38
Vespasian, Emperor 41, 112
Vespucci, Amerigo 136

Victoria, Queen 164
Vietnam 170, 172
Vikings 74, 84, 122, 123
Villa, Pancho 179
Viracocha 106, 107
Virginius, U.S. ship 176
Vivaldi, Captain 134
Voltaire 128

W
War of Spanish Succession 155
War of the Holy League 135
Warsaw pact 187
Wells, H.G. 167
Western Roman Empire 111, 112
Wilson, President Woodrow 179
Wood, Michael 34–35
Woolley, Leonard 12
Wordsworth, William 126
World War I 145, 148, 149, 153, 157, 164,
    168, 172
World War II 168, 170
Wudi, Emperor 49, 50
Wuzon, Emperor 59
Wycliffe, John 130

X
Xenophon 31
Xerxes, King 30, 32
Xiandi, Emperor 51
Xiu, Liu, Emperor 48
Xuanzong, Emperor 59

Y
Yalta Conference 185
Yamamoto, Admiral 175
Yazdegerd I 44
Yazdegerd II 44
Yazdegerd III 45
yellow journalism 177
Yellow Turbans uprising 51
Yemen 65

Z
Zacharias, Pope 73
Zetian, Wu, Empress 47, 56
Zhou, Dong 51
ziggurats 15, 22
Zoroastrianism 28, 42, 43
Zoser, Pharaoh 17